EVERYMAN, I will go with thee,
and be thy guide,
In thy most need to go by thy side

JOHN MILLINGTON SYNGE

Born at Rathfarnham, near Dublin, on 16 April
1871. Educated privately, and at Trinity College,
Dublin. Travelled on Continent, spending much
time at Paris, 1893–8, and intermittently to 1902,
when he gave up his Paris room. Returned to Ireland, where he wrote his plays and other works. A
director of the Abbey Theatre, Dublin, 1904–9.
Died at Dublin on 24 March 1909.

J. M. SYNGE

Plays, Poems and Prose

Introduction by Micheál Mac Liammóir

Dent: London and Melbourne
EVERYMAN'S LIBRARY

© Introduction, J. M. Dent & Sons Ltd, 1958
All rights reserved
Made in Great Britain by
Guernsey Press Co. Ltd, Guernsey, C.I. for
J. M. Dent & Sons Ltd
Aldine House, 33 Welbeck Street, London W1M 8LX

First included in Everyman's Library 1941
Last reprinted 1985

No 968 Hardback ISBN 0 460 00968 0
No 1968 Paperback ISBN 0 460 11968 0

INTRODUCTION

THE appearance of Synge in the Dublin of the early nineteen hundreds was a greater shock in fact than was commonly felt even by the very uncommon people into whose hands the city, for a brief period of magic, had fallen.   Ireland, always a little late for appointments, was having her fruitful decade at the opening of the new century, transforming that *fin de siècle* already celebrated and buried in France and England to a *début d'époque*.   The air, blowing listlessly over the quaysides of the Liffey, grew heavy with whisperings and murmurings, and Yeats, who some twelve years earlier had discovered in twilight Ireland's supreme moment among the circling hours, much as Van Gogh had discovered in the noonday sun the supreme moment of Provence, was at the end of his first achievement.   The temple of mystery had become, paradoxically, an established fact, with himself as high priest and with A. E. and a host of lesser men as attendant though passionately independent druids and bards, and with Lady Gregory as a dignified and cosily frosty Hebe to minister to the needs of the mystic circle.   By 1904—the year, significantly enough, of Leopold Bloom's Odyssey—all seemed ready for an uninterrupted voyage of poetry and poetical plays, of calm minstrelsy upon the shadowy waters, of endless 'dreamy kind delights,' with an occasional pleasant small comedy (to be supplied at intervals by Hebe) filled with gentle laughter.

All in the temple was indeed gentle and remote, and curiously uninsistent on anything but beauty and the essentially dreamlike quality of beauty, when this gaunt, laughing shadow fell abruptly across the threshold, and the trancelike mood was disturbed.   But the newcomer was of that race of modest men of delicate health and supremely reserved manners and habits who are born to disturb.   He shook people to their foundations by the sheer reality of his mind, by the strange unrealistic reality of his ear and of his method, by the relentless rich reality of his solitude. He must, I think, have been one of the strangest students ever to enter Trinity College where he was educated and where he seems to have left but few memories—a thin, dark-haired, gloomy-eyed young man, with broad, ashen-coloured cheekbones, and 'not very much to say for himself' is all the description I have gleaned from those few elderly men who remember him and with whom, one suspects, he was not expansive—and we can be fairly certain that he was not in his element there. Like so many young Irishmen of individuality he disappeared for a time to Paris, where most reasonable and unreasonable people feel at home, and it was here chiefly that he stayed during the nineties making some sort of a living—he had an income of sixty pounds a year—and working meanwhile on those translations from the French which, as George Moore has told us, Yeats dismissed by saying: 'You will never know as much about French poetry as Arthur Symons. Come to Ireland and write plays for me.'

It was strange that Yeats, who knew the Aran Islands but slightly and whose knowledge of their language was slighter still, should have felt so insistently that Aran was where his new discovery should go in quest of his medium. The poet's own passion at that time was to discover a master of living speech, one of the few gifts the Muse had denied to himself, and to him, as to most of his generation, Ireland's future expression seemed inevitably to be in English. Yet it had to be, he felt, an English not altogether English, but a speech such as one hears in the mouths of the people in Ireland to this day in all those places where the older tongue is still alive or partially alive, and where the imported language is profoundly influenced by it. It is in the enthusiasm for this speech that one can trace much of the strength and all of the weakness of what is usually called the Irish dramatic renaissance, of what, in reality, is the history of the Abbey Theatre. Its strength lies in the fact that Anglo-Irish, by translating to English so much that is commonplace in Gaelic syntax and idiom, acquires in the process a most uncommon richness of flavour, a savage, salty tang, a sudden barbed yet kindly brilliance of imagery that falls upon the ear of an audience—especially it may be on the ear of an audience that is not Irish—with all the delight of the unexpected.   Its weakness lies, I think, in the fact that by its very position in time this speech, a freakish and eloquent hybrid, is doomed to the briefest existence, especially if the well, which is the Irish language itself and from which the magic water has flowed, should run dry. Wherever this has happened, in Dublin and in all districts where Irish has been dead for more than a hundred years, the common speech had grown and is growing not less voluble but less coloured, not less expressive but far less rich; in fact more and more like the language of the newspaper and the radio, less and less like the language of Synge; and one comes at last to understand that the use that has been made of it and has proved one of the most potent attractions of modern dramatic literature in Ireland can but lead at last to a blind alley.

Perhaps no writer, the expression of whose genius was at once so wide and so clearly defined, could have been expected to trouble his head with speculation as to what is to come when the mode he has discovered or created has passed, not merely out of fashion, but out of existence.   Certainly Synge had no such thought in his head when he made 'The Shadow of the Glen,' or 'The Playboy of the Western World,' or 'Riders to the Sea,' for he allowed those wild and turbulent people and places to take such possession of his imagination that to see them at their best upon the stage, or to read of them in the sober pages of a book, is to pass, no matter what the mood of the spectator or the reader before the spell has begun its work, into a world so crammed with violence and energy, so melodious with wild splendour, that one feels one has parted the curtains of a quiet lamp-lit room, and seen the lightning leap among the hill-tops at the dawn of day.

Professor Corkery has lamented the fact that Synge was not a native speaker, which would have thrust him into the position of the heir and the saviour of the Gaelic tradition of literature. Had he written the poetry and plays that are contained in this book in the language which has so shaped his style that one might almost say he had created in one tongue and set down in another, it is indeed not unlikely that the Irish language would be nearer its rescue than it is to-day. Yet one wonders would he have had the same temper had he been born of the world that enchanted him instead of discovering it. For it is as the discoverer of an ancient world in flame and ruin that he appears in the imagination, and I cannot help believing that he delighted in the spectacle of that fiery wreckage as fiercely as he did in the contemplation of the bonfire's ingredients.

When audiences in Ireland and in America hooted at 'The Playboy' they told themselves that their national susceptibilities were outraged by the injustice of a libellous and immoral caricature. In fact they were shaken by the unaccustomed spectacle of truth, and indeed, if one's sympathies with human vanity and weakness be not as unbending as the Spartans' steel, one can sympathize with them. Nothing is more alarming to the sentimentalist than passion, nothing more disturbing than the lack of confusion between the one quality and the other, for sentimentality after all is but a mistaken identification for passion, and if there is no sentimentality in Synge it is simply that there is no confusion and no mistake.

Much has been made of the bitterness of his mind, and certainly one finds everywhere in his work—more frequently, as it seems to me, in the poetry than in the plays or in those diaries he kept in Aran and in Wicklow and West Kerry— the vision and the revelation of all that is bitterest in life, yet it is in the spectacle, not in the spectator, that the bitterness lies. He shared no more in that *dranntaíl*, that continuous dog-like grinning snarl for which the English language can supply no one word and which is such a feature of what I may call the darker aspect of the Gaelic temper, than he shared in his century's mania for what is commonly known as progress, but he took a ferocious pleasure in the study of the one as he regarded the existence of the other with a silent disdain. He

held himself apart from all things but contemplation and the
dramatic or lyrical chronicling of that contemplation, and
when he seems impatient with what to him is an over-sweet-
ness, a too facile idealization in the work of a contemporary
craftsman, instead of brooding long over it he bids it farewell
and turns swiftly to what gives him his keenest pleasure, to
'Red Dan Sally's ditch' where he will 'stretch'

> And drink in Tubber fair,
> Or poach with Red Dan Philly's bitch
> The badger and the hare.

Like so many who seem destined to become major artists
and are cut off in early life by a mysterious fate—for he died
at the age of thirty-eight after many years of ill health—he
was haunted by a sense of doom and of the coming of death,
and even in the momentary radiance of some poem about the
morning sunshine in Kerry he is confronted by the image of
'this stack of thigh-bones, jaws, and shins.' Nor had he that
love of death that consoles so many to whom it appears
luminously as friend or lover: to him it is

> . . . death that changes happy things . . .

an enemy with whom he is fated 'to lie,'

> . . . poor wretch,
> With worms eternally.

And in a mood at once reminiscent and prophetic he writes:

> They'll say I came in Eighteen-seventy-one,
> And died in Dublin. . . . What year will they write
> For my poor passage to the stall of night?

It is in this mood that his masterpiece, or what was to have
been his masterpiece, 'Deirdre of the Sorrows,' was written,
and it is this mood, born of the ever present dread of parting
from some beloved secret life held for him, that underlies the
wildest merriments of 'The Playboy' or 'The Tinker's
Wedding.' Nobody could love life with all its harshness and
grotesque ignominious familiarities as he did without the
knowledge that some unknown and dreaded thing was waiting
to tear him from its side; the hinted promise of some greater

beauty or happiness meant as little to him as it did to Catherine Earnshaw when she awoke from her dream of heaven to find herself at Wuthering Heights 'sobbing for joy.' Yet for all his horror of the unknown, so great is his power of merriment and pleasure that one feels that he might even yet awaken, young and alive and well once more, among the glens of Wicklow or the Kerry mountains, laughing for joy.

The minor dramatist echoes his age; the dramatist of genius is he who stands outside his age or, it may be, creates it. John Millington Synge came close to creating an age in Ireland: he more than any other changed the shape of Irish dramatic writing; he more than any other showed Ireland to the world, and it was an Ireland neither of fact nor of fiction but of a creative revelation. That Ireland, and indeed the rest of the world, chose to misunderstand him in the very moment of applauding him is not his loss or the world's but Ireland's. But Ireland is an adept in the art of misunderstanding, of losing, of carelessly leaving things lying about anywhere—did she not leave even her language and a dozen other less valuable things lying about like so many parcels till she found herself incapable of using them any longer?—and that perhaps is why she needed Synge to interpret her. A personal success as an artist held, of course, some interest for him; a successful entity, a busy prosperous countryside or community to be moulded into a subject-matter for his art would have bored him to death; for in his own words he was one of those for whom the important things served as a prelude to that wild and lonely mood in earth and sky that lies beyond the success or failure of the lives of men.

> I knew the stars, the flowers, and the birds,
> The grey and wintry sides of many glens,
> And did but half remember human words,
> In converse with the mountains, moors, and fens.

MICHEÁL MAC LIAMMÓIR.

Gate Theatre, Dublin, 1958.

SELECT BIBLIOGRAPHY

SEPARATE PLAYS. *The Shadow of the Glen*, 1905; *The Well of the Saints*, 1905; *The Playboy of the Western World*, 1907; *The Tinker's Wedding*, 1908; *Deirdre of the Sorrows*, 1910; *When the Moon Has Set* (first published in vol. iii of the Collected Works, 1968). The Collected Edition, 1910, was revised in 1932 with some changes of dialogue in the third Act of *The Well of the Saints*.

VERSE. *Poems and Translations*, 1909.

PROSE. *The Aran Islands*, 1907; *In Wicklow, West Kerry, and Connemara*, 1911.

COLLECTED WORKS. Vols. i and ii (Prose and Verse), edited by R. Skelton and A. Price, 1962 and 1966; vols. iii and iv (Plays), edited by Ann Saddlemeyer, 1968.

BIOGRAPHY AND CRITICISM. W. B. Yeats, *Synge and the Ireland of his Time*, 1911; P. P. Howe, *J. M. Synge: A Critical Study*, 1912; F. L. Bickley, *J. M. Synge and the Irish Dramatic Movement*, 1912; M. Bourgeois, *John Millington Synge and the Irish Theatre*, 1913; J. Masefield, *John Millington Synge: A Few Personal Recollections, with Biographical Notes*, 1915; D. Corkery, *Synge and Anglo-Irish Literature*, 1931; L. A. G. Strong, *John Millington Synge*, 1941; D. H. Greene and E. M. Stephens, *J. M. Synge, 1871–1909*, 1959; A. Price, *Synge and Anglo-Irish Drama*, 1961; D. Johnston, *John Millington Synge*, 1966; Robin Skelton, *J. M. Synge and His World*, Pictorial Biography Series, 1971; W. B. Yeats, *Synge and the Ireland of His Time*, 1972; Nicholas Grene, *Synge: A Critical Study of his Plays*, 1976; E. H. Mikhail, *J. M. Synge: Interviews and Recollections*, 1977; W. Thornton, *J. M. Synge and the Western Mind*, 1979; E. Benson, *J. M. Synge*, 1982.

BIBLIOGRAPHY AND REFERENCE. Paul Levitt (ed.), *J. M. Synge: A Bibliography of Published Criticism*, 1973; E. H. Mikhail (ed.), *J. M. Synge: A Bibliography of Criticism*, 1975; Edward A. Kopper (ed.), *John Millington Synge: A Reference Guide*, 1979.

CONTENTS

THE SHADOW OF THE GLEN

PERSONS IN THE PLAY

Dan Burke, farmer and herd
Nora Burke, his wife
Michael Dara, a young herd
A Tramp

Scene. *The last cottage at the head of a long glen in
County Wicklow*

THE SHADOW OF THE GLEN

*Cottage kitchen; turf fire on the right; a bed near it against
the wall, with a body lying on it covered with a sheet. A
door is at the other end of the room, with a low table near it,
and stools, or wooden chairs. There are a couple of glasses on
the table, and a bottle of whisky, as if for a wake, with two
cups, a tea-pot, and a home-made cake. There is another
small door near the bed. Nora Burke is moving about the
room, settling a few things, and lighting candles on the table,
looking now and then at the bed with an uneasy look. Someone knocks softly at the door. She takes up a stocking with
money from the table and puts it in her pocket. Then she
opens the door.*

TRAMP. [*Outside.*] Good evening to you, lady of the house.

NORA. Good evening kindly, stranger; it 's a wild night, God
help you, to be out in the rain falling.

TRAMP. It is, surely, and I walking to Brittas from the
Aughrim fair.

NORA. Is it walking on your feet, stranger?

TRAMP. On my two feet, lady of the house, and when I saw
the light below I thought maybe if you 'd a sup of new milk
and a quiet, decent corner where a man could sleep . . .
[*He looks in past her and sees the dead man.*] The Lord
have mercy on us all!

NORA. It doesn't matter anyway, stranger; come in out of
the rain.

TRAMP. [*Coming in slowly and going towards the bed.*] Is it
departed he is?

NORA. It is, stranger. He 's after dying on me, God forgive
him, and there I am now with a hundred sheep beyond on
the hills, and no turf drawn for the winter.

TRAMP. [*Looking closely at the dead man.*] It 's a queer look
is on him for a man that 's dead.

3

NORA. [*Half humorously.*] He was always queer, stranger;
and I suppose them that 's queer and they living men will
be queer bodies after.

TRAMP. Isn't it a great wonder you 're letting him lie there,
and he not tidied, or laid out itself?

NORA. [*Coming to the bed.*] I was afeard, stranger, for he put
a black curse on me this morning if I 'd touch his body the
time he 'd die sudden, or let any one touch it except his
sister only, and it 's ten miles away she lives, in the big
glen over the hill.

TRAMP. [*Looking at her and nodding slowly.*] It 's a queer
story he wouldn't let his own wife touch him, and he dying
quiet in his bed.

NORA. He was an old man, and an odd man, stranger, and
it 's always upon the hills he was, thinking thoughts in the
dark mist. . . . [*She pulls back a bit of the sheet.*] Lay
your hand on him now, and tell me if it 's cold he is
surely.

TRAMP. Is it getting the curse on me you 'd be, woman of
the house? I wouldn't lay my hand on him for the Lough
Nahanagan and it filled with gold.

NORA. [*Looking uneasily at the body.*] Maybe cold would be
no sign of death with the like of him, for he was always
cold, every day since I knew him . . . and every night,
stranger . . . [*she covers up his face and comes away from
the bed*]; but I 'm thinking it 's dead he is surely, for he 's
complaining a while back of a pain in his heart, and this
morning, the time he was going off to Brittas for three days
or four, he was taken with a sharp turn. Then he went
into his bed, and he was saying it was destroyed he was, the
time the shadow was going up through the glen, and when
the sun set on the bog beyond he made a great lep, and let
a great cry out of him, and stiffened himself out the like of
a dead sheep.

TRAMP. [*Crosses himself.*] God rest his soul.

NORA. [*Pouring him out a glass of whisky.*] Maybe that would
do you better than the milk of the sweetest cow in County
Wicklow.

TRAMP. The Almighty God reward you and may it be to
your good health. [*He drinks.*

NORA. [*Giving him a pipe and tobacco.*] I 've no pipes saving
his own, stranger, but they 're sweet pipes to smoke.

TRAMP. Thank you kindly, lady of the house.

NORA. Sit down now, stranger, and be taking your rest.

TRAMP. [*Filling a pipe and looking about the room.*] I 've
walked a great way through the world, lady of the house,
and seen great wonders, but I never seen a wake till this day
with fine spirits, and good tobacco, and the best of pipes,
and no one to taste them but a woman only.

NORA. Didn't you hear me say it was only after dying on me
he was when the sun went down, and how would I go out
into the glen and tell the neighbours, and I a lone woman
with no house near me?

TRAMP. [*Drinking.*] There 's no offence, lady of the house?

NORA. No offence in life, stranger. How would the like of
you, passing in the dark night, know the lonesome way I
was with no house near me at all?

TRAMP. [*Sitting down.*] I knew rightly. [*He lights his pipe,
so that there is a sharp light beneath his haggard face.*] And I
was thinking, and I coming in through the door, that it 's
many a lone woman would be afeard of the like of me in
the dark night, in a place wouldn't be as lonesome as this
place, where there aren't two living souls would see the
little light you have shining from the glass.

NORA. [*Slowly.*] I 'm thinking many would be afeard, but I
never knew what way I 'd be afeard of beggar or bishop or
any man of you at all. . . . [*She looks towards the window
and lowers her voice.*] It 's other things than the like of
you, stranger, would make a person afeard.

TRAMP. [*Looking round with a half shudder.*] It is surely,
God help us all!

NORA. [*Looking at him for a moment with curiosity.*] You 're
saying that, stranger, as if you were easy afeard.

TRAMP [*Speaking mournfully.*] Is it myself, lady of the house,
that does be walking round in the long nights, and crossing
the hills when the fog is on them, the time a little stick

would seem as big as your arm, and a rabbit as big as a bay horse, and a stack of turf as big as a towering church in the city of Dublin? If myself was easy afeard, I 'm telling you, it 's long ago I 'd have been locked into the Richmond Asylum, or maybe have run up into the back hills with nothing on me but an old shirt, and been eaten by the crows the like of Patch Darcy—the Lord have mercy on him—in the year that 's gone.

NORA. [*With interest.*] You knew Darcy?

TRAMP. Wasn't I the last one heard his living voice in the whole world?

NORA. There were great stories of what was heard at that time, but would any one believe the things they do be saying in the glen?

TRAMP. It was no lie, lady of the house. . . . I was passing below on a dark night the like of this night, and the sheep were lying under the ditch and every one of them coughing and choking like an old man, with the great rain and the fog. Then I heard a thing talking—queer talk, you wouldn't believe it at all, and you out of your dreams—and 'Merciful God,' says I, 'if I begin hearing the like of that voice out of the thick mist, I 'm destroyed surely.' Then I run and I run till I was below in Rathvanna. I got drunk that night, I got drunk in the morning, and drunk the day after—I was coming from the races beyond—and the third day they found Darcy. . . . Then I knew it was himself I was after hearing, and I wasn't afeard any more.

NORA. [*Speaking sorrowfully and slowly.*] God spare Darcy; he 'd always look in here and he passing up or passing down, and it 's very lonesome I was after him a long while [*she looks over at the bed and lowers her voice, speaking very slowly*], and then I got happy again—if it 's ever happy we are, stranger—for I got used to being lonesome.

[*A short pause; then she stands up.*

NORA. Was there any one on the last bit of the road, stranger, and you coming from Aughrim?

TRAMP. There was a young man with a drift of mountain ewes, and he running after them this way and that.

NORA. [*With a half smile.*] Far down, stranger?

TRAMP. A piece only.

> [*Nora fills the kettle and puts it on the fire.*

NORA. Maybe, if you 're not easy afeard, you 'd stay here a short while alone with himself.

TRAMP. I would surely.   A man that 's dead can do no hurt.

NORA. [*Speaking with a sort of constraint.*] I 'm going a little back to the west, stranger, for himself would go there one night and another and whistle at that place, and then the young man you 're after seeing—a kind of a farmer has come up from the sea to live in a cottage beyond—would walk round to see if there was a thing we 'd have to be done, and I 'm wanting him this night, the way he can go down into the glen when the sun goes up and tell the people that himself is dead.

TRAMP. [*Looking at the body in the sheet.*] It 's myself will go for him, lady of the house, and let you not be destroying yourself with the great rain.

NORA. You wouldn't find your way, stranger, for there 's a small path only, and it running up between two sluigs where an ass and cart would be drowned. [*She puts a shawl over her head.*] Let you be making yourself easy, and saying a prayer for his soul, and it 's not long I 'll be coming again.

TRAMP. [*Moving uneasily.*] Maybe if you 'd a piece of a grey thread and a sharp needle—there 's great safety in a needle, lady of the house—I 'd be putting a little stitch here and there in my old coat, the time I 'll be praying for his soul, and it going up naked to the saints of God.

NORA. (*Takes a needle and thread from the front of her dress and gives it to him.*] There 's the needle, stranger, and I 'm thinking you won't be lonesome, and you used to the back hills, for isn't a dead man itself more company than to be sitting alone, and hearing the winds crying, and you not knowing on what thing your mind would stay?

TRAMP. (*Slowly.*) It 's true, surely, and the Lord have mercy on us all!

> [*Nora goes out. The tramp begins stitching one of the tags in his coat, saying the 'De Profundis' under his breath.*

In an instant the sheet is drawn slowly down, and Dan Burke looks out. The tramp moves uneasily, then looks up, and springs to his feet with a movement of terror.

DAN. [*With a hoarse voice.*] Don't be afeard, stranger; a man that's dead can do no hurt.

TRAMP. [*Trembling.*] I meant no harm, your honour; and won't you leave me easy to be saying a little prayer for your soul?　　　　　　　　　　[*A long whistle is heard outside.*

DAN. [*Sitting up in his bed and speaking fiercely.*] Ah, the devil mend her. . . . Do you hear that, stranger? Did ever you hear another woman could whistle the like of that with two fingers in her mouth? [*He looks at the table hurriedly.*] I'm destroyed with the drouth, and let you bring me a drop quickly before herself will come back.

TRAMP. [*Doubtfully.*] Is it not dead you are?

DAN. How would I be dead, and I as dry as a baked bone, stranger?

TRAMP. [*Pouring out the whisky.*] What will herself say if she smells the stuff on you, for I'm thinking it's not for nothing you're letting on to be dead?

DAN. It is not, stranger; but she won't be coming near me at all, and it's not long now I'll be letting on, for I've a cramp in my back, and my hip's asleep on me, and there's been the devil's own fly itching my nose. It's near dead I was wanting to sneeze, and you blathering about the rain, and Darcy [*bitterly*]—the devil choke him—and the towering church. [*Crying out impatiently.*] Give me that whisky. Would you have herself come back before I taste a drop at all?　　　　　[*Tramp gives him the glass.*

DAN. [*After drinking.*] Go over now to that cupboard, and bring me a black stick you'll see in the west corner by the wall.

TRAMP. [*Taking a stick from the cupboard.*] Is it that, your honour?

DAN. It is, stranger; it's a long time I'm keeping that stick, for I've a bad wife in the house.

TRAMP. [*With a queer look.*] Is it herself, master of the house, and she a grand woman to talk?

DAN. It 's herself, surely, it 's a bad wife she is—a bad wife for an old man, and I 'm getting old, God help me, though I 've an arm to me still. [*He takes the stick in his hand.*] Let you wait now a short while, and it 's a great sight you 'll see in this room in two hours or three. [*He stops to listen.*] Is that somebody above?

TRAMP. [*Listening.*] There 's a voice speaking on the path.

DAN. Put that stick here in the bed and smooth the sheet the way it was lying. [*He covers himself up hastily.*] Be falling to sleep now, and don't let on you know anything, or I 'll be having your life. I wouldn't have told you at all but it 's destroyed with the drouth I was.

TRAMP. [*Covering his head.*] Have no fear, master of the house. What is it I know of the like of you that I 'd be saying a word or putting out my hand to stay you at all?
> [*He goes back to the fire, sits down on a stool with his back to the bed, and goes on stitching his coat.*]

DAN. [*Under the sheet, querulously.*] Stranger!

TRAMP. [*Quickly.*] Whisht! whisht! Be quiet, I 'm telling you; they 're coming now at the door.
> [*Nora comes in with Michael Dara, a tall, innocent young man, behind her.*

NORA. I wasn't long at all, stranger, for I met himself on the path.

TRAMP. You were middling long, lady of the house.

NORA. There was no sign from himself?

TRAMP. No sign at all, lady of the house.

NORA. [*To Michael.*] Go over now and pull down the sheet, and look on himself, Michael Dara, and you 'll see it 's the truth I 'm telling you.

MICHAEL. I will not, Nora; I do be afeard of the dead.
> [*He sits down on a stool next the table, facing the tramp. Nora puts the kettle on a lower hook of the pot-hooks, and piles turf under it.*]

NORA. [*Turning to tramp.*] Will you drink a sup of tea with myself and the young man, stranger, or [*speaking more persuasively*] will you go into the little room and stretch yourself a short while on the bed? I 'm thinking it 's destroyed

you are walking the length of that way in the great
rain.

TRAMP. Is it go away and leave you, and you having a wake,
lady of the house? I will not, surely. [*He takes a drink
from his glass, which he has beside him.*] And it 's none of
your tea I 'm asking either.
                    [*He goes on stitching.   Nora makes the tea.*

MICHAEL. [*After looking at the tramp rather scornfully for a
moment.*] That 's a poor coat you have, God help you,
and I 'm thinking it 's a poor tailor you are with it.

TRAMP. If it 's a poor tailor I am, I 'm thinking it 's a poor
herd does be running backward and forward after a little
handful of ewes, the way I seen yourself running this day,
young fellow, and you coming from the fair.
                    [*Nora comes back to the table.*

NORA. [*To Michael, in a low voice.*] Let you not mind him
at all, Michael Dara; he has a drop taken, and it 's soon
he 'll be falling asleep.

MICHAEL. It 's no lie he 's telling; I was destroyed, surely.
They were that wilful they were running off into one man's
bit of oats, and another man's bit of hay, and tumbling into
the red bog till it 's more like a pack of old goats than sheep
they were. . . . Mountain ewes is a queer breed, Nora
Burke, and I not used to them at all.

NORA. [*Settling the tea-things.*] There 's no one can drive a
mountain ewe but the men do be reared in the Glenmalure,
I 've heard them say, and above by Rathvanna, and the
Glen Imaal—men the like of Patch Darcy, God spare his
soul, who would walk through five hundred sheep and miss
one of them, and he not reckoning them at all.

MICHAEL. [*Uneasily.*] Is it the man went queer in his head
the year that 's gone?

NORA. It is, surely.

TRAMP. [*Plaintively.*] That was a great man, young fellow
—a great man, I 'm telling you. There was never a lamb
from his own ewes he wouldn't know before it was marked,
and he 'd run from this to the city of Dublin and never
catch for his breath.

NORA. [*Turning round quickly.*] He was a great man surely, stranger; and isn't it a grand thing when you hear a living man saying a good word of a dead man, and he mad dying?

TRAMP. It's the truth I'm saying, God spare his soul.

[*He puts the needle under the collar of his coat, and settles himself to sleep in the chimney corner. Nora sits down at the table: Nora and Michael's backs are turned to the bed.*

MICHAEL. [*Looking at her with a queer look.*] I heard tell this day, Nora Burke, that it was on the path below Patch Darcy would be passing up and passing down, and I heard them say he'd never pass it night or morning without speaking with yourself.

NORA. [*In a low voice.*] It was no lie you heard, Michael Dara.

MICHAEL. I'm thinking it's a power of men you're after knowing if it's in a lonesome place you live itself.

NORA. [*Giving him his tea.*] It's in a lonesome place you do have to be talking with someone, and looking for someone, in the evening of the day, and if it's a power of men I'm after knowing they were fine men, for I was a hard child to please, and a hard girl to please [*she looks at him a little sternly*], and it's a hard woman I am to please this day, Michael Dara, and it's no lie I'm telling you.

MICHAEL. [*Looking over to see that the tramp is asleep, and then pointing to the dead man.*] Was it a hard woman to please you were when you took himself for your man?

NORA. What way would I live, and I an old woman, if I didn't marry a man with a bit of a farm, and cows on it, and sheep on the back hills?

MICHAEL. [*Considering.*] That's true, Nora, and maybe it's no fool you were, for there's good grazing on it, if it is a lonesome place, and I'm thinking it's a good sum he's left behind.

NORA. [*Taking the stocking with the money from her pocket, and putting it on the table.*] I do be thinking in the long nights it was a big fool I was that time, Michael Dara; for what good is a bit of a farm with cows on it, and sheep on the back hills, when you do be sitting looking out from a door the like of that door, and seeing nothing but the mists rolling down the bog, and the mists again and they rolling up the bog, and hearing nothing but the wind crying out in the bits of broken trees were left from the great storm, and the streams roaring with the rain.

MICHAEL. [*Looking at her uneasily.*] What is it ails you this night, Nora Burke? I 've heard tell it 's the like of that talk you do hear from men, and they after being a great while on the back hills.

NORA. [*Putting out the money on the table.*] It 's a bad night, and a wild night, Michael Dara, and isn't it a great while I am at the foot of the back hills, sitting up here boiling food for himself, and food for the brood sow, and baking a cake when the night falls? [*She puts up the money listlessly in little piles on the table.*] Isn't it a long while I am sitting here in the winter and the summer, and the fine spring, with the young growing behind me and the old passing, saying to myself one time to look on Mary Brien, who wasn't that height [*holding out her hand*], and I a fine girl growing up, and there she is now with two children, and another coming on her in three months or four.   [*She pauses.*

MICHAEL. [*Moving over three of the piles.*] That 's three pounds we have now, Nora Burke.

NORA. [*Continuing in the same voice.*] And saying to myself another time, to look on Peggy Cavanagh, who had the lightest hand at milking a cow that wouldn't be easy, or turning a cake, and there she is now walking round on the roads, or sitting in a dirty old house, with no teeth in her mouth, and no sense, and no more hair than you 'd see on a bit of hill and they after burning the furze from it.

MICHAEL. That 's five pounds and ten notes, a good sum, surely! . . . It 's not that way you 'll be talking when you marry a young man, Nora Burke, and they were saying in the fair my lambs were the best lambs, and I got a grand price, for I 'm no fool now at making a bargain when my lambs are good.

NORA. What was it you got?

MICHAEL. Twenty pounds for the lot, Nora Burke. . . .
We 'd do right to wait now till himself will be quiet awhile
in the Seven Churches, and then you 'll marry me in the
chapel of Rathvanna, and I 'll bring the sheep up on the
bit of a hill you have on the back mountain, and we won't
have anything we 'd be afeard to let our minds on when
the mist is down.

NORA. [*Pouring him out some whisky.*] Why would I marry
you, Mike Dara? You 'll be getting old and I 'll be
getting old, and in a little while, I 'm telling you, you 'll be
sitting up in your bed—the way himself was sitting—with
a shake in your face, and your teeth falling, and the white
hair sticking out round you like an old bush where sheep do
be leaping a gap.

> [*Dan Burke sits up noiselessly from under the sheet, with his
> hand to his face. His white hair is sticking out
> round his head. Nora goes on slowly without
> hearing him.*

It 's a pitiful thing to be getting old, but it 's a queer thing
surely. It 's a queer thing to see an old man sitting up
there in his bed with no teeth in him, and a rough word in
his mouth, and his chin the way it would take the bark
from the edge of an oak board you 'd have building a door.
. . . God forgive me, Michael Dara, we 'll all be getting
old, but it 's a queer thing surely.

MICHAEL. It 's too lonesome you are from living a long time
with an old man, Nora, and you 're talking again like a
herd that would be coming down from the thick mist [*he
puts his arm round her*], but it 's a fine life you 'll have now
with a young man—a fine life, surely. . . .

> [*Dan sneezes violently. Michael tries to get to the door,
> but before he can do so Dan jumps out of the bed in
> queer white clothes, with the stick in his hand, and
> goes over and puts his back against it.*

MICHAEL. Son of God deliver us!

> [*Crosses himself, and goes backward across the room.*

DAN. [*Holding up his hand at him.*] Now you 'll not marry
her the time I 'm rotting below in the Seven Churches,

and you 'll see the thing I 'll give you will follow you on the back mountains when the wind is high.

MICHAEL. [*To Nora.*] Get me out of it, Nora, for the love of God. He always did what you bid him, and I 'm thinking he would do it now.

NORA. [*Looking at the tramp.*] Is it dead he is or living?

DAN. [*Turning towards her.*] It 's little you care if it 's dead or living I am; but there 'll be an end now of your fine times, and all the talk you have of young men and old men, and of the mist coming up or going down. [*He opens the door.*] You 'll walk out now from that door, Nora Burke; and it 's not to-morrow, or the next day, or any day of your life, that you 'll put in your foot through it again.

TRAMP. [*Standing up.*] It 's a hard thing you 're saying for an old man, master of the house; and what would the like of her do if you put her out on the roads?

DAN. Let her walk round the like of Peggy Cavanagh below, and be begging money at the cross-roads, or selling songs to the men. [*To Nora.*] Walk out now, Nora Burke, and it 's soon you 'll be getting old with that life, I 'm telling you; it 's soon your teeth 'll be falling and your head 'll be the like of a bush where sheep do be leaping a gap.

[*He pauses; Nora looks round at Michael.*

MICHAEL. [*Timidly*]. There 's a fine Union below in Rathdrum.

DAN. The like of her would never go there. . . . It 's lonesome roads she 'll be going and hiding herself away till the end will come, and they find her stretched like a dead sheep with the frost on her, or the big spiders maybe, and they putting their webs on her, in the butt of a ditch.

NORA. [*Angrily*]. What way will yourself be that day, Daniel Burke? What way will you be that day and you lying down a long while in your grave? For it 's bad you are living, and it 's bad you 'll be when you 're dead. [*She looks at him a moment fiercely, then half turns away and speaks plaintively again.*] Yet, if it is itself, Daniel Burke, who can help it at all, and let you be getting up into your bed, and not be taking your death with the wind blowing on you, and the rain with it, and you half in your skin.

DAN. It's proud and happy you'd be if I was getting my death the day I was shut of yourself. [*Pointing to the door.*] Let you walk out through that door, I'm telling you, and let you not be passing this way it it's hungry you are, or wanting a bed.

TRAMP. [*Pointing to Michael.*] Maybe himself would take her.

NORA. What would he do with me now?

TRAMP. Give you the half of a dry bed, and good food in your mouth.

DAN. Is it a fool you think him, stranger, or is it a fool you were born yourself? Let her walk out of that door, and let you go along with her, stranger—if it's raining itself—for it's too much talk you have surely.

TRAMP. [*Going over to Nora.*] We'll be going now, lady of the house; the rain is falling, but the air is kind, and maybe it'll be a grand morning, by the grace of God.

NORA. What good is a grand morning when I'm destroyed surely, and I going out to get my death walking the roads?

TRAMP. You'll not be getting your death with myself, lady of the house, and I knowing all the ways a man can put food in his mouth. . . . We'll be going now, I'm telling you, and the time you'll be feeling the cold, and the frost, and the great rain, and the sun again, and the south wind blowing in the glens, you'll not be sitting up on a wet ditch, the way you're after sitting in this place, making yourself old with looking on each day, and it passing you by. You'll be saying one time: 'It's a grand evening, by the grace of God,' and another time, 'It's a wild night, God help us; but it'll pass, surely.' You'll be saying . . .

DAN. [*Goes over to them, crying out impatiently.*] Go out of that door, I'm telling you, and do your blathering below in the glen. [*Nora gathers a few things into her shawl.*

TRAMP. [*At the door.*] Come along with me now, lady of the house, and it's not my blather you'll be hearing only, but you'll be hearing the herons crying out over the black lakes, and you 'll be hearing the grouse and the owls with them, and the larks and the big thrushes when the days are warm; and it 's not from the like of them you 'll be hearing a tale of getting old like Peggy Cavanagh, and losing the hair off you, and the light of your eyes, but it 's fine songs you 'll be hearing when the sun goes up, and there 'll be no old fellow wheezing, the like of a sick sheep, close to your ear.

NORA. I 'm thinking it 's myself will be wheezing that time with lying down under the heavens when the night is cold; but you 've a fine bit of talk, stranger, and it 's with yourself I 'll go. [*She goes towards the door, then turns to Dan.*] You think it 's a grand thing you 're after doing with your letting on to be dead, but what is it at all? What way would a woman live in a lonesome place the like of this place, and she not making a talk with the men passing? And what way will yourself live from this day, with none to care you? What is it you 'll have now but a black life, Daniel Burke; and it 's not long, I 'm telling you, till you 'll be lying again under that sheet, and you dead surely.

[*She goes out with the tramp. Michael is slinking after them, but Dan stops him.*

DAN. Sit down now and take a little taste of the stuff, Michael Dara. There 's a great drouth on me, and the night is young.

MICHAEL. [*Coming back to the table.*] And it 's very dry I am, surely, with the fear of death you put on me, and I after driving mountain ewes since the turn of the day.

DAN. [*Throwing away his stick.*] I was thinking to strike you, Michael Dara; but you 're a quiet man, God help you, and I don't mind you at all. [*He pours out two glasses of whisky, and gives one to Michael.*] Your good health, Michael Dara.

MICHAEL. God reward you, Daniel Burke, and may you have a long life and a quiet life, and good health with it.

[*They drink.*

CURTAIN

RIDERS TO THE SEA

PERSONS IN THE PLAY

MAURYA, an old woman
BARTLEY, her son
CATHLEEN, her daughter
NORA, a younger daughter
MEN AND WOMEN

SCENE. *An Island off the West of Ireland*

*Cottage kitchen, with nets, oilskins, spinning-wheel, some new
boards standing by the wall, etc. Cathleen, a girl of about
twenty, finishes kneading cake, and puts it down in the pot-
oven by the fire; then wipes her hands, and begins to spin at
the wheel. Nora, a young girl, puts her head in at the door.*

NORA. [*In a low voice.*] Where is she?

CATHLEEN. She 's lying down, God help her, and maybe
sleeping, if she 's able.

　　[*Nora comes in softly, and takes a bundle from under her
　　　shawl.*

CATHLEEN. [*Spinning the wheel rapidly.*] What is it you
have?

NORA. The young priest is after bringing them.   It 's a shirt
and a plain stocking were got off a drowned man in
Donegal.

　　[*Cathleen stops her wheel with a sudden movement, and
　　　leans out to listen.*

NORA. We 're to find out if it 's Michael's they are, some
time herself will be down looking by the sea.

CATHLEEN. How would they be Michael's, Nora?   How
would he go the length of that way to the far north?

NORA. The young priest says he 's known the like of it.   'If
it 's Michael's they are,' says he, 'you can tell herself he 's
got a clean burial, by the grace of God; and if they 're not
his, let no one say a word about them, for she 'll be getting
her death,' says he, 'with crying and lamenting.'

　　[*The door which Nora half closed is blown open by a gust
　　　of wind.*

CATHLEEN. [*Looking out anxiously.*] Did you ask him would
he stop Bartley going this day with the horses to the Galway fair?

NORA. 'I won't stop him,' says he; 'but let you not be

afraid. Herself does be saying prayers half through the night, and the Almighty God won't leave her destitute,' says he, 'with no son living.'

CATHLEEN. Is the sea bad by the white rocks, Nora?

NORA. Middling bad, God help us. There's a great roaring in the west, and it's worse it'll be getting when the tide's turned to the wind. [*She goes over to the table with the bundle.*] Shall I open it now?

CATHLEEN. Maybe she'd wake up on us, and come in before we'd done. [*Coming to the table.*] It's a long time we'll be, and the two of us crying.

NORA. [*Goes to the inner door and listens.*] She's moving about on the bed. She'll be coming in a minute.

CATHLEEN. Give me the ladder, and I'll put them up in the turf loft, the way she won't know of them at all, and maybe when the tide turns she'll be going down to see would he be floating from the east.

[*They put the ladder against the gable of the chimney; Cathleen goes up a few steps and hides the bundle in the turf loft. Maurya comes from the inner room.*

MAURYA. [*Looking up at Cathleen and speaking querulously.*] Isn't it turf enough you have for this day and evening?

CATHLEEN. There's a cake baking at the fire for a short space [*throwing down the turf*], and Bartley will want it when the tide turns if he goes to Connemara.

[*Nora picks up the turf and puts it round the pot-oven.*

MAURYA. [*Sitting down on a stool at the fire.*] He won't go this day with the wind rising from the south and west. He won't go this day, for the young priest will stop him surely.

NORA. He'll not stop him, mother; and I heard Eamon Simon and Stephen Pheety and Colum Shawn saying he would go.

MAURYA. Where is he itself?

NORA. He went down to see would there be another boat sailing in the week, and I'm thinking it won't be long till he's here now, for the tide's turning at the green head, and the hooker's tacking from the east.

CATHLEEN. I hear someone passing the big stones.

NORA. [*Looking out.*] He 's coming now, and he in a hurry.

BARTLEY. [*Comes in and looks round the room. Speaking sadly and quietly.*] Where is the bit of new rope, Cathleen, was bought in Connemara?

CATHLEEN. [*Coming down.*] Give it to him, Nora; it 's on a nail by the white boards. I hung it up this morning, for the pig with the black feet was eating it.

NORA. [*Giving him a rope.*] Is that it, Bartley?

MAURYA. You 'd do right to leave that rope, Bartley, hanging by the boards. [*Bartley takes the rope.*] It will be wanting in this place, I 'm telling you, if Michael is washed up to-morrow morning, or the next morning, or any morning in the week; for it 's a deep grave we 'll make him, by the grace of God.

BARTLEY. [*Beginning to work with the rope.*] I 've no halter the way I can ride down on the mare, and I must go now quickly. This is the one boat going for two weeks or beyond it, and the fair will be a good fair for horses, I heard them saying below.

MAURYA. It 's a hard thing they 'll be saying below if the body is washed up and there 's no man in it to make the coffin, and I after giving a big price for the finest white boards you 'd find in Connemara.

                                  [*She looks round at the boards.*

BARTLEY. How would it be washed up, and we after looking each day for nine days, and a strong wind blowing a while back from the west and south?

MAURYA. If it isn't found itself, that wind is raising the sea, and there was a star up against the moon, and it rising in the night. If it was a hundred horses, or a thousand horses you had itself, what is the price of a thousand horses against a son where there is one son only?

BARTLEY. [*Working at the halter, to Cathleen.*] Let you go down each day, and see the sheep aren't jumping in on the rye, and if the jobber comes you can sell the pig with the black feet if there is a good price going.

MAURYA. How would the like of her get a good price for a pig?

BARTLEY. [*To Cathleen.*] If the west winds holds with the last bit of the moon let you and Nora get up weed enough for another cock for the kelp. It 's hard set we 'll be from this day with no one in it but one man to work.

MAURYA. It 's hard set we 'll be surely the day you 're drowned with the rest. What way will I live and the girls with me, and I an old woman looking for the grave?

[*Bartley lays down the halter, takes off his old coat, and puts on a newer one of the same flannel.*

BARTLEY. [*To Nora.*] Is she coming to the pier?

NORA. [*Looking out.*] She 's passing the green head and letting fall her sails.

BARTLEY. [*Getting his purse and tobacco.*] I 'll have half an hour to go down, and you 'll see me coming again in two days, or in three days, or maybe in four days if the wind is bad.

MAURYA. [*Turning round to the fire, and putting her shawl over her head.*] Isn't it a hard and cruel man won't hear a word from an old woman, and she holding him from the sea?

CATHLEEN. It 's the life of a young man to be going on the sea, and who would listen to an old woman with one thing and she saying it over?

BARTLEY. [*Taking the halter*]. I must go now quickly. I 'll ride down on the red mare, and the grey pony 'ill run behind me. . . . The blessing of God on you.

[*He goes out.*

MAURYA. [*Crying out as he is in the door.*] He 's gone now, God spare us, and we 'll not see him again. He 's gone now, and when the black night is falling I 'll have no son left me in the world.

CATHLEEN. Why wouldn't you give him your blessing and he looking round in the door? Isn't it sorrow enough is on every one in this house without your sending him out with an unlucky word behind him, and a hard word in his ear?

[*Maurya takes up the tongs and begins raking the fire aimlessly without looking round.*

NORA. [*Turning towards her.*] You 're taking away the turf from the cake.

CATHLEEN. [*Crying out.*] The Son of God forgive us, Nora, we 're after forgetting his bit of bread.

[*She comes over to the fire.*

NORA. And it 's destroyed he 'll be going till dark night, and he after eating nothing since the sun went up.

CATHLEEN. [*Turning the cake out of the oven.*] It 's destroyed he 'll be surely. There 's no sense left on any person in a house where an old woman will be talking for ever.   [*Maurya sways herself on her stool.*

CATHLEEN. [*Cutting off some of the bread and rolling it in a cloth; to Maurya.*] Let you go down now to the spring well and give him this and he passing. You 'll see him then and the dark word will be broken, and you can say 'God speed you,' the way he 'll be easy in his mind.

MAURYA. [*Taking the bread.*] Will I be in it as soon as himself?

CATHLEEN. If you go now quickly.

MAURYA. [*Standing up unsteadily.*] It 's hard set I am to walk.

CATHLEEN. [*Looking at her anxiously.*] Give her the stick, Nora, or maybe she 'll slip on the big stones.

NORA. What stick?

CATHLEEN. The stick Michael brought from Connemara.

MAURYA. [*Taking a stick Nora gives her.*] In the big world the old people do be leaving things after them for their sons and children, but in this place it is the young men do be leaving things behind for them that do be old.

[*She goes out slowly. Nora goes over to the ladder.*

CATHLEEN. Wait, Nora, maybe she 'd turn back quickly. She 's that sorry, God help her, you wouldn't know the thing she 'd do.

NORA. Is she gone round by the bush?

CATHLEEN. [*Looking out.*] She 's gone now. Throw it down quickly, for the Lord knows when she 'll be out of

NORA. [*Getting the bundle from the loft.*] The young priest said he 'd be passing to-morrow, and we might go down and speak to him below if it 's Michael's they are surely.

CATHLEEN. [*Taking the bundle.*] Did he say what way they were found?

NORA. [*Coming down.*] 'There were two men,' said he, 'and they rowing round with poteen before the cocks crowed, and the oar of one of them caught the body, and they passing the black cliffs of the north.'

CATHLEEN. [*Trying to open the bundle.*] Give me a knife, Nora; the string 's perished with the salt water, and there 's a black knot on it you wouldn't loosen in a week.

NORA. [*Giving her a knife.*] I 've heard tell it was a long way to Donegal.

CATHLEEN. [*Cutting the string.*] It is surely. There was a man in here a while ago—the man sold us that knife—and he said if you set off walking from the rocks beyond, it would be in seven days you 'd be in Donegal.

NORA. And what time would a man take, and he floating?
    [*Cathleen opens the bundle and takes out a bit of a shirt
    and a stocking. They look at them eagerly.*

CATHLEEN. [*In a low voice.*] The Lord spare us, Nora! isn't it a queer hard thing to say if it 's his they are surely?

NORA. I 'll get his shirt off the hook the way we can put the one flannel on the cther. [*She looks through some clothes hanging in the corner.*] It 's not with them, Cathleen, and where will it be?

CATHLEEN. I 'm thinking Bartley put it on him in the morning, for his own shirt was heavy with the salt in it. [*Pointing to the corner.*] There 's a bit of a sleeve was of the same stuff. Give me that and it will do.

    [*Nora brings it to her and they compare the flannel.*

CATHLEEN. It 's the same stuff, Nora; but if it is itself, aren't there great rolls of it in the shops of Galway, and isn't it many another man may have a shirt of it as well as Michael himself?

NORA. [*Who has taken up the stocking and counted the stitches, crying out.*] It 's Michael, Cathleen, it 's Michael; God

spare his soul, and what will herself say when she hears
this story, and Bartley on the sea?

CATHLEEN. [*Taking the stocking.*] It's a plain stocking.

NORA. It's the second one of the third pair I knitted,
and I put up three-score stitches, and I dropped four
of them.

CATHLEEN. [*Counts the stitches.*] It's that number is in it.
[*Crying out.*] Ah, Nora, isn't it a bitter thing to think of
him floating that way to the far north, and no one to keen
him but the black hags that do be flying on the sea?

NORA. [*Swinging herself half round, and throwing out her
arms on the clothes.*] And isn't it a pitiful thing when there
is nothing left of a man who was a great rower and fisher
but a bit of an old shirt and a plain stocking?

CATHLEEN. [*After an instant.*] Tell me is herself coming,
Nora? I hear a little sound on the path.

NORA. [*Looking out.*] She is, Cathleen. She's coming up
to the door.

CATHLEEN. Put these things away before she'll come in.
Maybe it's easier she'll be after giving her blessing to
Bartley, and we won't let on we've heard anything the
time he's on the sea.

NORA. [*Helping Cathleen to close the bundle.*] We'll put
them here in the corner.

[*They put them into a hole in the chimney corner. Cathleen goes back to the spinning-wheel.*

NORA. Will she see it was crying I was?

CATHLEEN. Keep your back to the door the way the light 'll
not be on you.

[*Nora sits down at the chimney corner, with her back to the
door. Maurya comes in very slowly, without looking
at the girls, and goes over to her stool at the other side
of the fire. The cloth with the bread is still in her
hand. The girls look at each other, and Nora points
to the bundle of bread.*

CATHLEEN. [*After spinning for a moment.*] You didn't give
him his bit of bread?

[*Maurya begins to keen softly, without turning round.*

CATHLEEN. Did you see him riding down?

[*Maurya goes on keening.*

CATHLEEN. [*A little impatiently.*] God forgive you; isn't it a better thing to raise your voice and tell what you seen, than to be making lamentation for a thing that's done? Did you see Bartley, I'm saying to you?

MAURYA. [*With a weak voice.*] My heart's broken from this day.

CATHLEEN. [*As before.*] Did you see Bartley?

MAURYA. I seen the fearfullest thing.

CATHLEEN. [*Leaves her wheel and looks out.*] God forgive you; he's riding the mare now over the green head, and the grey pony behind him.

MAURYA. [*Starts so that her shawl falls back from her head and shows her white tossed hair. With a frightened voice.*] The grey pony behind him. . . .

CATHLEEN. [*Coming to the fire.*] What is it ails you at all?

MAURYA. [*Speaking very slowly.*] I've seen the fearfullest thing any person has seen since the day Bride Dara seen the dead man with the child in his arms.

CATHLEEN and NORA. Uah.

[*They crouch down in front of the old woman at the fire.*

NORA. Tell us what it is you seen.

MAURYA. I went down to the spring well, and I stood there saying a prayer to myself. Then Bartley came along, and he riding on the red mare with the grey pony behind him. [*She puts up her hands, as if to hide something from her eyes.*] The Son of God spare us, Nora!

CATHLEEN. What is it you seen?

MAURYA. I seen Michael himself.

CATHLEEN. [*Speaking softly.*] You did not, mother. It wasn't Michael you seen, for his body is after being found in the far north, and he's got a clean burial, by the grace of God.

MAURYA. [*A little defiantly.*] I'm after seeing him this day, and he riding and galloping. Bartley came first on the red mare, and I tried to say 'God speed you,' but something choked the words in my throat. He went by quickly; and

'The blessing of God on you,' says he, and I could say nothing. I looked up then, and I crying, at the grey pony, and there was Michael upon it—with fine clothes on him, and new shoes on his feet.

CATHLEEN. [*Begins to keen.*] It 's destroyed we are from this day. It 's destroyed, surely.

NORA. Didn't the young priest say the Almighty God won't leave her destitute with no son living?

MAURYA. [*In a low voice, but clearly.*] It 's little the like of him knows of the sea. . . . Bartley will be lost now, and let you call in Eamon and make me a good coffin out of the white boards, for I won't live after them. I 've had a husband, and a husband's father, and six sons in this house —six fine men, though it was a hard birth I had with every one of them and they coming into the world—and some of them were found and some of them were not found, but they 're gone now the lot of them. . . . There were Stephen and Shawn were lost in the great wind, and found after in the Bay of Gregory of the Golden Mouth, and carried up the two of them on one plank, and in by that door.

> [*She pauses for a moment, the girls start as if they heard something through the door that is half open behind them.*

NORA. [*In a whisper.*] Did you hear that, Cathleen? Did you hear a noise in the north-east?

CATHLEEN [*In a whisper.*] There 's someone after crying out by the seashore.

MAURYA. [*Continues without hearing anything.*] There was Sheamus and his father, and his own father again, were lost in a dark night, and not a stick or sign was seen of them when the sun went up. There was Patch after was drowned out of a curragh that turned over. I was sitting here with Bartley, and he a baby lying on my two knees, and I seen two women, and three women, and four women coming in, and they crossing themselves and not saying a word. I looked out then, and there were men coming after them, and they holding a thing in the half of a red sail, and water dripping out of it—it was a dry day, Nora—and leaving a track to the door.

[*She pauses again with her hand stretched out towards the door. It opens softly and old women begin to come in, crossing themselves on the threshold, and kneeling down in front of the stage with red petticoats over their heads.*

MAURYA. [*Half in a dream, to Cathleen.*] Is it Patch, or Michael, or what is it at all?

CATHLEEN. Michael is after being found in the far north, and when he is found there how could he be here in this place?

MAURYA. There does be a power of young men floating round in the sea, and what way would they know if it was Michael they had, or another man like him, for when a man is nine days in the sea, and the wind blowing, it's hard set his own mother would be to say what man was in it.

CATHLEEN. It's Michael, God spare him, for they're after sending us a bit of his clothes from the far north.

[*She reaches out and hands Maurya the clothes that belonged to Michael. Maurya stands up slowly, and takes them in her hands. Nora looks out.*

NORA. They're carrying a thing among them, and there's water dripping out of it and leaving a track by the big stones.

CATHLEEN. [*In a whisper to the women who have come in.*] Is it Bartley it is?

ONE OF THE WOMEN. It is, surely, God rest his soul.

[*Two younger women come in and pull out the table. Then men carry in the body of Bartley, laid on a plank, with a bit of a sail over it, and lay it on the table.*

CATHLEEN. [*To the women as they are doing so.*] What way was he drowned?

ONE OF THE WOMEN. The grey pony knocked him over into the sea, and he was washed out where there is a great surf on the white rocks.

[*Maurya has gone over and knelt down at the head of the table. The women are keening softly and swaying*

*themselves with a slow movement. Cathleen and
Nora kneel at the other end of the table. The men
kneel near the door.*

MAURYA. [*Raising her head and speaking as if she did not see
the people around her.*] They 're all gone now, and there
isn't anything more the sea can do to me. . . . I 'll have
no call now to be up crying and praying when the wind
breaks from the south, and you can hear the surf is in the
east, and the surf is in the west, making a great stir with the
two noises, and they hitting one on the other. I 'll have
no call now to be going down and getting Holy Water in
the dark nights after Samhain, and I won't care what way
the sea is when the other women will be keening. [*To
Nora.*] Give me the Holy Water, Nora; there 's a small
sup still on the dresser. [*Nora gives it to her.*

MAURYA. [*Drops Michael's clothes across Bartley's feet, and
sprinkles the Holy Water over him.*] It isn't that I haven't
prayed for you, Bartley, to the Almighty God. It isn't
that I haven't said prayers in the dark night till you
wouldn't know what I 'd be saying; but it 's a great rest
I 'll have now, and it 's time, surely. It 's a great rest I 'll
have now, and great sleeping in the long nights after Samhain, if it 's only a bit of wet flour we do have to eat, and
maybe a fish that would be stinking.

[*She kneels down again, crossing herself, and saying
prayers under her breath.*

CATHLEEN. [*To an old man.*] Maybe yourself and Eamon
would make a coffin when the sun rises. We have fine
white boards herself bought, God help her, thinking
Michael would be found, and I have a new cake you can
eat while you 'll be working.

THE OLD MAN. [*Looking at the boards.*] Are there nails
with them?

CATHLEEN. There are not, Colum; we didn't think of the
nails.

ANOTHER MAN. It 's a great wonder she wouldn't think of
the nails, and all the coffins she 's seen made already.

CATHLEEN. It 's getting old she is, and broken.

[*Maurya stands up again very slowly and spreads out the pieces of Michael's clothes beside the body, sprinkling them with the last of the Holy Water.*

NORA. [*In a whisper to Cathleen.*] She's quiet now and easy; but the day Michael was drowned you could hear her crying out from this to the spring well. It's fonder she was of Michael, and would any one have thought that?

CATHLEEN. [*Slowly and clearly.*] An old woman will be soon tired with anything she will do, and isn't it nine days herself is after crying and keening, and making great sorrow in the house?

MAURYA. [*Puts the empty cup mouth downwards on the table, and lays her hands together on Bartley's feet.*] They're all together this time, and the end is come. May the Almighty God have mercy on Bartley's soul, and on Michael's soul, and on the souls of Sheamus and Patch, and Stephen and Shawn [*bending her head*]; and may He have mercy on my soul, Nora, and on the soul of every one is left living in the world.

[*She pauses, and the keen rises a little more loudly from the women, then sinks away.*

MAURYA. [*Continuing.*] Michael has a clean burial in the far north, by the grace of the Almighty God. Bartley will have a fine coffin out of the white boards, and a deep grave surely. What more can we want than that? No man at all can be living for ever, and we must be satisfied.

[*She kneels down again and the curtain falls slowly.*

THE TINKER'S WEDDING

PERSONS IN THE PLAY

MICHAEL BYRNE, a tinker
MARY BYRNE, an old woman, his mother
SARAH CASEY, a young tinker woman
A PRIEST

SCENE. *A village roadside after nightfall*

PREFACE

*The drama is made serious—in the French sense of the word—
not by the degree in which it is taken up with problems that are
serious in themselves, but by the degree in which it gives the
nourishment, not very easy to define, on which our imaginations
live. We should not go to the theatre as we go to a chemist's or
a dram-shop, but as we go to a dinner where the food we need is
taken with pleasure and excitement. This was nearly always so
in Spain and England and France when the drama was at its
richest—the infancy and decay of the drama tend to be didactic
—but in these days the playhouse is too often stocked with the
drugs of many seedy problems, or with the absinthe or vermouth
of the last musical comedy.*

*The drama, like the symphony, does not teach or prove any-
thing. Analysts with their problems, and teachers with their
systems, are soon as old-fashioned as the pharmacopoeia of Galen
—look at Ibsen and the Germans—but the best plays of Ben
Jonson and Molière can no more go out of fashion than the
blackberries on the hedges.*

*Of the things which nourish the imagination humour is one of
the most needful, and it is dangerous to limit or destroy it.
Baudelaire calls laughter the greatest sign of the Satanic
element in man; and where a country loses its humour, as some
towns in Ireland are doing, there will be morbidity of mind, as
Baudelaire's mind was morbid.*

*In the greater part of Ireland, however, the whole people,
from the tinkers to the clergy, have still a life, and view of life,
that are rich and genial and humorous. I do not think that these
country people, who have so much humour themselves, will mind
being laughed at without malice, as the people in every country
have been laughed at in their own comedies.*

J. M. S.

2nd December 1907.

Note.—*The Tinker's Wedding* was first written a few years ago,
about the time I was working at *Riders to the Sea* and *In the Shadow
of the Glen.* I have re-written it since.

33

THE TINKER'S WEDDING

Act I

A village roadside after nightfall.   A fire of sticks is burning near the ditch a little to the right.   Michael is working beside it.   In the background, on the left, a sort of tent and ragged clothes drying on the hedge.   On the right a chapel gate.

SARAH CASEY. [*Coming in on right, eagerly.*] We'll see his reverence this place, Michael Byrne, and he passing backward to his house to-night.

MICHAEL. [*Grimly.*] That'll be a sacred and a sainted joy!

SARAH. [*Sharply.*] It'll be small joy for yourself if you aren't ready with my wedding ring. [*She goes over to him.*] Is it near done this time, or what way is it at all?

MICHAEL. A poor way only, Sarah Casey, for it's the divil's job making a ring, and you'll be having my hands destroyed in a short while the way I'll not be able to make a tin can at all maybe at the dawn of day.

SARAH. [*Sitting down beside him and throwing sticks on the fire.*] If it's the divil's job, let you mind it, and leave your speeches that would choke a fool.

MICHAEL. [*Slowly and glumly.*] And it's you'll go talking of fools, Sarah Casey, when no man did ever hear a lying story even of your like unto this mortal day.   You to be going beside me a great while, and rearing a lot of them, and then to be setting off with your talk of getting married, and your driving me to it, and I not asking it at all.

[*Sarah turns her back to him and arranges something in the ditch.*

MICHAEL. [*Angrily.*] Can't you speak a word when I'm asking what is it ails you since the moon did change?

SARAH. [*Musingly.*] I'm thinking there isn't anything ails

35

me, Michael Byrne; but the springtime is a queer time, and it 's queer thoughts maybe I do think at whiles.

MICHAEL. It 's hard set you 'd be to think queerer than welcome, Sarah Casey; but what will you gain dragging me to the priest this night, I 'm saying, when it 's new thoughts you 'll be thinking at the dawn of day?

SARAH. [Teasingly.] It 's at the dawn of day I do be thinking I 'd have a right to be going off to the rich tinkers do be travelling from Tibradden to the Tara Hill; for it 'd be a fine life to be driving with young Jaunting Jim, where there wouldn't be any big hills to break the back of you, with walking up and walking down.

MICHAEL. [With dismay.] It 's the like of that you do be thinking!

SARAH. The like of that, Michael Byrne, when there is a bit of sun in it, and a kind air, and a great smell coming from the thorn-trees is above your head.

MICHAEL. [Looks at her for a moment with horror and then hands her the ring.] Will that fit you now?

SARAH. [Trying it on.] It 's making it tight you are, and the edges sharp on the tin.

MICHAEL. [Looking at it carefully.] It 's the fat of your own finger, Sarah Casey; and isn't it a mad thing I 'm saying again that you 'd be asking marriage of me, or making a talk of going away from me, and you thriving and getting your good health by the grace of the Almighty God?

SARAH. [Giving it back to him.] Fix it now, and it 'll do, if you 're wary you don't squeeze it again.

MICHAEL. [Moodily, working again.] It 's easy saying be wary; there 's many things easy said, Sarah Casey, you 'd wonder a fool even would be saying at all. [He starts violently.] The divil mend you, I 'm scalded again!

SARAH. [Scornfully.] If you are, it 's a clumsy man you are this night, Michael Byrne [raising her voice]; and let you make haste now, or herself will be coming with the porter.

MICHAEL. [Defiantly, raising his voice.] Let me make haste? I 'll be making haste maybe to hit you a great clout; for I 'm thinking it 's the like of that you want. I 'm think-

ing on the day I got you above at Rathvanna, and the way
you began crying out and we coming down off the hill,
crying out and saying 'I 'll go back to my ma'; and I 'm
thinking on the way I came behind you that time, and hit
you a great clout in the lug, and how quiet and easy it was
you came along with me from that hour to this present·day.

SARAH. [*Standing up and throwing all her sticks into the
fire.*] And a big fool I was, too, maybe; but we 'll be seeing
Jaunting Jim to-morrow in Ballinaclash, and he after
getting a great price for his white foal in the horse fair of
Wicklow, the way it 'll be a great sight to see him squander-
ing his share of gold, and he with a grand eye for a fine
horse, and a grand eye for a woman.

MICHAEL. [*Working again with impatience.*] The divil do
him good with the two of them.

SARAH. [*Kicking up the ashes with her foot.*] Ah, he 's a great
lad, I 'm telling you, and it 's proud and happy I 'll be to
see him, and he the first one called me the Beauty of
Ballinacree, a fine name for a woman.

MICHAEL. [*With contempt.*] It 's the like of that name they
do be putting on the horses they have below racing in
Arklow. It 's easy pleased you are, Sarah Casey, easy
pleased with a big word, or the liar speaks it.

SARAH. Liar!

MICHAEL. Liar, surely.

SARAH. [*Indignantly.*] Liar, is it? Didn't you ever hear tell
of the peelers followed me ten miles along the Glen Malure,
and they talking love to me in the dark night; or of the
children you 'll meet coming from school and they saying
one to the other: 'It 's this day we seen Sarah Casey, the
Beauty of Ballinacree, a great sight, surely.'

MICHAEL. God help the lot of them.

SARAH. It 's yourself you 'll be calling God to help, in two
weeks or three, when you 'll be waking up in the dark night
and thinking you see me coming with the sun on me, and I
driving a high cart with Jaunting Jim going behind. It 's
lonesome and cold you 'll be feeling the ditch where you 'll
be lying down that night, I 'm telling you, and you hearing

the old woman making a great noise in her sleep, and the
bats squeaking in the trees.

MICHAEL. Whisht. I hear someone coming the road.

SARAH. [*Looking out right.*] It 's someone coming forward
from the doctor's door.

MICHAEL. It 's often his reverence does be in there playing
cards, or drinking a sup, or singing songs, until the dawn
of day.

SARAH. It 's a big boast of a man with a long step on him and
a trumpeting voice. It 's his reverence, surely; and if you
have the ring down, it 's a great bargain we 'll make now
and he after drinking his glass.

MICHAEL. [*Going to her and giving her the ring.*] There 's
your ring, Sarah Casey; but I 'm thinking he 'll walk by
and not stop to speak with the like of us at all.

SARAH. [*Tidying herself, in great excitement.*] Let you be
sitting here and keeping a great blaze; the way he can look
on my face; and let you seem to be working, for it 's great
love the like of him have to talk of work.

MICHAEL. [*Moodily, sitting down and beginning to work at a
tin can*]. Great love, surely.

SARAH. [*Eagerly.*] Make a great blaze now, Michael Byrne.
[*The Priest comes in on right; she comes forward in front
of him.*

SARAH. [*In a very plausible voice.*] Good evening, your
reverence. It 's a grand fine night, by the grace of God.

PRIEST. The Lord have mercy on us! What kind of a
living woman is it that you are at all?

SARAH. It 's Sarah Casey I am, your reverence, the Beauty
of Ballinacree, and it 's Michael Byrne is below in the ditch.

PRIEST. A holy pair surely! Let you get out of my way.
[*He tries to pass by.*

SARAH. [*Keeping in front of him.*] We are wanting a little
word with your reverence.

PRIEST. I haven't a halfpenny at all. Leave the road, I 'm
saying.

SARAH. It isn't a halfpenny we 're asking, holy father; but
we were thinking maybe we 'd have a right to be getting

married; and we were thinking it 's yourself would marry
us for not a halfpenny at all; for you 're a kind man, your
reverence, a kind man with the poor.

PRIEST. [*With astonishment.*] Is it marry you for nothing
at all?

SARAH. It is, your reverence; and we were thinking maybe
you 'd give us a little small bit of silver to pay for the ring.

PRIEST. [*Loudly.*] Let you hold your tongue; let you be
quiet, Sarah Casey. I 've no silver at all for the like of
you; and if you want to be married, let you pay your pound.
I 'd do it for a pound only, and that 's making it a sight
cheaper than I 'd make it for one of my own pairs is living
here in the place.

SARAH. Where would the like of us get a pound, your
reverence?

PRIEST. Wouldn't you easy get it with your selling asses, and
making cans, and your stealing east and west in Wicklow
and Wexford and the county Meath? [*He tries to pass her.*]
Let you leave the road, and not be plaguing me more.

SARAH. [*Pleadingly, taking money from her pocket.*] Wouldn't
you have a little mercy on us, your reverence? [*Holding out
money.*] Wouldn't you marry us for a half a sovereign, and
it a nice shiny one with a view on it of the living king's
mamma?

PRIEST. If it 's ten shillings you have, let you get ten more
the same way, and I 'll marry you then.

SARAH. [*Whining.*] It 's two years we are getting that bit,
your reverence, with our pence and our halfpence and an
odd threepenny bit; and if you don't marry us now, himself and the old woman, who has a great drouth, will be
drinking it to-morrow in the fair [*she puts her apron to her
eyes, half sobbing*], and then I won't be married any time,
and I 'll be saying till I 'm an old woman: 'It 's a cruel and
a wicked thing to be bred poor.'

PRIEST. [*Turning up towards the fire.*] Let you not be crying, Sarah Casey. It 's a queer woman you are to be
crying at the like of that, and you your whole life walking
the roads.

SARAH. [*Sobbing.*] It 's two years we are getting the gold, your reverence, and now you won't marry us for that bit, and we hard-working poor people do be making cans in the dark night, and blinding our eyes with the black smoke from the bits of twigs we do be burning.

> [*An old woman is heard singing tipsily on the left.*

PRIEST. [*Looking at the can Michael is making.*] When will you have that can done, Michael Byrne?

MICHAEL. In a short space only, your reverence, for I 'm putting the last dab of solder on the rim.

PRIEST. Let you get a crown along with the ten shillings and the gallon can, Sarah Casey, and I will wed you so.

MARY. [*Suddenly shouting behind, tipsily.*] Larry was a fine lad, I 'm saying; Larry was a fine lad, Sarah Casey——

MICHAEL. Whisht, now, the two of you. There 's my mother coming, and she 'd have us destroyed if she heard the like of that talk the time she 's been drinking her fill.

MARY. [*Comes in singing.*]

> And when he asked him what way he 'd die,
>   And he hanging unrepented,
> 'Begob,' says Larry, 'that 's all in my eye,
>   By the clergy first invented.'

SARAH. Give me the jug now, or you 'll have it spilt in the ditch.

MARY. [*Holding the jug with both her hands, in a stilted voice.*] Let you leave me easy, Sarah Casey. I won't spill it, I 'm saying. God help you; are you thinking it 's frothing full to the brim it is at this hour of the night, and I after carrying it in my two hands a long step from Jemmy Neill's?

MICHAEL. [*Anxiously.*] Is there a sup left at all?

SARAH. [*Looking into the jug.*] A little small sup only, I 'm thinking.

MARY. [*Sees the Priest, and holds out jug towards him.*] God save your reverence. I 'm after bringing down a smart drop; and let you drink it up now, for it 's a middling drouthy man you are at all times, God forgive you, and this night is cruel dry.

[*She tries to go towards him.   Sarah holds her back.*

PRIEST. [*Waving her away.*] Let you not be falling to the flames.   Keep off, I 'm saying.

MARY. [*Persuasively.*] Let you not be shy of us, your reverence.   Aren't we all sinners, God help us!   Drink a sup now, I 'm telling you; and we won't let on a word about it till the Judgment Day.

[*She takes up a tin mug, pours some porter into it, and gives it to him.*

MARY. [*Singing, and holding the jug in her hand.*]

> A lonesome ditch in Ballygan
> The day you 're beating a tenpenny can;
> A lonesome bank in Ballyduff
> The time . . .

[*She breaks off.*

It 's a bad, wicked song, Sarah Casey; and let you put me down now in the ditch, and I won't sing it till himself will be gone; for it 's bad enough he is, I 'm thinking, without ourselves making him worse.

SARAH. [*Putting her down, to the Priest, half laughing.*] Don't mind her at all, your reverence.   She 's no shame the time she 's a drop taken; and if it was the Holy Father from Rome was in it, she 'd give him a little sup out of her mug, and say the same as she 'd say to yourself.

MARY. [*To the Priest.*] Let you drink it up, holy father. Let you drink it up, I 'm saying, and not be letting on you wouldn't do the like of it, and you with a stack of pint bottles above reaching the sky.

PRIEST. [*With resignation.*] Well, here 's to your good health and God forgive us all.   [*He drinks.*

MARY. That 's right now, your reverence, and the blessing of God be on you.   Isn't it a grand thing to see you sitting down, with no pride in you, and drinking a sup with the like of us, and we the poorest, wretched, starving creatures you 'd see any place on the earth?

PRIEST. If it 's starving you are itself, I 'm thinking it 's well for the like of you that do be drinking when there 's drouth on you, and lying down to sleep when your legs are stiff. [*He sighs gloomily.*] What would you do if it was the like of myself you were, saying Mass with your mouth dry, and running east and west for a sick call maybe, and hearing the rural people again and they saying their sins?

MARY. [*With compassion.*] It 's destroyed you must be hearing the sins of the rural people on a fine spring.

PRIEST. [*With despondency.*] It 's a hard life, I 'm telling you, a hard life, Mary Byrne, and there 's the bishop coming in the morning, and he an old man, would have you destroyed if he seen a thing at all.

MARY. [*With great sympathy*.] It 'd break my heart to hear you talking and sighing the like of that, your reverence. [*She pats him on the knee.*] Let you rouse up now, if it 's a poor, single man you are itself, and I 'll be singing you songs unto the dawn of day.

PRIEST. [*Interrupting her.*] What is it I want with your songs when it 'd be better for the like of you, that 'll soon die, to be down on your two knees saying prayers to the Almighty God?

MARY. If it 's prayers I want, you 'd have a right to say one yourself, holy father; for we don't have them at all, and I 've heard tell a power of times it 's that you 're for. Say one now, your reverence; for I 've heard a power of queer things and I walking the world, but there 's one thing I never heard any time, and that 's a real priest saying a prayer.

PRIEST. The Lord protect us!

MARY. It 's no lie, holy father. I often heard the rural people making a queer noise and they going to rest; but who 'd mind the like of them? And I 'm thinking it should be great game to hear a scholar, the like of you, speaking Latin to the saints above.

PRIEST. [*Scandalized.*] Stop your talking, Mary Byrne; you 're an old, flagrant heathen, and I 'll stay no more with the lot of you. [*He rises.*

MARY. [*Catching hold of him.*] Stop till you say a prayer,

your reverence; stop till you say a little prayer, I 'm telling you, and I 'll give you my blessing and the last sup from the jug.

PRIEST. [*Breaking away.*] Leave me go, Mary Byrne; for I never met your like for hard abominations the score and two years I 'm living in the place.

MARY. [*Innocently.*] Is that the truth?

PRIEST. It is, then, and God have mercy on your soul.

[*The Priest goes towards the left, and Sarah follows him.*

SARAH. [*In a low voice.*] And what time will you do the thing I 'm asking, holy father? for I 'm thinking you 'll do it surely, and not have me growing into an old, wicked heathen like herself.

MARY. [*Calling out shrilly.*] Let you be walking back here, Sarah Casey, and not be talking whisper-talk with the like of him in the face of the Almighty God.

SARAH. [*To the Priest.*] Do you hear her now, your reverence? Isn't it true, surely, she 's an old, flagrant heathen, would destroy the world?

PRIEST. [*To Sarah, moving off.*] Well, I 'll be coming down early to the chapel, and let you come to me a while after you see me passing, and bring the bit of gold along with you, and the tin can. I'll marry you for them two, though it 's a pitiful small sum; for I wouldn't be easy in my soul if I left you growing into an old, wicked heathen the like of her.

SARAH. [*Following him out.*] The blessing of the Almighty God be on you, holy father, and that He may reward and watch you from this present day.

MARY. [*Nudging Michael.*] Did you see that, Michael Byrne? Didn't you hear me telling you she 's flighty a while back since the change of the moon? With her fussing for marriage, and she making whisper-talk with one man or another man along by the road.

MICHAEL. Whisht now, or she 'll knock the head of you the time she comes back.

MARY. Ah, it 's a bad, wicked way the world is this night, if there 's a fine air in it itself. You 'd never have seen me,

and I a young woman, making whisper-talk with the like
of him, and he the fearfullest old fellow you 'd see any
place walking the world.   [*Sarah comes back quickly.*

MARY. [*Calling out to her.*] What is it you 're after whispering above with himself?

SARAH. [*Exultingly.*] Lie down, and leave us in peace.
    [*She whispers with Michael.*

MARY. [*Poking out her pipe with a straw, sings.*]

She 'd whisper with one, and she 'd whisper with two——

[*written in margin: pipe & booze for a female*]

[*She breaks off coughing.*] My singing voice is gone for this
night, Sarah Casey. [*She lights her pipe.*] But if it 's flighty
you are itself, you 're a grand, handsome woman, the glory
of tinkers, the pride of Wicklow, the Beauty of Ballinacree.
I wouldn't have you lying down and you lonesome to sleep
this night in a dark ditch when the spring is coming in the
trees; so let you sit down there by the big bough, and I 'll
be telling you the finest story you 'd hear any place from
Dundalk to Ballinacree, with great queens in it, making
themselves matches from the start to the end, and they
with shiny silks on them the length of the day, and white
shifts for the night.

MICHAEL. [*Standing up with the tin can in his hand.*] Let
you go asleep, and not have us destroyed.

MARY. [*Lying back sleepily.*] Don't mind him, Sarah Casey.
Sit down now, and I 'll be telling you a story would be fit
to tell a woman the like of you in the springtime of the
year.

SARAH. [*Taking the can from Michael, and tying it up in a
piece of sacking.*] That 'll not be rusting now in the dews of
night.   I 'll put it up in the ditch the way it will be handy
in the morning; and now we 've that done, Michael Byrne,
I 'll go along with you and welcome for Tim Flaherty's
hens.   [*She puts the can in the ditch.*

MARY. [*Sleepily.*] I 've a grand story of the great queens of
Ireland, with white necks on them the like of Sarah Casey,
and fine arms would hit you a slap the way Sarah Casey
would hit you.

SARAH. [*Beckoning on the left.*] Come along now, Michael, while she's falling asleep.

> [*He goes towards left.   Mary sees that they are going, starts up suddenly, and turns over on her hands and knees.*

MARY. [*Piteously.*] Where is it you're going? Let you walk back here, and not be leaving me lonesome when the night is fine.

SARAH. Don't be waking the world with your talk when we're going up through the back wood to get two of Tim Flaherty's hens are roosting in the ash-tree above at the well.

MARY. And it's leaving me lone you are? Come back here, Sarah Casey. Come back here, I'm saying; or if it's off you must go, leave me the two little coppers you have, the way I can walk up in a short while, and get another pint for my sleep.

SARAH. It's too much you have taken. Let you stretch yourself out and take a long sleep; for isn't that the best thing any woman can do, and she an old drinking heathen like yourself?   [*She and Michael go out left.*

MARY. [*Standing up slowly.*] It's gone they are and I with my feet that weak under me you'd knock me down with a rush; and my head with a noise in it the like of what you'd hear in a stream and it running between two rocks and rain falling. [*She goes over to the ditch where the can is tied in sacking, and takes it down.*] What good am I this night, God help me? What good are the grand stories I have when it's few would listen to an old woman, few but a girl maybe would be in great fear the time her hour was come, or a little child wouldn't be sleeping with the hunger on a cold night? [*She takes the can from the sacking, and fits in three empty bottles and straw in its place, and ties them up.*] Maybe the two of them have a good right to be walking out the little short while they'd be young; but if they have itself they'll not keep Mary Byrne from her full pint when the night's fine, and there's a dry moon in the sky. [*She takes up the can, and puts the package back in the ditch.*] Jemmy Neill 's a decent lad; and he 'll give me a good drop for the can; and maybe if I keep near the peelers to-morrow for the first bit of the fair, herself won't strike me at all; and if she does itself, what 's a little stroke on your head beside sitting lonesome on a fine night, hearing the dogs barking, and the bats squeaking, and you saying over, it 's a short while only till you die.

[*She goes out singing ' The night before Larry was stretched.'*

CURTAIN

Act II

The same scene as before. Early morning. Sarah is washing her face in an old bucket; then plaits her hair. Michael is tidying himself also. Mary Byrne is asleep against the ditch.

SARAH. [*To Michael, with pleased excitement.*] Go over, now, to the bundle beyond, and you 'll find a kind of a red handkerchief to put upon your neck, and a green one for myself.

MICHAEL. [*Getting them.*] You 're after spending more money on the like of them. Well, it 's a power we 're losing this time, and we not gaining a thing at all. [*With the handkerchief.*] Is it them two?

SARAH. It is, Michael. [*She takes one of them.*] Let you tackle that one round under your chin; and let you not forget to take your hat from your head when we go up into the church. I asked Biddy Flynn below, that 's after marrying her second man, and she told me it 's the like of that they do. [*Mary yawns, and turns over in her sleep.*

SARAH. [*With anxiety.*] There she is waking up on us, and I thinking we 'd have the job done before she 'd know of it at all.

MICHAEL. She 'll be crying out now, and making game of us, and saying it 's fools we are surely.

SARAH. I 'll send her to her sleep again, or get her out of it one way or another; for it 'd be a bad case to have a divil's scholar the like of her turning the priest against us maybe with her godless talk.

MARY. [*Waking up, and looking at them with curiosity, blandly.*] That 's fine things you have on you, Sarah Casey; and it 's a great stir you 're making this day, washing your face. I 'm that used to the hammer, I wouldn't hear it at all; but washing is a rare thing, and you 're after waking me up, and I having a great sleep in the sun.

[*She looks around cautiously at the bundle in which she has hidden the bottles.*

SARAH. [*Coaxingly.*] Let you stretch out again for a sleep, Mary Byrne; for it 'll be a middling time yet before we go to the fair.

MARY. [*With suspicion.*] That 's a sweet tongue you have, Sarah Casey; but if sleep 's a grand thing, it 's a grand thing to be waking up a day the like of this, when there 's a warm sun in it, and a kind air, and you 'll hear the cuckoos singing and crying out on the top of the hills.

SARAH. If it 's that gay you are, you 'd have a right to walk down and see would you get a few halfpence from the rich men do be driving early to the fair.

MARY. When rich men do be driving early it 's queer tempers they have, the Lord forgive them; the way it 's little but bad words and swearing out you 'd get from them all.

SARAH. [*Losing her temper and breaking out fiercely.*] Then if you 'll neither beg nor sleep, let you walk off from this place where you 're not wanted, and not have us waiting for you maybe at the turn of day.

MARY. [*Rather uneasy, turning to Michael.*] God help our spirits, Michael; there she is again rousing cranky from the break of dawn. Oh! isn't she a terror since the moon did change? [*She gets up slowly.*] And I 'd best be going forward to sell the gallon can.

[*She goes over and takes up the bundle.*

SARAH. [*Crying out angrily.*] Leave that down, Mary Byrne. Oh! aren't you the scorn of women to think that you 'd have that drouth and roguery on you that you 'd go drinking the can and the dew not dried from the grass?

MARY. [*In a feigned tone of pacification with the bundle still in her hand.*] It 's not a drouth but a heartburn I have this day, Sarah Casey, so I 'm going down to cool my gullet at the blessed well; and I 'll sell the can to the parson's daughter below, a harmless poor creature would fill your hand with shillings for a brace of lies.

SARAH. Leave down the tin can, Mary Byrne, for I hear the drouth upon your tongue to-day.

MARY. There 's not a drink-house from this place to the

fair, Sarah Casey; the way you 'll find me below with the full price, and not a farthing gone. [*She turns to go off left.*

SARAH. [*Jumping up, and picking up the hammer threateningly.*] Put down that can, I 'm saying.

MARY. [*Looking at her for a moment in terror, and putting down the bundle in the ditch.*] Is it raving mad you 're going, Sarah Casey, and you the pride of women to destroy the world?

SARAH. [*Going up to her, and giving her a push off left.*] I 'll show you if it 's raving mad I am. Go on from this place, I 'm saying, and be wary now.

MARY. [*Turning back after her.*] If I go, I 'll be telling old and young you 're a weathered heathen savage, Sarah Casey, the one did put down a head of the parson's cabbage to boil in the pot with your clothes [*the Priest comes in behind her, on the left, and listens*], and quenched the flaming candles on the throne of God the time your shadow fell within the pillars of the chapel door.

[*Sarah turns on her, and she springs round nearly into the Priest's arms. When she sees him, she claps her shawl over her mouth, and goes up towards the ditch, laughing to herself.*

PRIEST. [*Going to Sarah, half terrified at the language that he has heard.*] Well, aren't you a fearful lot? I 'm thinking it 's only humbug you were making at the fall of night, and you won't need me at all.

SARAH. [*With anger still in her voice.*] Humbug is it! Would you be turning back upon your spoken promise in the face of God?

PRIEST. [*Dubiously.*] I 'm thinking you were never christened, Sarah Casey; and it would be a queer job to go dealing Christian sacraments unto the like of you. [*Persuasively, feeling in his pocket.*] So it would be best, maybe, I 'd give you a shilling for to drink my health, and let you walk on, and not trouble me at all.

SARAH. That 's your talking, is it? If you don't stand to your spoken word, holy father, I 'll make my own complaint to the mitred bishop in the face of all.

PRIEST. You 'd do that!

SARAH. I would surely, holy father, if I walked to the city of Dublin with blood and blisters on my naked feet.

PRIEST. [*Uneasily scratching his ear.*] I wish this day was done, Sarah Casey; for I 'm thinking it 's a risky thing getting mixed in any matters with the like of you.

SARAH. Be hasty then, and you 'll have us done with before you 'd think at all.

PRIEST. [*Giving in.*] Well, maybe it 's right you are, and let you come up to the chapel when you see me looking from the door. [*He goes up into the chapel.*

SARAH. [*Calling after him.*] We will, and God preserve you, holy father.

MARY. [*Coming down to them, speaking with amazement and consternation, but without anger.*] Going to the chapel! It 's at marriage you 're fooling again, maybe? [*Sarah turns her back on her.*] It was for that you were washing your face, and you after sending me for porter at the fall of night the way I 'd drink a good half from the jug? [*Going round in front of Sarah.*] Is it at marriage you 're fooling again?

SARAH. [*Triumphantly.*] It is, Mary Byrne. I 'll be married now in a short while; and from this day there will no one have a right to call me a dirty name, and I selling cans in Wicklow or Wexford or the city of Dublin itself.

MARY. [*Turning to Michael.*] And it 's yourself is wedding her, Michael Byrne?

MICHAEL. [*Gloomily.*] It is, God spare us.

MARY. [*Looks at Sarah for a moment, and then bursts out into a laugh of derision.*] Well, she 's a tight, hardy girl, and it 's no lie; but I never knew till this day it was a black born fool I had for a son. You 'll breed asses, I 've heard them say, and poaching dogs, and horses 'd go licking the wind, but it 's a hard thing, God help me, to breed sense in a son.

MICHAEL. [*Gloomily.*] If I didn't marry her, she 'd be walking off to Jaunting Jim maybe at the fall of night; and it 's well yourself knows there isn't the like of her for getting money and selling songs to the men.

MARY. And you 're thinking it 's paying gold to his reverence would make a woman stop when she 's a mind to go?

SARAH. [*Angrily.*] Let you not be destroying us with your talk when I 've as good a right to a decent marriage as any speckled female does be sleeping in the black hovels above, would choke a mule.

MARY. [*Soothingly.*] It 's as good a right you have, surely, Sarah Casey, but what good will it do? Is it putting that ring on your finger will keep you from getting an aged woman and losing the fine face you have, or be easing your pains; when it 's the grand ladies do be married in silk dresses, with rings of gold, that do pass any woman with their share of torment in the hour of birth, and do be paying the doctors in the city of Dublin a great price at that time, the like of what you 'd pay for a good ass and a cart?

[*She sits down.*

SARAH. [*Puzzled.*] Is that the truth?

MARY. [*Pleased with the point she has made.*] Wouldn't any know it 's the truth? Ah, it 's few short years you are yet in the world, Sarah Casey, and it 's little or nothing at all maybe you know about it.

SARAH. [*Vehement but uneasy.*] What is it yourself knows of the fine ladies when they wouldn't let the like of you go near to them at all?

MARY. If you do be drinking a little sup in one town and another town, it 's soon you get great knowledge and a great sight into the world. You 'll see men there, and women there, sitting up on the ends of barrels in the dark night, and they making great talk would soon have the like of you, Sarah Casey, as wise as a March hare.

MICHAEL. [*To Sarah.*] That 's the truth she 's saying, and maybe, if you 've sense in you at all you 'd have a right still to leave your fooling, and not be wasting our gold.

SARAH. [*Decisively.*] If it 's wise or fool I am, I 've made a good bargain, and I 'll stand to it now.

MARY. What is it he 's making you give?

MICHAEL. The ten shillings in gold, and the tin can is above tied in the sack.

MARY. [*Looking at the bundle with surprise and dread.*] The bit of gold and the tin can, is it?

MICHAEL. The half a sovereign and the gallon can.

MARY. [*Scrambling to her feet quickly.*] Well, I think I 'll be walking off the road to the fair the way you won't be destroying me going too fast on the hills. [*She goes a few steps towards the left, then turns and speaks to Sarah very persuasively.*] Let you not take the can from the sack, Sarah Casey; for the people is coming above would be making game of you, and pointing their fingers if they seen you do the like of that. Let you leave it safe in the bag, I 'm saying, Sarah darling. It 's that way will be best.

[*She goes towards left, and pauses for a moment, looking about her with embarrassment.*

MICHAEL. [*In a low voice.*] What ails her at all?

SARAH. [*Anxiously.*] It 's real wicked she does be when you hear her speaking as easy as that.

MARY. [*To herself.*] I 'd be safer in the chapel, I 'm thinking; for if she caught me after on the road, maybe she would kill me then.

[*She comes hobbling back towards the right.*

SARAH. Where is it you 're going? It isn't that way we 'll be walking to the fair.

MARY. I 'm going up into the chapel to give you my blessing and hear the priest saying his prayers. It 's a lonesome road is running below to Grianan, and a woman would never know the things might happen her and she walking single in a lonesome place.

[*As she reaches the chapel gate, the Priest comes to it in his surplice.*

PRIEST. [*Crying out.*] Come along now. Is it the whole day you 'd keep me here saying my prayers, and I getting my death with not a bit in my stomach, and my breakfast in ruins, and the Lord Bishop maybe driving on the road to-day?

SARAH. We 're coming now, holy father.

PRIEST. Give me the bit of gold into my hand.

SARAH. It 's here, holy father.

[*She gives it to him.   Michael takes the bundle from the ditch and brings it over, standing a little behind Sarah.   He feels the bundle and looks at Mary with a meaning look.*

PRIEST. [*Looking at the gold.*] It's a good one, I'm thinking, wherever you got it.   And where is the can?

SARAH. [*Taking the bundle.*] We have it here in a bit of clean sack, your reverence.   We tied it up in the inside of that to keep it irom rusting in the dews of night, and let you not open it now or you'll have the people making game of us and telling the story on us, east and west to the butt of the hills.

PRIEST. [*Taking the bundle.*] Give it here into my hand, Sarah Casey.   What is it any person would think of a tinker making a can?   [*He begins opening the bundle.*

SARAH. It's a fine can, your reverence; for if it's poor, simple people we are, it's fine cans we can make, and himself, God help him, is a great man surely at the trade.

    [*Priest opens the bundle; the three empty bottles fall out.*

SARAH. Glory to the saints of joy!

PRIEST. Did ever any man see the like of that?   To think you'd be putting deceit on me, and telling lies to me, and I going to marry you for a little sum wouldn't marry a child.

SARAH. [*Crestfallen and astonished.*] It's the divil did it, your reverence, and I wouldn't tell you a lie. [*Raising her hands.*] May the Lord Almighty strike me dead if the divil isn't after hooshing the tin can from the bag.

PRIEST. [*Vehemently.*] Go along now, and don't be swearing your lies.   Go along now, and let you not be thinking I'm big fool enough to believe the like of that when it's after selling it you are, or making a swap for drink of it, maybe, in the darkness of the night.

MARY. [*In a peacemaking voice, putting her hand on the Priest's left arm.*] She wouldn't do the like of that, your reverence, when she hasn't a decent standing drouth on her at all; and she setting great store on her marriage the way you'd have a right to be taking her easy, and not minding the can. What differ would an empty can make with a fine, rich, hardy man the like of you?

SARAH. [*Imploringly.*] Marry us, your reverence, for the ten shillings in gold, and we 'll make you a grand can in the evening—a can would be fit to carry water for the holy man of God. Marry us now and I 'll be saying fine prayers for you, morning and night, if it 'd be raining itself and it 'd be in two black pools I 'd be setting my knees.

PRIEST. [*Loudly.*] It 's a wicked, thieving, lying, scheming lot you are, the pack of you. Let you walk off now and take every stinking rag you have there from the ditch.

MARY. [*Putting her shawl over her head.*] Marry her, your reverence, for the love of God, for there 'll be queer doings below if you send her off the like of that and she swearing crazy on the road.

SARAH. [*Angrily.*] It 's the truth she 's saying; for it 's herself, I 'm thinking, is after swapping the tin can for a pint, the time she was raging mad with the drouth, and ourselves above walking the hill.

MARY. [*Crying out with indignation.*] Have you no shame, Sarah Casey, to tell lies unto a holy man?

SARAH. [*To Mary, working herself into a rage.*] It 's making game of me you 'd be, and putting a fool's head on me in the face of the world; but if you were thinking to be mighty cute walking off, or going up to hide in the church, I 've got you this time, and you 'll not run from me now.

[*She seizes one of the bottles.*

MARY. [*Hiding behind the Priest.*] Keep her off, your reverence; keep her off, for the love of the Almighty God. What at all would the Lord Bishop say if he found me here lying with my head broken across, or the two of yous maybe digging a bloody grave for me at the door of the church?

PRIEST. [*Waving Sarah off.*] Go along, Sarah Casey. Would you be doing murder at my feet? Go along from me now, and wasn't I a big fool to have to do with you when it 's nothing but distraction and torment I get from the kindness of my heart?

SARAH. [*Shouting.*] I 've bet a power of strong lads east and west through the world, and are you thinking I 'd turn back from a priest? Leave the road now, or maybe I would strike yourself.

PRIEST. You would not, Sarah Casey. I 've no fear for the lot of you; but let you walk off, I 'm saying, and not be coming where you 've no business, and screeching tumult and murder at the doorway of the church.

SARAH. I 'll not go a step till I have her head broke, or till I 'm wed with himself. If you want to get shut of us, let you marry us now, for I 'm thinking the ten shillings in gold is a good price for the like of you, and you near burst with the fat.

PRIEST. I wouldn't have you coming in on me and soiling my church; for there 's nothing at all, I 'm thinking, would keep the like of you from hell. [*He throws down the ten shillings on the ground.*] Gather up your gold now, and begone from my sight, for if ever I set an eye on you again you 'll hear me telling the peelers who it was stole the black ass belonging to Philly O'Cullen, and whose hay it is the grey ass does be eating.

SARAH. You 'd do that?

PRIEST. I would surely.

SARAH. If you do, you 'll be getting all the tinkers from Wicklow and Wexford, and the county Meath, to put up block tin in the place of glass to shield your windows where you do be looking out and blinking at the girls. It 's hard set you 'll be that time, I 'm telling you, to fill the depth of your belly the long days of Lent; for we wouldn't leave a laying pullet in your yard at all.

PRIEST. [*Losing his temper finally.*] Go on, now, or I 'll send the Lords of Justice a dated story of your villainies—burning, stealing, robbing, raping to this mortal day. Go on now, I 'm saying, if you 'd run from Kilmainham or the rope itself.

MICHAEL. [*Taking off his coat.*] Is it run from the like of you, holy father? Go up to your own shanty, or I 'll beat you with the ass's reins till the world would hear you roaring from this place to the coast of Clare.

PRIEST. Is it lift your hand upon myself when the Lord would blight your members if you 'd touch me now? Go on from this.   [*He gives him a shove.*

MICHAEL. Blight me, is it? Take it then, your reverence, and God help you so.   [*He runs at him with the reins.*

PRIEST. [*Runs up to ditch, crying out.*] There are the peelers passing, by the grace of God. Hey, below!

MARY. [*Clapping her hand over his mouth.*] Knock him down on the road; they didn't hear him at all.

                        [*Michael pulls him down.*

SARAH. Gag his jaws.

MARY. Stuff the sacking in his teeth.

      [*They gag him with the sack that had the can in it.*

SARAH. Tie the bag around his head, and if the peelers come, we 'll put him head first in the bog-hole is beyond the ditch.   [*They tie him up in some sacking.*

MICHAEL. [*To Mary.*] Keep him quiet, and the rags tight on him for fear he 'd screech. [*He goes back to their camp.*] Hurry with the things, Sarah Casey. The peelers aren't coming this way, and maybe we 'll get off from them now.

    [*They bundle the things together in wild haste, the Priest wriggling and struggling about on the ground, with old Mary trying to keep him quiet.*

MARY. [*Patting his head.*] Be quiet, your reverence. What is it ails you, with your wrigglings now? Is it choking maybe? [*She puts her hand under the sack, and feels his mouth, patting him on the back.*] It 's only letting on you are, holy father, for your nose is blowing back and forward as easy as an east wind on an April day. [*In a soothing voice.*] There now, holy father, let you stay easy, I 'm telling you, and learn a little sense and patience, the way you 'll not be so airy again going to rob poor sinners of their scraps of gold. [*He gets quieter.*] That 's a good boy you are now, your reverence, and let you not be uneasy, for we wouldn't hurt you at all. It 's sick and sorry we are to tease you; but what did you want meddling with the like of us, when it 's a long time we are going our own ways—father and son, and his son after him, or mother and daughter, and her own daughter again; and it's little need we ever had of going up into a church and swearing—I'm told there's swearing with it—a word no man would beleive, or with drawing rings on our fingers, would be cutting our skins maybe when we'd be taking the ass from the shafts, and pulling the straps the time they'd be slippy with going around beneath the heavens in rains falling.

MICHAEL. [*Who has finished bundling up the things, comes over with Sarah.*] We're fixed now; and I have a mind to run him in a bog-hole the way he'll not be tattling to the peelers of our games to-day.

SARAH. You'd have a right too, I'm thinking.

MARY. [*Soothingly.*] Let you not be rough with him, Sarah Casey, and he after drinking his sup of porter with us at the fall of night. Maybe he'd swear a mighty oath he wouldn't harm us, and then we'd safer loose him; for if we went to drown him, they'd maybe hang the batch of us, man and child and woman, and the ass itself.

MICHAEL. What would he care for an oath?

MARY. Don't you know his like do live in terror of the wrath of God? [*Putting her mouth to the Priest's ear in the sacking.*] Would you swear an oath, holy father, to leave us in our freedom, and not talk at all? [*Priest nods in sacking.*] Didn't I tell you? Look at the poor fellow nodding his head off in the bias of the sacks. Strip them off from him, and he'll be easy now.

MICHAEL. [*As if speaking to a horse.*] Hold up, holy father.
   [*He pulls the sacking off, and shows the Priest with his hair on end. They free his mouth.*

MARY. Hold him till he swears.

PRIEST. [*In a faint voice.*] I swear, surely. If you let me go in peace, I'll not inform against you or say a thing at all, and may God forgive me for giving heed unto your like to-day.

SARAH. [*Puts the ring on his finger.*] There's the ring, holy father, to keep you minding of your oath until the end of time; for my heart's scalded with your fooling; and it'll be a long day till I go making talk of marriage or the like of that.

MARY. [*Complacently, standing up slowly.*] She 's vexed now, your reverence; and let you not mind her at all, for she 's right, surely, and it 's little need we ever had of the like of you to get us our bit to eat, and our bit to drink, and our time of love when we were young men and women, and were fine to look at.

MICHAEL. Hurry on now. He 's a great man to have kept us from fooling our gold; and we 'll have a great time drinking that bit with the trampers on the green of Clash.

[*They gather up their things. The Priest stands up.*

PRIEST. [*Lifting up his hand.*] I 've sworn not to call the hand of man upon your crimes to-day; but I haven't sworn I wouldn't call the fire of heaven from the hand of the Almighty God.

[*He begins saying a Latin malediction in a loud ecclesiastical voice.*

MARY. There 's an old villain.

ALL. [*Together.*] Run, run. Run for your lives.

[*They rush out, leaving the Priest master of the situation.*

CURTAIN

THE WELL OF THE SAINTS

PERSONS IN THE PLAY

MARTIN DOUL, weather-beaten blind beggar

MARY DOUL, his wife, weather-beaten, ugly woman, blind also, nearly fifty

TIMMY, a middle-aged, almost elderly, but vigorous smith

MOLLY BYRNE, fine-looking girl with fair hair

BRIDE, another handsome girl

MAT SIMON

THE SAINT, a wandering friar

OTHER GIRLS AND MEN

SCENE. *Some lonely mountainous district in the east of Ireland one or more centuries ago*

THE WELL OF THE SAINTS

Act I

*Roadside with big stones, etc., on the right; low loose wall at
back with gap near centre; at left, ruined doorway of church
with bushes beside it. Martin Doul and Mary Doul grope
in on left and pass over to stones on right, where they sit.*

MARY DOUL. What place are we now, Martin Doul?

MARTIN DOUL. Passing the gap.

MARY DOUL. [*Raising her head.*] The length of that! Well,
the sun's coming warm this day if it's late autumn itself.

MARTIN DOUL. [*Putting out his hands in sun.*] What way
wouldn't it be warm and it getting high up in the south?
You were that length plaiting your yellow hair you have
the morning lost on us, and the people are after passing to
the fair of Clash.

MARY DOUL. It isn't going to the fair, the time they do be
driving their cattle and they with a litter of pigs maybe
squealing in their carts, they'd give us a thing at all. [*She sits
down.*] It's well you know that, but you must be talking.

MARTIN DOUL. [*Sitting down beside her and beginning to
shred rushes she gives him.*] If I didn't talk I'd be destroyed
in a short while listening to the clack you do be making,
for you've a queer cracked voice, the Lord have mercy on
you, if it's fine to look on you are itself.

MARY DOUL. Who wouldn't have a cracked voice sitting out
all the year in the rain falling? It's a bad life for the voice,
Martin Doul, though I've heard tell there isn't anything
like the wet south wind does be blowing upon us for keeping a white beautiful skin—the like of my skin—on your
neck and on your brows, and there isn't anything at all like
a fine skin for putting splendour on a woman.

61

MARTIN DOUL. [*Teasingly, but with good humour.*] I do be thinking odd times we don't know rightly what way you have your splendour, or asking myself, maybe, if you have it at all, for the time I was a young lad, and had fine sight, it was the ones with sweet voices were the best in face.

MARY DOUL. Let you not be making the like of that talk when you 've heard Timmy the smith, and Mat Simon, and Patch Ruadh, and a power besides saying fine things of my face, and you know rightly it was 'the beautiful dark woman' they did call me in Ballinatone.

MARTIN DOUL. [*As before.*] If it was itself I heard Molly Byrne saying at the fall of night it was little more than a fright you were.

MARY DOUL. [*Sharply.*] She was jealous, God forgive her, because Timmy the smith was after praising my hair——

MARTIN DOUL. [*With mock irony.*] Jealous!

MARY DOUL. Ay, jealous, Martin Doul; and if she wasn't itself, the young and silly do be always making game of them that 's dark, and they 'd think it a fine thing if they had us deceived, the way we wouldn't know we were so fine-looking at all.

[*She puts her hand to her face with a complacent gesture.*

MARTIN DOUL. [*A little plaintively.*] I do be thinking in the long nights it 'd be a grand thing if we could see ourselves for one hour, or a minute itself, the way we 'd know surely we were the finest man and the finest woman of the seven counties of the east—[*bitterly*] and then the seeing rabble below might be destroying their souls telling bad lies, and we' d never heed a thing they 'd say.

MARY DOUL. If you weren't a big fool you wouldn't heed them this hour, Martin Doul, for they 're a bad lot those that have their sight, and they do have great joy, the time they do be seeing a grand thing, to let on they don't see it at all, and to be telling fool's lies, the like of what Molly Byrne was telling to yourself.

MARTIN DOUL. If it 's lies she does be telling she 's a sweet, beautiful voice you 'd never tire to be hearing, if it was only the pig she 'd be calling, or crying out in the long grass, maybe, after her hens. [*Speaking pensively.*] It should be a fine, soft, rounded woman, I 'm thinking, would have a voice the like of that.

MARY DOUL. [*Sharply again, scandalized.*] Let you not be minding if it 's flat or rounded she is; for she 's a flighty, foolish woman you 'll hear when you 're off a long way, and she making a great noise and laughing at the well.

MARTIN DOUL. Isn't laughing a nice thing the time a woman 's young?

MARY DOUL. [*Bitterly.*] A nice thing is it? A nice thing to hear a woman making a loud braying laugh the like of that? Ah, she 's a great one for drawing the men, and you 'll hear Timmy himself, the time he does be sitting in his forge, getting mighty fussy if she 'll come walking from Grianan, the way you 'll hear his breath going, and he wringing his hands.

MARTIN DOUL. [*Slightly piqued.*] I 've heard him say a power of times it 's nothing at all she is when you see her at the side of you, and yet I never heard any man's breath getting uneasy the time he 'd be looking on yourself.

MARY DOUL. I 'm not the like of the girls do be running round on the roads, swinging their legs, and they with their necks out looking on the men. . . . Ah, there 's a power of villainy walking the world, Martin Doul, among them that do be gadding around, with their gaping eyes, and their sweet words, and they with no sense in them at all.

MARTIN DOUL [*Sadly.*] It 's the truth, maybe, and yet I 'm told it 's a grand thing to see a young girl walking the road.

MARY DOUL. You 'd be as bad as the rest of them if you had your sight, and I did well, surely, not to marry a seeing man —it 's scores would have had me and welcome—for the seeing is a queer lot, and you 'd never know the thing they 'd do. [*A moment's pause.*

MARTIN DOUL. [*Listening.*] There 's someone coming on the road.

MARY DOUL. Let you put the pith away out of their sight, or they 'll be picking it out with the spying eyes they have,

and saying it 's rich we are, and not sparing us a thing at all.
[*They bundle away the rushes.   Timmy the smith comes in
    on left.*

MARTIN DOUL. [*With a begging voice.*] Leave a bit of silver
for blind Martin, your honour.   Leave a bit of silver, or a
penny copper itself, and we 'll be praying the Lord to bless
you and you going the way.

TIMMY. [*Stopping before them.*] And you letting on a while
back you knew my step!   [*He sits down.*

MARTIN DOUL. [*With his natural voice.*] I know it when
Molly Byrne 's walking in front, or when she 's two perches
maybe, lagging behind; but it 's few times I 've heard you
walking up the like of that, as if you 'd met a thing wasn't
right and you coming on the road.

TIMMY. [*Hot and breathless, wiping his face.*] You 've good
ears, God bless you, if you 're a liar itself; for I 'm after
walking up in great haste from hearing wonders in the fair.

MARTIN DOUL. [*Rather contemptuously.*] You 're always
hearing queer wonderful things, and the lot of them
nothing at all; but I 'm thinking, this time, it 's a strange
thing surely you 'd be walking up before the turn of day,
and not waiting below to look on them lepping, or dancing,
or playing shows on the green of Clash.

TIMMY. [*Huffed.*] I was coming to tell you it 's in this place
there 'd be a bigger wonder done in a short while [*Martin
Doul stops working*] than was ever done on the green of
Clash, or the width of Leinster itself; but you 're thinking,
maybe, you 're too cute a little fellow to be minding me
at all.

MARTIN DOUL. [*Amused, but incredulous.*] There 'll be
wonders in this place, is it?

TIMMY. Here at the crossing of the roads.

MARTIN DOUL. I never heard tell of anything to happen in
this place since the night they killed the old fellow going
home with his gold, the Lord have mercy on him, and
threw down his corpse into the bog.   Let them not be
doing the like of that this night, for it 's ourselves have a
right to the crossing roads, and we don't want any of your

bad tricks, or your wonders either, for it 's wonder enough
we are ourselves.

TIMMY. If I 'd a mind I 'd be telling you of a real wonder
this day, and the way you 'll be having a great joy, maybe,
you 're not thinking on at all.

MARTIN DOUL. [*Interested.*] Are they putting up a still behind in the rocks? It 'd be a grand thing if I 'd a sup
handy the way I wouldn't be destroying myself groping
up across the bogs in the rain falling.

TIMMY. [*Still moodily.*] It 's not a still they 're bringing, or
the like of it either.

MARY DOUL. [*Persuasively, to Timmy.*] Maybe they 're
hanging a thief, above at the bit of a tree. I 'm told it 's
a great sight to see a man hanging by his neck; but what joy
would that be to ourselves, and we not seeing it at all?

TIMMY. [*More pleasantly.*] They 're hanging no one this
day, Mary Doul, and yet, with the help of God, you 'll
see a power hanged before you die.

MARY DOUL. Well, you 've queer humbugging talk. . . .
What way would I see a power hanged, and I a dark
woman since the seventh year of my age?

TIMMY. Did you ever hear tell of a place across a bit of the
sea, where there is an island, and the grave of the four
beautiful saints?

MARY DOUL. I 've heard people have walked round from
the west and they speaking of that.

TIMMY. [*Impressively.*] There 's a green ferny well, I 'm
told, behind of that place, and if you put a drop of the water
out of it on the eyes of a blind man, you 'll make him see as
well as any person is walking the world.

MARTIN DOUL. [*With excitement.*] Is that the truth, Timmy?
I 'm thinking you 're telling a lie.

TIMMY. [*Gruffly.*] That 's the truth, Martin Doul, and you
may believe it now, for you 're after believing a power of
things weren't as likely at all.

MARY DOUL. Maybe we could send a young lad to bring us
the water. I could wash a naggin bottle in the morning,
and I 'm thinking Patch Ruadh would go for it, if we gave

him a good drink, and the bit of money we have hid in the thatch.

TIMMY. It 'd be no good to be sending a sinful man the like of ourselves, for I 'm told the holiness of the water does be getting soiled with the villainy of your heart, the time you 'd be carrying it, and you looking round on the girls, maybe, or drinking a small sup at a still.

MARTIN DOUL. [*With disappointment.*] It 'd be a long terrible way to be walking ourselves, and I 'm thinking that 's a wonder will bring small joy to us at all.

TIMMY. [*Turning on him impatiently.*] What is it you want with your walking? It 's as deaf as blind you 're growing if you 're not after hearing me say it 's in this place the wonder would be done.

MARTIN DOUL. [*With a flash of anger.*] If it is can't you open the big slobbering mouth you have and say what way it 'll be done, and not be making blather till the fall of night.

TIMMY. [*Jumping up.*] I 'll be going on now [*Mary Doul rises*], and not wasting time talking civil talk with the like of you.

MARY DOUL. [*Standing up, disguising her impatience.*] Let you come here to me, Timmy, and not be minding him at all. [*Timmy stops, and she gropes up to him and takes him by the coat.*] You 're not huffy with myself, and let you tell me the whole story and don't be fooling me more. . . . Is it yourself has brought us the water?

TIMMY. It is not, surely.

MARY DOUL. Then tell us your wonder, Timmy. . . . What person 'll bring it at all?

TIMMY. [*Relenting.*] It 's a fine holy man will bring it, a saint of the Almighty God.

MARY DOUL. [*Overawed.*] A saint is it?

TIMMY. Ay, a fine saint, who 's going round through the churches of Ireland, with a long cloak on him, and naked feet, for he 's brought a sup of the water slung at his side, and, with the like of him, any little drop is enough to cure the dying, or to make the blind see as clear as the grey hawks do be high up, on a still day, sailing the sky.

MARTIN DOUL. [*Feeling for his stick.*] What place is he, Timmy? I 'll be walking to him now.

TIMMY. Let you stay quiet, Martin.   He 's straying around saying prayers at the churches and high crosses, between this place and the hills, and he with a great crowd going behind—for it 's fine prayers he does be saying, and fasting with it, till he 's as thin as one of the empty rushes you have there on your knee; then he 'll be coming after to this place to cure the two of you—we 're after telling him the way you are—and to say his prayers in the church.

MARTIN DOUL. [*Turning suddenly to Mary Doul.*] And we 'll be seeing ourselves this day.   Oh, glory be to God, is it true surely?

MARY DOUL. [*Very pleased, to Timmy.*] Maybe I 'd have time to walk down and get the big shawl I have below, for I do look my best, I 've heard them say, when I 'm dressed up with that thing on my head.

TIMMY. You 'd have time surely.

MARTIN DOUL. [*Listening.*] Whisht now. . . . I hear people again coming by the stream.

TIMMY. [*Looking out left, puzzled.*] It 's the young girls I left walking after the Saint. . . . They 're coming now [*goes up to entrance*] carrying things in their hands, and they walking as easy as you 'd see a child walk who 'd have a dozen eggs hid in her bib.

MARTIN DOUL. [*Listening.*] That 's Molly Byrne, I 'm thinking.

[*Molly Byrne and Bride come on left and cross to Martin Doul, carrying water can, Saint's bell, and cloak.*

MOLLY. [*Volubly.*] God bless you, Martin.   I 've holy water here, from the grave of the four saints of the west, will have you cured in a short while and seeing like ourselves——

TIMMY. [*Crosses to Molly, interrupting her.*] He 's heard that, God help you!   But where at all is the Saint, and what way is he after trusting the holy water with the likes of you?

MOLLY BYRNE. He was afeard to go a far way with the

clouds is coming beyond, so he 's gone up now through the thick woods to say a prayer at the crosses of Grianan, and he 's coming on this road to the church.

TIMMY. [*Still astonished.*] And he 's after leaving the holy water with the two of you? It 's a wonder, surely.

[*Comes down left a little.*

MOLLY BYRNE. The lads told him no person could carry them things through the briers, and steep, slippy-feeling rocks he 'll be climbing above, so he looked round then, and gave the water, and his big cloak, and his bell to the two of us, for young girls, says he, are the cleanest holy people you 'd see walking the world. [*Mary Doul goes near seat.*

MARY DOUL. [*Sits down, laughing to herself.*] Well, the Saint 's a simple fellow, and it 's no lie.

MARTIN DOUL. [*Leaning forward, holding out his hands.*] Let you give me the water in my hand, Molly Byrne, the way I 'll know you have it surely.

MOLLY BYRNE. [*Giving it to him.*] Wonders is queer things, and maybe it 'd cure you, and you holding it alone.

MARTIN DOUL. [*Looking round.*] It does not, Molly. I 'm not seeing at all. [*He shakes the can.*] There 's a small sup only. Well, isn't it a great wonder the little trifling thing would bring seeing to the blind, and be showing us the big women and the young girls, and all the fine things is walking the world.

[*He feels for Mary Doul and gives her the can.*

MARY DOUL. [*Shaking it.*] Well, glory be to God——

MARTIN DOUL. [*Pointing to Bride.*] And what is it herself has, making sounds in her hand?

BRIDE. [*Crossing to Martin Doul.*] It 's the Saint's bell; you 'll hear him ringing out the time he 'll be going up some place, to be saying his prayers.

[*Martin Doul holds out his hands; she gives it to him.*

MARTIN DOUL. [*Ringing it.*] It 's a sweet beautiful sound.

MARY DOUL. You 'd know, I 'm thinking, by the little silvery voice of it, a fasting holy man was after carrying it a great way at his side.

[*Bride crosses a little right behind Martin Doul.*

MOLLY BYRNE. [*Unfolding Saint's cloak.*] Let you stand up now, Martin Doul, till I put his big cloak on you. [*Martin Doul rises, comes forward, centre a little.*] The way we 'd see how you 'd look, and you a saint of the Almighty God.

MARTIN DOUL. [*Standing up, a little diffidently.*] I 've heard the priests a power of times making great talk and praises of the beauty of the saints.

[*Molly Byrne slips cloak round him.*

TIMMY. [*Uneasily.*] You 'd have a right to be leaving him alone, Molly.   What would the Saint say if he seen you making game with his cloak?

MOLLY BYRNE. [*Recklessly.*] How would he see us, and he saying prayers in the wood? [*She turns Martin Doul round.*] Isn't that a fine, holy-looking saint, Timmy the smith? [*Laughing foolishly.*] There 's a grand, handsome fellow, Mary Doul; and if you seen him now you 'd be as proud, I 'm thinking, as the archangels below, fell out with the Almighty God.

MARY DOUL. [*With quiet confidence going to Martin Doul and feeling his cloak.*] It 's proud we 'll be this day, surely.

[*Martin Doul is still ringing.*

MOLLY BYRNE. [*To Martin Doul.*] Would you think well to be all your life walking round the like of that, Martin Doul, and you bell-ringing with the saints of God?

MARY DOUL. [*Turning on her, fiercely.*] How would he be bell-ringing with the saints of God and he wedded with myself.

MARTIN DOUL. It 's the truth she 's saying, and if bell-ringing is a fine life, yet I 'm thinking, maybe, it 's better I am wedded with the beautiful dark woman of Ballinatone.

MOLLY BYRNE. [*Scornfully.*] You 're thinking that, God help you; but it 's little you know of her at all.

MARTIN DOUL. It 's little surely, and I 'm destroyed this day waiting to look upon her face.

TIMMY. [*Awkwardly.*] It 's well you know the way she is; for the like of you do have great knowledge in the feeling of your hands.

MARTIN DOUL. [*Still feeling the cloak.*] We do, maybe.

Yet it 's little I know of faces, or of fine beautiful cloaks, for it 's few cloaks I 've had my hand to, and few faces [*plaintively*]; for the young girls is mighty shy, Timmy the smith, and it isn't much they heed me, though they do be saying I 'm a handsome man.

MARY DOUL. [*Mockingly, with good humour.*] Isn't it a queer thing the voice he puts on him, when you hear him talking of the skinny-looking girls, and he married with a woman he 's heard called the wonder of the western world?

TIMMY. [*Pityingly.*] The two of you will see a great wonder this day, and it 's no lie.

MARTIN DOUL. I 've heard tell her yellow hair, and her white skin, and her big eyes are a wonder, surely——

BRIDE. [*Who has looked out left.*] Here 's the Saint coming from the selvage of the wood. . . . Strip the cloak from him, Molly, or he 'll be seeing it now.

MOLLY BYRNE. [*Hastily to Bride.*] Take the bell and put herself by the stones.   [*To Martin Doul.*] Will you hold your head up till I loosen the cloak? [*She pulls off the cloak and throws it over her arm.   Then she pushes Martin Doul over and stands him beside Mary Doul.*] Stand there now, quiet, and let you not be saying a word.

   [*She and Bride stand a little on their left, demurely, with bell, etc., in their hands.*]

MARTIN DOUL. [*Nervously arranging his clothes.*] Will he mind the way we are, and not tidied or washed cleanly at all?

MOLLY BYRNE. He 'll not see what way you are. . . . He 'd walk by the finest woman in Ireland, I 'm thinking, and not trouble to raise his two eyes to look upon her face. . . . Whisht!   [*The Saint comes left, with crowd.*

SAINT. Are these the two poor people?

TIMMY. [*Officiously.*] They are, holy father; they do be always sitting here at the crossing of the roads, asking a bit of copper from them that do pass, or stripping rushes for lights, and they not mournful at all, but talking out straight with a full voice, and making game with them that likes it.

SAINT. [*To Martin Doul and Mary Doul*] It 's a hard life

you 've had not seeing sun or moon, or the holy priests itself praying to the Lord, but it 's the like of you who are brave in a bad time will make a fine use of the gift of sight the Almighty God will bring to you to-day. [*He takes his cloak and puts it about him.*] It 's on a bare starving rock that there 's the grave of the four beauties of God, the way it 's little wonder, I 'm thinking, if it 's with bare starving people the water should be used. [*He takes the water and bell and slings them round his shoulders.*] So it 's to the like of yourselves I do be going, who are wrinkled and poor, a thing rich men would hardly look at at all, but would throw a coin to or a crust of bread.

MARTIN DOUL. [*Moving uneasily.*] When they look on herself, who is a fine woman——

TIMMY. [*Shaking him.*] Whisht now, and be listening to the Saint.

SAINT. [*Looks at them a moment, continues.*] If it 's raggy and dirty you are itself, I 'm saying, the Almighty God isn't at all like the rich men of Ireland; and, with the power of the water I 'm after bringing in a little curragh into Cashla Bay, He 'll have pity on you, and put sight into your eyes.

MARTIN DOUL. [*Taking off his hat.*] I 'm ready now, holy father——

SAINT. [*Taking him by the hand.*] I 'll cure you first, and then I 'll come for your wife. We 'll go up now into the church, for I must say a prayer to the Lord. [*To Mary Doul, as he moves off.*] And let you be making your mind still and saying praises in your heart, for it 's a great wonderful thing when the power of the Lord of the world is brought down upon your like.

PEOPLE. [*Pressing after him.*] Come on till we watch.

BRIDE. Come, Timmy.

SAINT. [*Waving them back.*] Stay back where you are, for I 'm not wanting a big crowd making whispers in the church. Stay back there, I 'm saying, and you 'd do well to be thinking on the way sin has brought blindness to the world, and to be saying a prayer for your own sakes against false prophets and heathens, and the words of women and smiths, and all knowledge that would soil the soul or the body of a man.

> [*People shrink back. He goes into church. Mary Doul gropes half-way towards the door and kneels near path. People form a group at right.*

TIMMY. Isn't it a fine, beautiful voice he has, and he a fine, brave man if it wasn't for the fasting?

BRIDE. Did you watch him moving his hands?

MOLLY BYRNE. It 'd be a fine thing if someone in this place could pray the like of him, for I 'm thinking the water from our own blessed well would do rightly if a man knew the way to be saying prayers, and then there 'd be no call to be bringing water from that wild place, where, I 'm told, there are no decent houses, or fine-looking people at all.

BRIDE. [*Who is looking in at door from right.*] Look at the great trembling Martin has shaking him, and he on his knees.

TIMMY. [*Anxiously*]. God help him. . . . What will he be doing when he sees his wife this day? I 'm thinking it was bad work we did when we let on she was fine-looking, and not a wrinkled, wizened hag the way she is.

MAT SIMON. Why would he be vexed, and we after giving him great joy and pride, the time he was dark?

MOLLY BYRNE. [*Sitting down in Mary Doul's seat and tidying her hair.*] If it 's vexed he is itself, he 'll have other things now to think on as well as his wife; and what does any man care for a wife, when it 's two weeks, or three, he is looking on her face?

MAT SIMON. That 's the truth now, Molly, and it 's more joy dark Martin got from the lies we told of that hag is kneeling by the path than your own man will get from you, day or night, and he living at your side.

MOLLY BYRNE. [*Defiantly.*] Let you not be talking, Mat Simon, for it 's not yourself will be my man, though you 'd be crowing and singing fine songs if you 'd that hope in you at all.

TIMMY. [*Shocked, to Molly Byrne.*] Let you not be raising your voice when the Saint 's above at his prayers.

BRIDE. [*Crying out.*] Whisht. . . . Whisht. . . . I 'm thinking he 's cured.

MARTIN DOUL. [*Crying out in the church.*] Oh, glory be to God. . . .

SAINT. [*Solemnly.*]

> Laus Patri sit et Filio cum Spiritu Paraclito
> Qui suae dono gratiae misertus est Hiberniae. . . .

MARTIN DOUL. [*Ecstatically.*] Oh, glory be to God, I see now surely. . . . I see the walls of the church, and the green bits of ferns in them, and yourself, holy father, and the great width of the sky.

> [*He runs out half foolish with joy, and comes past Mary Doul as she scrambles to her feet, drawing a little away from her as he goes by.*

TIMMY. [*To the others.*] He doesn't know her at all.

> [*The Saint comes out behind Martin Doul, and leads Mary Doul into the church. Martin Doul comes on to the people. The men are between him and the girls; he verifies his position with his stick.*

MARTIN DOUL. [*Crying out joyfully.*] That's Timmy, I know Timmy by the black of his head. . . . That's Mat Simon, I know Mat by the length of his legs. . . . That should be Patch Ruadh, with the gamy eyes in him, and the fiery hair. [*He sees Molly Byrne on Mary Doul's seat, and his voice changes completely.*] Oh, it was no lie they told me, Mary Doul. Oh, glory to God and the seven saints I didn't die and not see you at all. The blessing of God on the water, and the feet carried it round through the land. The blessing of God on this day, and them that brought me the Saint, for it's grand hair you have [*she lowers her head a little confused*], and soft skin, and eyes would make the saints, if they were dark awhile, and seeing again, fall down out of the sky. [*He goes nearer to her.*] Hold up your head, Mary, the way I'll see it's richer I am than the great kings of the east. Hold up your head, I'm saying, for it's soon you'll be seeing me, and I not a bad one at all. [*He touches her and she starts up.*

MOLLY BYRNE. Let you keep away from me, and not be soiling my chin. [*People laugh loudly.*

MARTIN DOUL. [*Bewildered.*] It 's Molly's voice you have.

MOLLY BYRNE. Why wouldn't I have my own voice? Do you think I 'm a ghost?

MARTIN DOUL. Which of you all is herself? [*He goes up to Bride.*] Is it you is Mary Doul? I 'm thinking you 're more the like of what they said. [*Peering at her.*] For you 've yellow hair, and white skin, and it 's the smell of my own turf is rising from your shawl.

[*He catches her shawl.*

BRIDE. [*Pulling away her shawl.*] I 'm not your wife, and let you get out of my way. [*The people laugh again.*

MARTIN DOUL. [*With misgiving, to another girl.*] Is it yourself it is? You 're not so fine-looking, but I 'm thinking you 'd do, with the grand nose you have, and your nice hands and your feet.

GIRL. [*Scornfully.*] I never seen any person that took me for blind, and a seeing woman, I 'm thinking, would never wed the like of you.

[*She turns away, and the people laugh once more, drawing back a little and leaving him on their left.*

PEOPLE. [*Jeeringly.*] Try again, Martin, try again, and you 'll be finding her yet.

MARTIN DOUL. [*Passionately.*] Where is it you have her hidden away? Isn't it a black shame for a drove of pitiful beasts the like of you to be making game of me, and putting a fool's head on me the grand day of my life? Ah, you 're thinking you 're a fine lot, with your giggling, weeping eyes, a fine lot to be making game of myself and the woman I 've heard called the great wonder of the west.

[*During this speech, which he gives with his back towards the church, Mary Doul has come out with her sight cured, and come down towards the right with a silly simpering smile, till she is a little behind Martin Doul.*

MARY DOUL. [*When he pauses.*] Which of you is Martin Doul?

MARTIN DOUL. [*Wheeling round.*] It 's her voice surely.

[*They stare at each other blankly.*

MOLLY BYRNE. [*To Martin Doul.*] Go up now and take her under the chin and be speaking the way you spoke to myself.

MARTIN DOUL. [*In a low voice, with intensity.*] If I speak now, I'll speak hard to the two of you——

MOLLY BYRNE. [*To Mary Doul.*] You're not saying a word, Mary. What is it you think of himself, with the fat legs on him, and the little neck like a ram?

MARY DOUL. I'm thinking it's a poor thing when the Lord God gives you sight and puts the like of that man in your way.

MARTIN DOUL. It's on your two knees you should be thanking the Lord God you're not looking on yourself, for if it was yourself you seen you'd be running round in a short while like the old screeching madwoman is running round in the glen.

MARY DOUL. [*Beginning to realize herself.*] If I'm not so fine as some of them said, I have my hair, and big eyes, and my white skin——

MARTIN DOUL. [*Breaking out into a passionate cry.*] Your hair and your big eyes, is it? . . . I'm telling you there isn't a wisp on any grey mare on the ridge of the world isn't finer than the dirty twist on your head. There isn't two eyes in any starving sow isn't finer than the eyes you were calling blue like the sea.

MARY DOUL. [*Interrupting him.*] It's the devil cured you this day with your talking of sows; it's the devil cured you this day, I'm saying, and drove you crazy with lies.

MARTIN DOUL. Isn't it yourself is after playing lies on me, ten years, in the day and in the night; but what is that to you now the Lord God has given eyes to me, the way I see you an old, wizendy hag, was never fit to rear a child to me itself.

MARY DOUL. I wouldn't rear a crumpled whelp the like of you. It's many a woman is married with finer than yourself should be praising God if she's no child, and isn't loading the earth with things would make the heavens lonesome above, and they scaring the larks, and the crows, and the angels passing in the sky.

MARTIN DOUL. Go on now to be seeking a lonesome place where the earth can hide you away; go on now, I 'm saying, or you 'll be having men and women with their knees bled, and they screaming to God for a holy water would darken their sight, for there 's no man but would liefer be blind a hundred years or a thousand itself, than to be looking on your like.

MARY DOUL. [*Raising her stick.*] Maybe if I hit you a strong blow you 'd be blind again, and having what you want——
    [*The Saint is seen in church door with his head bent in prayer.*

MARTIN DOUL. [*Raising his stick and driving Mary Doul back towards left.*] Let you keep off from me now if you wouldn't have me strike out the little handful of brains you have about on the road.
    [*He is going to strike her, but Timmy catches him by the arm.*

TIMMY. Have you no shame to be making a great row, and the Saint above saying his prayers?

MARTIN DOUL. What is it I care for the like of him? [*Struggling to free himself.*] Let me hit her one good one, for the love of the Almighty God, and I 'll be quiet after till I die.

TIMMY. [*Shaking him.*] Will you whisht, I 'm saying.

SAINT. [*Coming forward, centre.*] Are their minds troubled with joy, or is their sight uncertain, the way it does often be the day a person is restored?

TIMMY. It 's too certain their sight is, holy father; and they 're after making a great fight, because they 're a pair of pitiful shows.

SAINT. [*Coming between them.*] May the Lord who has given you sight send a little sense into your heads, the way it won't be on your two selves you 'll be looking—on two pitiful sinners of the earth—but on the splendour of the Spirit of God, you 'll see an odd time shining out through the big hills, and steep streams falling to the sea. For if it 's on the like of that you do be thinking, you 'll not be minding the faces of men, but you 'll be saying prayers and great praises, till you 'll be living the way the great saints do be living, with little but old sacks, and skin covering their bones. [*To Timmy.*] Leave him go now, you 're seeing he 's quiet again. [*He frees Martin Doul.*] And let you [*he turns to Mary Doul*] not be raising your voice, a bad thing in a woman; but let the lot of you, who have seen the power of the Lord, be thinking on it in the dark night, and be saying to yourselves it 's great pity and love He has for the poor, starving people of Ireland. [*He gathers his cloak about him.*] And now the Lord send blessing to you all, for I am going on to Annagolan, where there is a deaf woman, and to Laragh, where there are two men without sense, and to Glenassil, where there are children blind from their birth; and then I 'm going to sleep this night in the bed of the holy Kevin, and to be praising God, and asking great blessing on you all.   [*He bends his head.*

CURTAIN

Act II

Village roadside, on left the door of a forge, with broken wheels, etc., lying about. A well near centre, with board above it, and room to pass behind it. Martin Doul is sitting near forge, cutting sticks.

TIMMY. [*Heard hammering inside forge, then calls.*] Let you make haste out there. . . . I 'll be putting up new fires at the turn of day, and you haven't the half of them cut yet.

MARTIN DOUL. [*Gloomily.*] It 's destroyed I 'll be whacking your old thorns till the turn of day, and I with no food in my stomach would keep the life in a pig. [*He turns towards the door.*] Let you come out here and cut them yourself if you want them cut, for there 's an hour every day when a man has a right to his rest.

TIMMY. [*Coming out with a hammer, impatiently.*] Do you want me to be driving you off again to be walking the roads? There you are now, and I giving you your food, and a corner to sleep, and money with it; and, to hear the talk of you, you 'd think I was after beating you, or stealing your gold.

MARTIN DOUL. You 'd do it handy, maybe, if I 'd gold to steal.

TIMMY. [*Throws down hammer, picks up some of the sticks already cut, and throws them into door.*] There 's no fear of your having gold—a lazy, basking fool the like of you.

MARTIN DOUL. No fear, maybe, and I here with yourself; for it 's more I got a while since, and I sitting blinded in Grianan, than I get in this place, working hard, and destroying myself, the length of the day.

TIMMY. [*Stopping with amazement.*] Working hard? [*He goes over to him.*] I 'll teach you to work hard, Martin Doul. Strip off your coat now, and put a tuck in your sleeves, and cut the lot of them, while I 'd rake the ashes from the forge, or I 'll not put up with you another hour itself.

MARTIN DOUL. [*Horrified.*] Would you have me getting my death sitting out in the black wintry air with no coat on me at all?

TIMMY. [*With authority.*] Strip it off now, or walk down upon the road.

MARTIN DOUL. [*Bitterly.*] Oh, God help me! [*He begins taking off his coat.*] I 've heard tell you stripped the sheet from your wife and you putting her down into the grave, and there isn't the like of you for plucking your living ducks, the short days, and leaving them running round in their skins, in the great rains and the cold. [*He tucks up his sleeves.*] Ah, I 've heard a power of queer things of yourself, and there isn't one of them I 'll not believe from this day, and be telling to the boys.

TIMMY. [*Pulling over a big stick.*] Let you cut that now, and give me rest from your talk, for I 'm not heeding you at all.

MARTIN DOUL. [*Taking stick.*] That 's a hard, terrible stick, Timmy; and isn't it a poor thing to be cutting strong timber the like of that, when it 's cold the bark is, and slippy with the frost of the air?

TIMMY. [*Gathering up another armful of sticks.*] What way wouldn't it be cold, and it freezing since the moon was changed? [*He goes into forge.*

MARTIN DOUL. [*Querulously, as he cuts slowly.*] What way, indeed, Timmy? For it 's a raw, beastly day we do have each day, till I do be thinking it 's well for the blind don't be seeing them grey clouds driving on the hill, and don't be looking on people with their noses red, the like of your nose, and their eyes weeping and watering, the like of your eyes, God help you, Timmy the smith.

TIMMY. [*Seen blinking in doorway.*] Is it turning now you are against your sight?

MARTIN DOUL. [*Very miserably.*] It 's a hard thing for a man to have his sight, and he living near to the like of you [*he cuts a stick and throws it away*], or wed with a wife [*cuts a stick*]; and I do be thinking it should be a hard thing for the Almighty God to be looking on the world, bad days, and on men the like of yourself walking around on it, and they slipping each way in the muck.

TIMMY. [*With pot-hooks which he taps on anvil.*] You 'd have a right to be minding, Martin Doul, for it 's a power the Saint cured lose their sight after a while. Mary Doul 's dimming again, I 've heard them say: and I 'm thinking the Lord, if He hears you making that talk, will have little pity left for you at all.

MARTIN DOUL. There 's not a bit of fear of me losing my sight, and if it 's a dark day itself it 's too well I see every wicked wrinkle you have round by your eye.

TIMMY. [*Looking at him sharply.*] The day 's not dark since the clouds broke in the east.

MARTIN DOUL. Let you not be tormenting yourself trying to make me afeard. You told me a power of bad lies the time I was blind, and it 's right now for you to stop, and be taking your rest [*Mary Doul comes in unnoticed on right with a sack filled with green-stuff on her arm*], for it 's little ease or quiet any person would get if the big fools of Ireland weren't weary at times. [*He looks up and sees Mary Doul.*] Oh, glory be to God, she 's coming again.

[*He begins to work busily with his back to her.*

TIMMY. [*Amused, to Mary Doul, as she is going by without looking at them.*] Look on him now, Mary Doul. You 'd be a great one for keeping him steady at his work, for he 's after idling and blathering to this hour from the dawn of day.

MARY DOUL. [*Stiffly.*] Of what is it you 're speaking, Timmy the smith?

TIMMY. [*Laughing.*] Of himself, surely. Look on him there, and he with the shirt on him ripping from his back. You 'd have a right to come round this night, I 'm thinking, and put a stitch into his clothes, for it 's long enough you are not speaking one to the other.

MARY DOUL. Let the two of you not torment me at all.

[*She goes out left, with her head in the air.*

MARTIN DOUL. [*Stops work and looks after her.*] Well, isn't it a queer thing she can't keep herself two days without looking on my face?

TIMMY. [*Jeeringly.*] Looking on your face is it? And she after going by with her head turned the way you 'd see a priest going where there 'd be a drunken man in the side ditch talking with a girl. [*Martin Doul gets up and goes to corner of forge, and looks out left.*] Come back here and don't mind her at all. Come back here, I 'm saying, you 've no call to be spying behind her since she went off and left you, in place of breaking her heart, trying to keep you in the decency of clothes and food.

MARTIN DOUL. [*Crying out indignantly.*] You know rightly, Timmy, it was myself drove her away.

TIMMY. That 's a lie you 're telling, yet it 's little I care which one of you was driving the other, and let you walk back here, I 'm saying, to your work.

MARTIN DOUL. [*Turning round.*] I 'm coming, surely.
    [*He stops and looks out right, going a step or two towards centre.*

TIMMY. On what is it you 're gaping, Martin Doul?

MARTIN DOUL. There 's a person walking above. . . . It 's Molly Byrne, I 'm thinking, coming down with her can.

TIMMY. If she is itself let you not be idling this day, or minding her at all, and let you hurry with them sticks, for I 'll want you in a short while to be blowing in the forge.
                    [*He throws down pot-hooks.*

MARTIN DOUL. [*Crying out.*] Is it roasting me now you 'd be? [*Turns back and sees pot-hooks; he takes them up.*] Pothooks? Is it over them you 've been inside sneezing and sweating since the dawn of day?

TIMMY. [*Resting himself on anvil, with satisfaction.*] I 'm making a power of things you do have when you 're settling with a wife, Martin Doul; for I heard tell last night the Saint 'll be passing again in a short while, and I 'd have him wed Molly with myself. . . . He 'd do it, I 've heard them say, for not a penny at all.

MARTIN DOUL. [*Lays down hooks and looks at him steadily.*] Molly 'll be saying great praises now to the Almighty God and He giving her a fine, stout, hardy man the like of you.

TIMMY. [*Uneasily.*] And why wouldn't she, if she's a fine woman itself?

MARTIN DOUL. [*Looking up right.*] Why wouldn't she, indeed, Timmy? . . . The Almighty God's made a fine match in the two of you, for if you went marrying a woman was the like of yourself you'd be having the fearfullest little children, I'm thinking, was ever seen in the world.

TIMMY. [*Seriously offended.*] God forgive you! if you're an ugly man to be looking at, I'm thinking your tongue's worse than your view.

MARTIN DOUL. [*Hurt also.*] Isn't it destroyed with the cold I am, and if I'm ugly itself I never seen any one the like of you for dreepiness this day, Timmy the smith, and I'm thinking now herself's coming above you'd have a right to step up into your old shanty, and give a rub to your face, and not be sitting there with your bleary eyes, and your big nose, the like of an old scarecrow stuck down upon the road.

TIMMY. [*Looking up the road uneasily.*] She's no call to mind what way I look, and I after building a house with four rooms in it above on the hill. [*He stands up.*] But it's a queer thing the way yourself and Mary Doul are after setting every person in this place, and up beyond to Rathvanna, talking of nothing, and thinking of nothing, but the way they do be looking in the face. [*Going towards forge.*] It's the devil's work you're after doing with your talk of fine looks, and I'd do right, maybe, to step in and wash the blackness from my eyes.

> [*He goes into forge. Martin Doul rubs his face furtively with the tail of his coat. Molly Byrne comes on right with a water can, and begins to fill it at the well.*

MARTIN DOUL. God save you, Molly Byrne.

MOLLY BYRNE. [*Indifferently.*] God save you.

MARTIN DOUL. That's a dark, gloomy day, and the Lord have mercy on us all.

MOLLY BYRNE. Middling dark.

MARTIN DOUL. It's a power of dirty days, and dark mornings, and shabby-looking fellows [*he makes a gesture over his shoulder*] we do have to be looking on when we have our sight, God help us, but there 's one fine thing we have, to be looking on a grand, white, handsome girl, the like of you . . . and every time I set my eyes on you I do be blessing the saints, and the holy water, and the power of the Lord Almighty in the heavens above.

MOLLY BYRNE. I 've heard the priests say it isn't looking on a young girl would teach many to be saying their prayers.

[*Bailing water into her can with a cup.*

MARTIN DOUL. It isn't many have been the way I was, hearing your voice speaking, and not seeing you at all.

MOLLY BYRNE. This should have been a queer time for an old, wicked, coaxing fool to be sitting there with your eyes shut, and not seeing a sight of a girl or woman passing the road.

MARTIN DOUL. If it was a queer time itself it was great joy and pride I had the time I 'd hear your voice speaking and you passing to Grianan [*beginning to speak with plaintive intensity*], for it 's of many a fine thing your voice would put a poor dark fellow in mind, and the day I 'd hear it it 's of little else at all I would be thinking.

MOLLY BYRNE. I 'll tell your wife if you talk to me the like of that. . . . You 've heard, maybe, she 's below picking nettles for the widow O'Flinn, who took great pity on her when she seen the two of you fighting, and yourself putting shame on her at the crossing of the roads.

MARTIN DOUL. [*Impatiently.*] Is there no living person can speak a score of words to me, or say 'God speed you' itself, without putting me in mind of the old woman or that day either at Grianan?

MOLLY BYRNE. [*Maliciously.*] I was thinking it should be a fine thing to put you in mind of the day you called the grand day of your life.

MARTIN DOUL. Grand day, is it? [*Plaintively again, throwing aside his work, and leaning towards her.*] Or a bad black day when I was roused up and found I was the like of the little children do be listening to the stories of an old woman, and do be dreaming after in the dark night that it's in grand houses of gold they are, with speckled horses to ride, and do be waking again, in a short while, and they destroyed with the cold, and the thatch dripping, maybe, and the starved ass braying in the yard?

MOLLY BYRNE. [*Working indifferently.*] You've great romancing this day, Martin Doul. Was it up at the still you were at the fall of night.

MARTIN DOUL. [*Stands up, comes towards her, but stands at far side of well.*] It was not, Molly Byrne, but lying down in a little rickety shed. . . . Lying down across a sop of straw, and I thinking I was seeing you walk, and hearing the sound of your step on a dry road, and hearing you again, and you laughing and making great talk in a high room with dry timber lining the roof. For it's a fine sound your voice has that time, and it's better I am, I'm thinking, lying down, the way a blind man does be lying, than to be sitting here in the grey light taking hard words of Timmy the smith.

MOLLY BYRNE. [*Looking at him with interest.*] It's queer talk you have if it's a little, old, shabby stump of a man you are itself.

MARTIN DOUL. I'm not so old as you do hear them say.

MOLLY BYRNE. You're old, I'm thinking, to be talking that talk with a girl.

MARTIN DOUL. [*Despondingly.*] It's not a lie you're telling maybe, for it's long years I'm after losing from the world, feeling love and talking love, with the old woman, and I fooled the whole while with the lies of Timmy the smith.

MOLLY BYRNE. [*Half invitingly.*] It's a fine way your wanting to pay Timmy the smith. . . . And it's not his *lies* you're making love to this day, Martin Doul.

MARTIN DOUL. It is not, Molly, and the Lord forgive us all. [*He passes behind her and comes near her left.*] For I've heard tell there are lands beyond in Cahir Iveraghig and the Reeks of Cork with warm sun in them, and fine light in the sky. [*Bending towards her.*] And light's a grand thing for a man ever was blind, or a woman, with a fine

neck, and a skin on her the like of you, the way we 'd
have a right to go off this day till we 'd have a fine life
passing abroad through them towns of the south, and we
telling stories, maybe, or singing songs at the fairs.

MOLLY BYRNE. [*Turning round half amused, and looking him
over from head to foot.*] Well, isn't it a queer thing when
your own wife 's after leaving you because you 're a pitiful
show, you 'd talk the like of that to me?

MARTIN DOUL. [*Drawing back a little, hurt, but indignant.*]
It 's a queer thing, maybe, for all things is queer in the
world. [*In a low voice with peculiar emphasis.*] But there 's
one thing I 'm telling you, if she walked off away from me,
it wasn't because of seeing me, and I no more than I am,
but because I was looking on her with my two eyes, and
she getting up, and eating her food, and combing her hair,
and lying down for her sleep.

MOLLY BYRNE. [*Interested, off her guard.*] Wouldn't any
married man you 'd have be doing the like of that?

MARTIN DOUL. [*Seizing the moment that he has her attention.*]
I 'm thinking by the mercy of God it 's few sees anything
but them is blind for a space [*with excitement*]. It 's few
sees the old women rotting for the grave, and it 's few
sees the like of yourself. [*He bends over her.*] Though it 's
shining you are, like a high lamp would drag in the ships
out of the sea.

MOLLY BYRNE. [*Shrinking away from him.*] Keep off from
me, Martin Doul.

MARTIN DOUL. [*Quickly with low, furious intensity.*] It 's the
truth I 'm telling you. [*He puts his hand on her shoulder and
shakes her.*] And you 'd do right not to marry a man is
after looking out a long while on the bad days of the world;
for what way would the like of him have fit eyes to look
on yourself, when you rise up in the morning and come out
of the little door you have above in the lane, the time it 'd
be a fine thing if a man would be seeing, and losing his
sight, the way he 'd have your two eyes facing him, and
he going the roads, and shining above him, and he looking
in the sky, and springing up from the earth, the time he 'd

lower his head, in place of the muck that seeing men do meet all roads spread on the world.

MOLLY BYRNE. [*Who has listened half mesmerized, starting away.*] It 's the like of that talk you 'd hear from a man would be losing his mind.

MARTIN DOUL. [*Going after her, passing to her right.*] It 'd be little wonder if a man near the like of you would be losing his mind. Put down your can now, and come along with myself, for I 'm seeing you this day, seeing you, maybe, the way no man has seen you in the world. [*He takes her by the arm and tries to pull her away softly to the right.*] Let you come on now, I 'm saying, to the lands of Iveragh and the Reeks of Cork, where you won't set down the width of your two feet and not be crushing fine flowers, and making sweet smells in the air.

MOLLY BYRNE. [*Laying down can, trying to free herself.*] Leave me go, Martin Doul! Leave me go, I 'm saying!

MARTIN DOUL. Let you not be fooling. Come along now the little path through the trees.

MOLLY BYRNE. [*Crying out towards forge.*] Timmy— Timmy the smith. [*Timmy comes out of forge, and Martin Doul lets her go. Molly Byrne, excited and breathless, pointing to Martin Doul.*] Did ever you hear that them that loses their sight loses their senses along with it, Timmy the smith!

TIMMY. [*Suspicious, but uncertain.*] He 's no sense, surely, and he 'll be having himself driven off this day from where he 's good sleeping, and feeding, and wages for his work.

MOLLY BYRNE. [*As before.*] He 's a bigger fool than that, Timmy. Look on him now, and tell me if that isn't a grand fellow to think he 's only to open his mouth to have a fine woman, the like of me, running along by his heels.

[*Martin Doul recoils towards centre, with his hand to his eyes; Mary Doul is seen on left coming forward softly.*]

TIMMY. [*With blank amazement.*] Oh, the blind is wicked people, and it 's no lie. But he 'll walk off this day and not be troubling us more.

[*Turns back left and picks up Martin Doul's coat and stick; some things fall out of coat pocket, which he gathers up again.*

MARTIN DOUL. [*Turns round, sees Mary Doul, whispers to Molly Byrne with imploring agony.*] Let you not put shame on me, Molly, before herself and the smith.   Let you not put shame on me and I after saying fine words to you, and dreaming . . . dreams . . . in the night. [*He hesitates, and looks round the sky.*] Is it a storm of thunder is coming, or the last end of the world? [*He staggers towards Mary Doul, tripping slightly over tin can.*] The heavens is closing, I 'm thinking, with darkness and great trouble passing in the sky. [*He reaches Mary Doul, and seizes her left arm with both his hands—with a frantic cry.*] Is it the darkness of thunder is coming, Mary Doul?   Do you see me clearly with your eyes?

MARY DOUL. [*Snatches her arm away, and hits him with empty sack across the face.*] I see you a sight too clearly, and let you keep off from me now.

MOLLY BYRNE. [*Clapping her hands.*] That 's right, Mary. That 's the way to treat the like of him is after standing there at my feet and asking me to go off with him, till I 'd grow an old wretched road-woman the like of yourself.

MARY DOUL. [*Defiantly.*] When the skin shrinks on your chin, Molly Byrne, there won't be the like of you for a shrunk hag in the four quarters of Ireland. . . . It 's a fine pair you 'd be, surely!

[*Martin Doul is standing at back right centre, with his back to the audience.*

TIMMY. [*Coming over to Mary Doul.*] Is it no shame you have to let on she 'd ever be the like of you?

MARY DOUL. It 's them that 's fat and flabby do be wrinkled young, and that whitish yellowy hair she has does be soon turning the like of a handful of thin grass you 'd see rotting, where the wet lies, at the north of a sty. [*Turning to go out on right.*] Ah, it 's a better thing to have a simple, seemly face, the like of my face, for twoscore years, or fifty itself, than to be setting fools mad a short while, and then to be turning a thing would drive off the little children from your feet.

[*She goes out; Martin Doul has come forward again, mastering himself, but uncertain.*

TIMMY. Oh, God protect us, Molly, from the words of the blind. [*He throws down Martin Doul's coat and stick.*] There's your old rubbish now, Martin Doul, and let you take it up, for it's all you have, and walk off through the world, for if ever I meet you coming again, if it's seeing or blind you are itself, I'll bring out the big hammer and hit you a welt with it will leave you easy till the Judgment Day.

MARTIN DOUL. [*Rousing himself with an effort.*] What call have you to talk the like of that with myself?

TIMMY. [*Pointing to Molly Byrne.*] It's well you know what call I have. It's well you know a decent girl, I'm thinking to wed, has no right to have her heart scalded with hearing talk—and queer, bad talk, I'm thinking—from a raggy-looking fool the like of you.

MARTIN DOUL. [*Raising his voice.*] It's making game of you she is, for what seeing girl would marry with yourself? Look on him, Molly, look on him, I'm saying, for I'm seeing him still, and let you raise your voice, for the time is come, and bid him go up into his forge, and be sitting there by himself, sneezing, and sweating, and he beating pot-hooks till the Judgment Day.

[*He seizes her arm again.*

MOLLY BYRNE. Keep him off from me, Timmy!

TIMMY. [*Pushing Martin Doul aside.*] Would you have me strike you, Martin Doul? Go along now after your wife, who's a fit match for you, and leave Molly with myself.

MARTIN DOUL. [*Despairingly.*] Won't you raise your voice, Molly, and lay hell's long curse on his tongue?

MOLLY BYRNE. [*On Timmy's left.*] I'll be telling him it's destroyed I am with the sight of you and the sound of your voice. Go off now after your wife, and if she beats you again, let you go after the tinker girls is above running the hills, or down among the sluts of the town, and you'll learn one day, maybe, the way a man should speak with a well-reared, civil girl the like of me. [*She takes Timmy by the arm.*] Come up now into the forge till he 'll be gone down a bit on the road, for it 's near afeard I am of the wild look he has come in his eyes.

[*She goes into the forge. Timmy stops in the doorway.*
TIMMY. Let me not find you here again, Martin Doul. [*He bares his arm.*] It 's well you know Timmy the smith has great strength in his arm, and it 's a power of things it has broken a sight harder than the old bone of your skull.

[*He goes into the forge and pulls the door after him.*
MARTIN DOUL. [*Stands a moment with his hand to his eyes.*] And that 's the last thing I 'm to set my sight on in the life of the world—the villainy of a woman and the bloody strength of a man. Oh, God, pity a poor blind fellow, the way I am this day with no strength in me to do hurt to them at all. [*He begins groping about for a moment, then stops.*] Yet if I 've no strength in me I 've a voice left for my prayers, and may God blight them this day, and my own soul the same hour with them, the way I 'll see them after, Molly Byrne and Timmy the smith, the two of them, on a high bed, and they screeching in hell. . . . It 'll be a grand thing that time to look on the two of them; and they twisting and roaring out, and twisting and roaring again, one day and the next day, and each day always and ever. It 's not blind I 'll be that time, and it won't be hell to me, I 'm thinking, but the like of heaven itself; and it 's fine care I 'll be taking the Lord Almighty doesn't know.

[*He turns to grope out.*

CURTAIN

Act III

The same scene as in first Act, but gap in centre has been filled with briers, or branches of some sort. Mary Doul, blind again, gropes her way in on left, and sits as before. She has a few rushes with her. It is an early spring day.

MARY DOUL. [*Mournfully.*] Ah, God help me . . . God help me; the blackness wasn't so black at all the other time as it is this time, and it 's destroyed I 'll be now, and hard set to get my living working alone, when it 's few are passing and the winds are cold. [*She begins shredding rushes.*] I 'm thinking short days will be long days to me from this time, and I sitting here, not seeing a blink, or hearing a word, and no thought in my mind but long prayers that Martin Doul 'll get his reward in a short while for the villainy of his heart. It 's great jokes the people 'll be making now, I 'm thinking, and they pass me by, pointing their fingers, maybe, and asking what place is himself, the way it 's no quiet or decency I 'll have from this day till I 'm an old woman with long white hair and it twisting from my brow. [*She fumbles with her hair, and then seems to hear something. Listens for a moment.*] There 's a queer slouching step coming on the road. . . . God help me, he 's coming surely.

> [*She stays perfectly quiet. Martin Doul gropes in on right, blind also.*

MARTIN DOUL. [*Gloomily.*] The devil mend Mary Doul for putting lies on me, and letting on she was grand. The devil mend the old Saint for letting me see it was lies. [*He sits down near her.*] The devil mend Timmy the smith for killing me with hard work, and keeping me with an empty, windy stomach in me, in the day and in the night. Ten thousand devils mend the soul of Molly Byrne—[*Mary Doul nods her head with approval*]—and the bad, wicked souls is hidden in all the women of the world. [*He rocks himself, with his hand over his face.*] It 's lonesome I 'll be from this day, and if living people is a bad lot, yet Mary Doul, herself, and she a dirty, wrinkled-looking hag, was better maybe to be sitting along with than no one at all. I 'll be getting my death now, I 'm thinking, sitting alone in the cold air, hearing the night coming, and the black-birds flying round in the briers crying to themselves, the time you 'll hear one cart getting off a long way in the east, and another cart getting off a long way in the west, and a dog barking maybe, and a little wind turning the sticks. [*He listens and sighs heavily.*] I 'll be destroyed sitting alone and losing my senses this time the way I 'm after losing my sight, for it 'd make any person afeard to be sitting up hearing the sound of his breath—[*he moves his feet on the stones*]—and the noise of his feet, when it 's a power of queer things do be stirring, little sticks breaking and the grass moving—[*Mary Doul half sighs, and he turns on her in horror*]—till you 'd take your dying oath on sun and moon a thing was breathing on the stones. [*He listens towards her for a moment, then starts up nervously and gropes about for his stick.*] I 'll be going now, I 'm thinking, but I 'm not sure what place my stick 's in, and I 'm destroyed with terror and dread. [*He touches her face as he is groping about and cries out.*] There 's a thing with a cold, living face on it sitting up at my side. [*He turns to run away, but misses his path and tumbles in against the wall.*] My road is lost on me now!   Oh, merciful God, set my foot on the path this day, and I 'll be saying prayers morn-ing and night, and not straining my ear after young girls, or doing any bad thing till I die——

MARY DOUL. [*Indignantly.*] Let you not be telling lies to the Almighty God.

MARTIN DOUL. Mary Doul, is it? [*Recovering himself with immense relief.*] Is it Mary Doul, I 'm saying?

MARY DOUL. There 's a sweet tone in your voice I 've not heard for a space.   You 're taking me for Molly Byrne, I 'm thinking.

MARTIN DOUL. [*Coming towards her, wiping sweat from his*

face.] Well, sight 's a queer thing for upsetting a man. It 's a queer thing to think I 'd live to this day to be fearing the like of you; but if it 's shaken I am for a short while, I 'll soon be coming to myself.

MARY DOUL. You 'll be grand then, and it 's no lie.

MARTIN DOUL. [*Sitting down shyly, some way off.*] You 've no call to be talking, for I 've heard tell you 're as blind as myself.

MARY DOUL. If I am I 'm bearing in mind I 'm married to a little dark stump of a fellow looks the fool of the world, and I 'll be bearing in mind from this day the great hullabaloo he 's after making from hearing a poor woman breathing quiet in her place.

MARTIN DOUL. And you 'll be bearing in mind, I 'm thinking, what you seen a while back when you looked down into a well, or a clear pool, maybe, when there was no wind stirring and a good light in the sky.

MARY DOUL. I 'm minding that surely, for if I 'm not the way the liars were saying below I seen a thing in them pools put joy and blessing in my heart.

[*She puts her hand to her hair again.*

MARTIN DOUL. [*Laughing ironically.*] Well, they were saying below I was losing my senses, but I never went any day the length of that. . . . God help you, Mary Doul, if you 're not a wonder for looks, you 're the maddest female woman is walking the counties of the east.

MARY DOUL. [*Scornfully.*] You were saying all times you 'd a great ear for hearing the lies in a word. A great ear, God help you, and you think you 're using it now.

MARTIN DOUL. If it 's not lies you 're telling would you have me think you 're not a wrinkled poor woman is looking like three scores, maybe, or two scores and a half!

MARY DOUL. I would not, Martin. [*She leans forward earnestly.*] For when I seen myself in them pools, I seen my hair would be grey or white, maybe, in a short while, and I seen with it that I 'd a face would be a great wonder when it 'll have soft white hair falling around it, the way when I 'm an old woman there won't be the like of me surely in the seven counties of the east.

MARTIN DOUL. [*With real admiration.*] You 're a cute thinking woman, Mary Doul, and it 's no lie.

MARY DOUL. [*Triumphantly.*] I am, surely, and I 'm telling you a beautiful white-haired woman is a grand thing to see, for I 'm told when Kitty Bawn was selling poteen below, the young men itself would never tire to be looking in her face.

MARTIN DOUL. [*Taking off his hat and feeling his head, speaking with hesitation.*] Did you think to look, Mary Doul, would there be a whiteness the like of that coming upon me?

MARY DOUL. [*With extreme contempt.*] On you, God help you! . . . In a short while you 'll have a head on you as bald as an old turnip you 'd see rolling round in the muck. You need never talk again of your fine looks, Martin Doul, for the day of that talk 's gone for ever.

MARTIN DOUL. That 's a hard word to be saying, for I was thinking if I 'd a bit of comfort, the like of yourself, it 's not far off we 'd be from the good days went before, and that 'd be a wonder surely. But I 'll never rest easy, thinking you 're a grey beautiful woman, and myself a pitiful show.

MARY DOUL. I can't help your looks, Martin Doul. It wasn't myself made you with your rat's eyes, and your big ears, and your griseldy chin.

MARTIN DOUL. [*Rubs his chin ruefully, then beams with delight.*] There 's one thing you 've forgot, if you 're a cute thinking woman itself.

MARY DOUL. Your slouching feet, is it? Or your hooky neck, or your two knees is black with knocking one on the other?

MARTIN DOUL. [*With delighted scorn.*] There 's talking for a cute woman. There 's talking, surely!

MARY DOUL. [*Puzzled at joy of his voice.*] If you 'd anything but lies to say you 'd be talking yourself.

MARTIN DOUL. [*Bursting with excitement.*] I 've this to say,

Mary Doul. I 'll be letting my beard grow in a short while, a beautiful, long, white, silken, streamy beard, you wouldn't see the like of in the eastern world. . . . Ah, a white beard 's a grand thing on an old man, a grand thing for making the quality stop and be stretching out their hands with good silver or gold, and a beard 's a thing you 'll never have, so you may be holding your tongue.

Mary Doul. [*Laughing cheerfully.*] Well, we 're a great pair, surely, and it 's great times we 'll have yet, maybe, and great talking before we die.

Martin Doul. Great times from this day, with the help of the Almighty God, for a priest itself would believe the lies of an old man would have a fine white beard growing on his chin.

Mary Doul. There 's the sound of one of them twittering yellow birds do be coming in the springtime from beyond the sea, and there 'll be a fine warmth now in the sun, and a sweetness in the air, the way it 'll be a grand thing to be sitting here quiet and easy, smelling the things growing up, and budding from the earth.

Martin Doul. I 'm smelling the furze a while back sprouting on the hill, and if you 'd hold your tongue you 'd hear the lambs of Grianan, though it 's near drowned their crying is with the full river making noises in the glen.

Mary Doul. [*Listens.*] The lambs is bleating, surely, and there 's cocks and laying hens making a fine stir a mile off on the face of the hill.   [*She starts.*

Martin Doul. What 's that is sounding in the west?

[*A faint sound of a bell is heard.*

Mary Doul. It 's not the churches, for the wind 's blowing from the sea.

Martin Doul. [*With dismay.*] It 's the old Saint, I 'm thinking, ringing his bell.

Mary Doul. The Lord protect us from the saints of God! [*They listen.*] He 's coming this road, surely.

Martin Doul. [*Tentatively.*] Will we be running off, Mary Doul?

Mary Doul. What place would we run?

MARTIN DOUL. There 's the little path going up through the sloughs. . . . If we reached the bank above, where the elders do be growing, no person would see a sight of us, if it was a hundred yeomen were passing itself; but I 'm afeard after the time we were with our sight we 'll not find our way to it at all.

MARY DOUL. [*Standing up.*] You 'd find the way, surely. You 're a grand man the world knows at finding your way winter or summer, if there was deep snow in it itself, or thick grass and leaves, maybe, growing from the earth.

MARTIN DOUL. [*Taking her hand.*] Come a bit this way; it 's here it begins. [*They grope about gap.*] There 's a tree pulled into the gap, or a strange thing happened, since I was passing it before.

MARY DOUL. Would we have a right to be crawling in below under the sticks?

MARTIN DOUL. It 's hard set I am to know what would be right. And isn't it a poor thing to be blind when you can't run off itself, and you fearing to see?

MARY DOUL. [*Nearly in tears.*] It 's a poor thing, God help us, and what good 'll our grey hairs be itself, if we have our sight, the way we 'll see them falling each day, and turning dirty in the rain? [*The bell sounds near by.*

MARTIN DOUL. [*In despair.*] He 's coming now, and we won't get off from him at all.

MARY DOUL. Could we hide in the bit of a brier is growing at the west butt of the church?

MARTIN DOUL. We 'll try that, surely. [*He listens a moment.*] Let you make haste; I hear them trampling in the wood. [*They grope over to church.*

MARY DOUL. It 's the words of the young girls making a great stir in the trees. [*They find the bush.*] Here 's the brier on my left, Martin; I 'll go in first, I 'm the big one, and I 'm easy to see.

MARTIN DOUL. [*Turning his head anxiously.*] It 's easy heard you are; and will you be holding your tongue?

MARY DOUL. [*Partly behind bush.*] Come in now beside of

me. [*They kneel down, still clearly visible.*] Do you think can they see us now, Martin Doul?

MARTIN DOUL. I 'm thinking they can't, but I 'm hard set to know; for the lot of them young girls, the devil save them, have sharp, terrible eyes, would pick out a poor man, I 'm thinking, and he lying below hid in his grave.

MARY DOUL. Let you not be whispering sin, Martin Doul, or maybe it 's the finger of God they 'd see pointing to ourselves.

MARTIN DOUL. It 's yourself is speaking madness, Mary Doul; haven't you heard the Saint say it 's the wicked do be blind?

MARY DOUL. If it is you 'd have a right to speak a big, terrible word would make the water not cure us at all.

MARTIN DOUL. What way would I find a big, terrible word, and I shook with the fear; and if I did itself, who 'd know rightly if it 's good words or bad would save us this day from himself?

MARY DOUL. They 're coming. I hear their feet on the stones.

[*The Saint comes in on right, with Timmy and Molly Byrne in holiday clothes, the others as before.*

TIMMY. I 've heard tell Martin Doul and Mary Doul were seen this day about on the road, holy father, and we were thinking you 'd have pity on them and cure them again.

SAINT. I would, maybe, but where are they at all? I 'll have little time left when I have the two of you wed in the church.

MAT SIMON. [*At their seat.*] There are the rushes they do have lying round on the stones. It 's not far off they 'll be, surely.

MOLLY BYRNE. [*Pointing with astonishment.*] Look beyond, Timmy.   [*They all look over and see Martin Doul.*

TIMMY. Well, Martin 's a lazy fellow to be lying in there at the height of the day. [*He goes over shouting.*] Let you get up out of that. You were near losing a great chance by your sleepiness this day, Martin Doul. . . . The two of them 's in it, God help us all!

MARTIN DOUL. [*Scrambling up with Mary Doul.*] What is it you want, Timmy, that you can't leave us in peace?

TIMMY. The Saint's come to marry the two of us, and I'm after speaking a word for yourselves, the way he'll be curing you now; for if you're a foolish man itself, I do be pitying you, for I've a kind heart, when I think of you sitting dark again, and you after seeing a while, and working for your bread.

[*Martin Doul takes Mary Doul's hand and tries to grope his way off right; he has lost his hat, and they are both covered with dust and grass seeds.*

PEOPLE. You're going wrong.   It's this way, Martin Doul.

[*They push him over in front of the Saint, near centre. Martin Doul and Mary Doul stand with piteous hang-dog dejection.*

SAINT. Let you not be afeard, for there's great pity with the Lord.

MARTIN DOUL. We aren't afeard, holy father.

SAINT. It's many a time those that are cured with the well of the four beauties of God lose their sight when a time is gone, but those I cured a second time go on seeing till the hour of death. [*He takes the cover from his can.*] I've a few drops only left of the water, but, with the help of God, it'll be enough for the two of you, and let you kneel down now upon the road.

[*Martin Doul wheels round with Mary Doul and tries to get away.*

SAINT. You can kneel down here, I'm saying, we'll not trouble this time going to the church.

TIMMY. [*Turning Martin Doul round, angrily.*] Are you going mad in your head, Martin Doul?   It's here you're to kneel.   Did you not hear his reverence, and he speaking to you now?

SAINT. Kneel down, I'm saying, the ground's dry at your feet.

MARTIN DOUL. [*With distress.*] Let you go on your own way, holy father.   We're not calling you at all.

SAINT. I'm not saying a word of penance, or fasting itself,

for I 'm thinking the Lord has brought you great teaching in the blinding of your eyes; so you 've no call now to be fearing me, but let you kneel down till I give you your sight.

MARTIN DOUL. [*More troubled.*] We 're not asking our sight, holy father, and let you walk on your own way, and be fasting, or praying, or doing anything that you will, but leave us here in our peace, at the crossing of the roads, for it 's best we are this way, and we 're not asking to see.

SAINT. [*To the people.*] Is his mind gone that he 's no wish to be cured this day, or to be living or working, or looking on the wonders of the world?

MARTIN DOUL. It 's wonders enough I seen in a short space for the life of one man only.

SAINT. [*Severely.*] I never heard tell of any person wouldn't have great joy to be looking on the earth, and the image of the Lord thrown upon men.

MARTIN DOUL. [*Raising his voice.*] Them is great sights, holy father. . . . What was it I seen when I first opened my eyes but your own bleeding feet, and they cut with the stones? That was a great sight, maybe, of the image of God. . . . And what was it I seen my last day but the villainy of hell looking out from the eyes of the girl you 're coming to marry—the Lord forgive you—with Timmy the smith. That was a great sight, maybe. And wasn't it great sights I seen on the roads when the north winds would be driving, and the skies would be harsh, till you 'd see the horses and the asses, and the dogs itself, maybe, with their heads hanging, and they closing their eyes——

SAINT. And did you never hear tell of the summer, and the fine spring, and the places where the holy men of Ireland have built up churches to the Lord? No man isn't a madman, I 'm thinking, would be talking the like of that, and wishing to be closed up and seeing no sight of the grand glittering seas, and the furze that is opening above, and will soon have the hills shining as if it was fine creels of gold they were, rising to the sky.

MARTIN DOUL. Is it talking now you are of Knock and

Ballavore? Ah, it 's ourselves had finer sights than the like of them, I 'm telling you, when we were sitting a while back hearing the birds and bees humming in every weed of the ditch, or when we 'd be smelling the sweet, beautiful smell does be rising in the warm nights, when you do hear the swift flying things racing in the air, till we 'd be looking up in our own minds into a grand sky, and seeing lakes, and big rivers, and fine hills for taking the plough.

SAINT. [*To People.*] There 's little use talking with the like of him.

MOLLY BYRNE. It 's lazy he is, holy father, and not wanting to work; for a while before you had him cured he was always talking, and wishing, and longing for his sight.

MARTIN DOUL. [*Turning on her.*] I was longing, surely, for sight; but I seen my fill in a short while with the look of my wife, and the look of yourself, Molly Byrne, when you 'd the queer wicked grin in your eyes you do have the time you 're making game with a man.

MOLLY BYRNE. Let you not mind him, holy father; for it 's bad things he was saying to me a while back—bad things for a married man, your reverence—and you 'd do right surely to leave him in darkness, if it 's that is best fitting the villainy of his heart.

TIMMY. [*To Saint.*] Would you cure Mary Doul, your reverence, who is a quiet poor woman, never did hurt to any, or said a hard word, saving only when she 'd be vexed with himself, or with young girls would be making game of her below.

SAINT. [*To Mary Doul.*] If you have any sense, Mary, kneel down at my feet, and I 'll bring the sight again into your eyes.

MARTIN DOUL. [*More defiantly.*] You will not, holy father. Would you have her looking on me, and saying hard words to me, till the hour of death?

SAINT. [*Severely.*] If she 's wanting her sight I wouldn't have the like of you stop her at all. [*To Mary Doul.*] Kneel down, I 'm saying.

MARY DOUL. [*Doubtfully.*] Let us be as we are, holy father,

and then we 'll be known again in a short while as the
people is happy and blind, and be having an easy time, with
no trouble to live, and we getting halfpence on the road.

MOLLY BYRNE. Let you not be a raving fool, Mary Doul.
Kneel down now, and let him give you your sight, and
himself can be sitting here if he likes it best, and taking
halfpence on the road.

TIMMY. That 's the truth, Mary; and if it 's choosing a
wilful blindness you are, I 'm thinking there isn't any one
in this place will ever be giving you a hand's turn or a
ha'p'orth of meal, or be doing the little things you do need
to keep you at all living in the world.

MAT SIMON. If you had your sight, Mary, you could be
walking up for him and down with him, and be stitching
his clothes, and keeping a watch on him day and night the
way no other woman would come near him at all.

MARY DOUL. [Half persuaded] That 's the truth,
maybe——

SAINT. Kneel down now, I 'm saying, for it 's in haste I am
to be going on with the marriage and be walking my own
way before the fall of night.

THE PEOPLE. Kneel down, Mary! Kneel down when
you 're bid by the Saint!

MARY DOUL. [Looking uneasily towards Martin Doul.]
Maybe it 's right they are, and I will if you wish it, holy
father.

> [She kneels down. The Saint takes off his hat and gives it
> to someone near him. All the men take off their hats.
> He goes forward a step to take Martin Doul's hand
> away from Mary Doul.

SAINT. [To Martin Doul.] Go aside now; we 're not wanting you here.

MARTIN DOUL. [Pushes him away roughly, and stands with
his left hand on Mary Doul's shoulder.] Keep off yourself,
holy father, and let you not be taking my rest from me in
the darkness of my wife. . . . What call has the like of
you to be coming between married people—that you 're
not understanding at all—and be making a great mess

with the holy water you have, and the length of your prayers? Go on now, I 'm saying, and leave us here on the road.

SAINT. If it was a seeing man I heard talking to me the like of that I 'd put a black curse on him would weigh down his soul till it 'd be falling to hell; but you 're a poor blind sinner, God forgive you, and I don't mind you at all. [*He raises his can.*] Go aside now till I give the blessing to your wife, and if you won't go with your own will, there are those standing by will make you, surely.

MARTIN DOUL. [*Pulling Mary Doul.*] Come along now, and don't mind him at all.

SAINT. [*Imperiously, to the people.*] Let you take that man and drive him down upon the road.

[*Some men seize Martin Doul.*

MARTIN DOUL. [*Struggling and shouting.*] Make them leave me go, holy father! Make them leave me go, I 'm saying, and you may cure her this day, or do anything that you will.

SAINT. [*To people.*] Let him be. . . . Let him be if his sense is come to him at all.

MARTIN DOUL. [*Shakes himself loose, feels for Mary Doul, sinking his voice to a plausible whine.*] You may cure herself surely, holy father; I wouldn't stop you at all—and it 's great joy she 'll have looking on your face—but let you cure myself along with her, the way I 'll see when it 's lies she 's telling, and be looking out day and night upon the holy men of God.   [*He kneels down a little before Mary Doul.*

SAINT. [*Speaking half to the people.*] Men who are dark a long while and thinking over queer thoughts in their heads, aren't the like of simple men, who do be working every day, and praying, and living like ourselves; so if he has found a right mind at the last minute itself, I 'll cure him, if the Lord will, and not be thinking of the hard, foolish words he 's after saying this day to us all.

MARTIN DOUL. [*Listening eagerly.*] I 'm waiting now, holy father.

SAINT. [*With can in his hand, close to Martin Doul.*] With the power of the water from the grave of the four beauties

of God, with the power of this water, I 'm saying, that I
put upon your eyes——   [*He raises can.*
MARTIN DOUL. [*With a sudden movement strikes the can from
the Saint's hand and sends it rocketing across stage.   He
stands up; people murmur loudly.*] If I 'm a poor dark
sinner I 've sharp ears, God help me, and it 's well I heard
the little splash of the water you had there in the can.   Go
on now, holy father, for if you 're a fine Saint itself, it 's
more sense is in a blind man, and more power maybe than
you 're thinking at all.   Let you walk on now with your
worn feet, and your welted knees, and your fasting, holy
ways have left you with a big head on you and a thin pitiful
arm. [*The Saint looks at him for a moment severely, then
turns away and picks up his can.   He pulls Mary Doul up.*]
For if it 's a right some of you have to be working and
sweating the like of Timmy the smith, and a right some of
you have to be fasting and praying and talking holy talk the
like of yourself, I 'm thinking it 's a good right ourselves
have to be sitting blind, hearing a soft wind turning round
the little leaves of the spring and feeling the sun, and we not
tormenting our souls with the sight of the grey days, and the
holy men, and the dirty feet is trampling the world.
          [*He gropes towards his stone with Mary Doul.*
MAT SIMON. It 'd be an unlucky fearful thing, I 'm thinking,
to have the like of that man living near us at all in the townland of Grianan.   Wouldn't he bring down a curse upon
us, holy father, from the heavens of God?
SAINT. [*Tying his girdle.*] God has great mercy, but great
wrath for them that sin.
THE PEOPLE. Go on now, Martin Doul.   Go on from this
place.   Let you not be bringing great storms or droughts
on us maybe from the power of the Lord.
          [*Some of them throw things at him.*
MARTIN DOUL. [*Turning round defiantly and picking up a
stone.*] Keep off now, the yelping lot of you, or it 's more
than one maybe will get a bloody head on him with the
pitch of my stone.   Keep off now, and let you not be
afeard; for we 're going on the two of us to the towns of

the south, where the people will have kind voices maybe, and we won't know their bad looks or their villainy at all. [*He takes Mary Doul's hand again.*] Come along now and we 'll be walking to the south, for we 've seen too much of every one in this place, and it 's small joy we 'd have living near them, or hearing the lies they do be telling from the grey of dawn till the night.

MARY DOUL. [*Despondingly.*] That 's the truth, surely; and we 'd have a right to be gone, if it 's a long way itself, as I 've heard them say, where you do have to be walking with a slough of wet on the one side and a slough of wet on the other, and you going a stony path with a north wind blowing behind.   [*They go out.*

TIMMY. There 's a power of deep rivers with floods in them where you do have to be lepping the stones and you going to the south, so I 'm thinking the two of them will be drowned together in a short while, surely.

SAINT. They have chosen their lot, and the Lord have mercy on their souls. [*He rings his bell.*] And let the two of you come up now into the church, Molly Byrne and Timmy the smith, till I make your marriage and put my blessing on you all.

[*He turns to the church; procession forms, and the curtain comes down as they go slowly into the church.*

THE PLAYBOY OF THE WESTERN WORLD

PERSONS IN THE PLAY

CHRISTOPHER MAHON

OLD MAHON, his father, a squatter

MICHAEL JAMES FLAHERTY (called MICHAEL JAMES), a publican

MARGARET FLAHERTY (called PEGEEN MIKE), his daughter

WIDOW QUIN, a woman of about thirty

SHAWN KEOGH, her cousin, a young farmer

PHILLY CULLEN and JIMMY FARRELL, small farmers

SARA TANSEY, SUSAN BRADY, and HONOR BLAKE, village girls

A BELLMAN

SOME PEASANTS

The action takes place near a village, on a wild coast of Mayo. The first Act passes on an evening of autumn, the other two Acts on the following day

PREFACE

In writing 'The Playboy of the Western World,' as in my other plays, I have used one or two words only that I have not heard among the country people of Ireland, or spoken in my own nursery before I could read the newspapers. A certain number of the phrases I employ I have heard also from herds and fishermen along the coast from Kerry to Mayo or from beggar-women and ballad-singers nearer Dublin; and I am glad to acknowledge how much I owe to the folk-imagination of these fine people. Any one who has lived in real intimacy with the Irish peasantry will know that the wildest sayings and ideas in this play are tame indeed, compared with the fancies one may hear in any little hillside cabin in Geesala, or Carraroe, or Dingle Bay. All art is a collaboration; and there is little doubt that in the happy ages of literature, striking and beautiful phrases were as ready to the story-teller's or the playwright's hand, as the rich cloaks and dresses of his time. It is probable that when the Elizabethan dramatist took his ink-horn and sat down to his work he used many phrases that he had just heard, as he sat at dinner, from his mother or his children. In Ireland, those of us who know the people have the same privilege. When I was writing 'The Shadow of the Glen,' some years ago, I got more aid than any learning could have given me from a chink in the floor of the old Wicklow house where I was staying, that let me hear what was being said by the servant girls in the kitchen. This matter, I think, is of importance, for in countries where the imagination of the people, and the language they use, is rich and living, it is possible for a writer to be rich and copious in his words, and at the same time to give the reality, which is the root of all poetry, in a comprehensive and natural form. In the modern literature of towns, however, richness is found only in sonnets, or prose poems, or in one or two elaborate books that are far away from the profound and common interests of life. One has, on one side, Mallarmé and

Huysmans producing this literature; and on the other, Ibsen and Zola dealing with the reality of life in joyless and pallid works. On the stage one must have reality, and one must have joy; and that is why the intellectual modern drama has failed, and people have grown sick of the false joy of the musical comedy, that has been given them in place of the rich joy found only in what is superb and wild in reality. In a good play every speech should be as fully flavoured as a nut or apple, and such speeches cannot be written by any one who works among people who have shut their lips on poetry. In Ireland, for a few years more, we have a popular imagination that is fiery, and magnificent, and tender; so that those of us who wish to write start with a chance that is not given to writers in places where the springtime of the local life has been forgotten, and the harvest is a memory only, and the straw has been turned into bricks.

J. M. S.

21st January 1907.

THE PLAYBOY OF THE WESTERN WORLD

Act I

Country public house or shebeen, very rough and untidy. There is a sort of counter on the right with shelves, holding many bottles and jugs, just seen above it. Empty barrels stand near the counter. At back, a little to left of counter, there is a door into the open air, then, more to the left, there is a settle with shelves above it, with more jugs, and a table beneath a window. At the left there is a large open fire-place, with turf fire, and a small door into inner room. Pegeen, a wild-looking but fine girl, of about twenty, is writing at table. She is dressed in the usual peasant dress.

PEGEEN. [*Slowly as she writes.*] Six yards of stuff for to make a yellow gown. A pair of lace boots with lengthy heels on them and brassy eyes. A hat is suited for a wedding-day. A fine-tooth comb. To be sent with three barrels of porter in Jimmy Farrell's creel cart on the evening of the coming Fair to Mister Michael James Flaherty. With the best compliments of this season. Margaret Flaherty.

SHAWN KEOGH. [*A fat and fair young man comes in as she signs, looks around awkwardly, when he sees she is alone.*] Where 's himself?

PEGEEN. [*Without looking at him.*] He 's coming. [*She directs letter.*] To Mister Sheamus Mulroy, Wine and Spirit Dealer, Castlebar.

SHAWN. [*Uneasily.*] I didn't see him on the road.

PEGEEN. How would you see him [*licks stamp and puts it on letter*] and it dark night this half-hour gone by?

SHAWN. [*Turning towards door again.*] I stood a while outside wondering would I have a right to pass on or to walk in and see you, Pegeen Mike [*comes to fire*], and I could hear

the cows breathing and sighing in the stillness of the air,
and not a step moving any place from this gate to the bridge.

PEGEEN. [*Putting letter in envelope.*] It 's above at the cross-
roads he is, meeting Philly Cullen and a couple more are
going along with him to Kate Cassidy's wake.

SHAWN. [*Looking at her blankly.*] And he 's going that length
in the dark night.

PEGEEN. [*Impatiently.*] He is surely, and leaving me lonesome on the scruff of the hill. [*She gets up and puts envelope on dresser, then winds clock.*] Isn't it long the nights
are now, Shawn Keogh, to be leaving a poor girl with her
own self counting the hours to the dawn of day?

SHAWN. [*With awkward humour.*] If it is, when we 're
wedded in a short while you 'll have no call to complain,
for I 've little will to be walking off to wakes or weddings
in the darkness of the night.

PEGEEN. [*With rather scornful good humour.*] You 're making mighty certain, Shaneen, that I 'll wed you now.

SHAWN. Aren't we after making a good bargain, the way
we 're only waiting these days on Father Reilly's dispensation from the bishops, or the Court of Rome.

PEGEEN. [*Looking at him teasingly, washing up at dresser.*]
It 's a wonder, Shaneen, the Holy Father 'd be taking notice
of the likes of you; for if I was him I wouldn't bother with
this place where you 'll meet none but Red Linahan, has a
squint in his eye, and Patcheen is lame in his heel, or the
mad Mulrannies were driven from California and they lost
in their wits. We 're a queer lot these times to go troubling
the Holy Father on his sacred seat.

SHAWN. [*Scandalized.*] If we are, we 're as good this place as
another, maybe, and as good these times as we were for ever.

PEGEEN. [*With scorn.*] As good is it? Where now will you
meet the like of Daneen Sullivan knocked the eye from a
peeler; or Marcus Quin, God rest him, got six months for
maiming ewes, and he a great warrant to tell stories of holy
Ireland till he 'd have the old women shedding down tears
about their feet. Where will you find the like of them,
I 'm saying?

SHAWN. [*Timidly.*] If you don't, it's a good job, maybe;
for [*with peculiar emphasis on the words*] Father Reilly has
small conceit to have that kind walking around and talking
to the girls.

PEGEEN. [*Impatiently throwing water from basin out of the
door.*] Stop tormenting me with Father Reilly [*imitating
his voice*] when I'm asking only what way I'll pass these
twelve hours of dark, and not take my death with the fear.
[*Looking out of door.*

SHAWN. [*Timidly.*] Would I fetch you the Widow Quin,
maybe?

PEGEEN. Is it the like of that murderer?   You'll not, surely.

SHAWN. [*Going to her, soothingly.*] Then I'm thinking himself will stop along with you when he sees you taking on;
for it'll be a long night-time with great darkness, and I'm
after feeling a kind of fellow above in the furzy ditch,
groaning wicked like a maddening dog, the way it's good
cause you have, maybe, to be fearing now.

PEGEEN. [*Turning on him sharply.*] What's that?   Is it a
man you seen?

SHAWN. [*Retreating.*] I couldn't see him at all; but I heard
him groaning out, and breaking his heart.   It should have
been a young man from his words speaking.

PEGEEN. [*Going after him.*] And you never went near to see
was he hurted or what ailed him at all?

SHAWN. I did not, Pegeen Mike.   It was a dark, lonesome
place to be hearing the like of him.

PEGEEN. Well, you're a daring fellow, and if they find his
corpse stretched above in the dews of dawn, what'll you
say then to the peelers, or the Justice of the Peace?

SHAWN. [*Thunderstruck.*] I wasn't thinking of that.   For
the love of God, Pegeen Mike, don't let on I was speaking
of him.   Don't tell your father and the men is coming
above; for if they heard that story they'd have great blabbing
this night at the wake.

PEGEEN. I'll maybe tell them, and I'll maybe not.

SHAWN. They are coming at the door.   Will you whisht,
I'm saying?

PEGEEN. Whisht yourself.

[*She goes behind counter. Michael James, fat, jovial publican, comes in followed by Philly Cullen, who is thin and mistrusting, and Jimmy Farrell, who is fat and amorous, about forty-five.*

MEN. [*Together.*] God bless you! The blessing of God on this place!

PEGEEN. God bless you kindly.

MICHAEL. [*To men, who go to the counter.*] Sit down now, and take your rest. [*Crosses to Shawn at the fire.*] And how is it you are, Shawn Keogh? Are you coming over the sands to Kate Cassidy's wake?

SHAWN. I am not, Michael James. I 'm going home the short cut to my bed.

PEGEEN. [*Speaking across the counter.*] He 's right, too, and have you no shame, Michael James, to be quitting off for the whole night, and leaving myself lonesome in the shop?

MICHAEL. [*Good-humouredly.*] Isn't it the same whether I go for the whole night or a part only? and I 'm thinking it 's a queer daughter you are if you 'd have me crossing backward through the Stooks of the Dead Women, with a drop taken.

PEGEEN. If I am a queer daughter, it 's a queer father 'd be leaving me lonesome these twelve hours of dark, and I piling the turf with the dogs barking, and the calves mooing, and my own teeth rattling with the fear.

JIMMY. [*Flatteringly.*] What is there to hurt you, and you a fine, hardy girl would knock the head of any two men in the place?

PEGEEN. [*Working herself up.*] Isn't there the harvest boys with their tongues red for drink, and the ten tinkers is camped in the east glen, and the thousand militia—bad cess to them!—walking idle through the land. There 's lots surely to hurt me, and I won't stop alone in it, let himself do what he will.

MICHAEL. If you 're that afeard, let Shawn Keogh stop along with you. It 's the will of God, I 'm thinking, himself should be seeing to you now. [*They all turn on Shawn.*

SHAWN. [*In horrified confusion.*] I would and welcome, Michael James, but I 'm afeard of Father Reilly; and what at all would the Holy Father and the Cardinals of Rome be saying if they heard I did the like of that?

MICHAEL. [*With contempt.*] God help you! Can't you sit in by the hearth with the light lit and herself beyond in the room? You 'll do that surely, for I 've heard tell there 's a queer fellow above, going mad or getting his death, maybe, in the gripe of the ditch, so she 'd be safer this night with a person here.

SHAWN. [*With plaintive despair.*] I 'm afeard of Father Reilly, I 'm saying. Let you not be tempting me, and we near married itself.

PHILLY. [*With cold contempt.*] Lock him in the west room. He 'll stay then and have no sin to be telling to the priest.

MICHAEL. [*To Shawn, getting between him and the door.*] Go up now.

SHAWN. [*At the top of his voice.*] Don't stop me, Michael James. Let me out of the door, I 'm saying, for the love of the Almighty God. Let me out. [*Trying to dodge past him.*] Let me out of it, and may God grant you His indulgence in the hour of need.

MICHAEL. [*Loudly.*] Stop your noising, and sit down by the hearth. [*Gives him a push and goes to counter laughing.*

SHAWN. [*Turning back, wringing his hands.*] Oh, Father Reilly, and the saints of God, where will I hide myself to-day? Oh, St Joseph and St Patrick and St Brigid and St James, have mercy on me now!

[*Shawn turns round, sees door clear, and makes a rush for it.*

MICHAEL. [*Catching him by the coat-tail.*] You 'd be going, is it?

SHAWN. [*Screaming.*] Leave me go, Michael James, leave me go, you old Pagan, leave me go, or I 'll get the curse of the priests on you, and of the scarlet-coated bishops of the Courts of Rome.

[*With a sudden movement he pulls himself out of his coat, and disappears out of the door, leaving his coat in Michael's hands.*

MICHAEL. [*Turning round, and holding up coat.*] Well, there's the coat of a Christian man. Oh, there's sainted glory this day in the lonesome west; and by the will of God I've got you a decent man, Pegeen, you'll have no call to be spying after if you've a score of young girls, maybe, weeding in your fields.

PEGEEN. [*Taking up the defence of her property.*] What right have you to be making game of a poor fellow for minding the priest, when it's your own the fault is, not paying a penny pot-boy to stand along with me and give me courage in the doing of my work.

[*She snaps the coat away from him, and goes behind counter with it.*

MICHAEL. [*Taken aback.*] Where would I get a pot-boy? Would you have me send the bell-man screaming in the streets of Castlebar?

SHAWN. [*Opening the door a chink and putting in his head, in a small voice.*] Michael James!

MICHAEL. [*Imitating him.*] What ails you?

SHAWN. The queer dying fellow's beyond looking over the ditch. He's come up, I'm thinking, stealing your hens. [*Looks over his shoulder.*] God help me, he's following me now [*he runs into room*], and if he's heard what I said, he'll be having my life, and I going home lonesome in the darkness of the night.

[*For a perceptible moment they watch the door with curiosity. Someone coughs outside. Then Christy Mahon, a slight young man, comes in very tired and frightened and dirty.*

CHRISTY. [*In a small voice.*] God save all here!

MEN. God save you kindly!

CHRISTY. [*Going to the counter.*] I'd trouble you for a glass of porter, woman of the house.   [*He puts down coin.*

PEGEEN. [*Serving him.*] You're one of the tinkers, young fellow, is beyond camped in the glen?

CHRISTY. I am not; but I'm destroyed walking.

MICHAEL. [*Patronizingly.*] Let you come up then to the fire. You're looking famished with the cold.

CHRISTY. God reward you. [*He takes up his glass and goes a little way across to the left, then stops and looks about him.*] Is it often the polis do be coming into this place, master of the house?

MICHAEL. If you 'd come in better hours, you 'd have seen 'Licensed for the Sale of Beer and Spirits, to be Consumed on the Premises,' written in white letters above the door, and what would the polis want spying on me, and not a decent house within four miles, the way every living Christian is a bona fide, saving one widow alone?

CHRISTY. [*With relief.*] It 's a safe house, so.

> [*He goes over to the fire, sighing and moaning. Then he sits down, putting his glass beside him, and begins gnawing a turnip, too miserable to feel the others staring at him with curiosity.*

MICHAEL. [*Going after him.*] Is it yourself is fearing the polis? You 're wanting, maybe?

CHRISTY. There 's many wanting.

MICHAEL. Many, surely, with the broken harvest and the ended wars. [*He picks up some stockings, etc., that are near the fire, and carries them away furtively.*] It should be larceny, I 'm thinking?

CHRISTY. [*Dolefully.*] I had it in my mind it was a different word and a bigger.

PEGEEN. There 's a queer lad. Were you never slapped in school, young fellow, that you don't know the name of your deed?

CHRISTY. [*Bashfully.*] I 'm slow at learning, a middling scholar only.

MICHAEL. If you 're a dunce itself, you 'd have a right to know that larceny 's robbing and stealing. Is it for the like of that you 're wanting?

CHRISTY. [*With a flash of family pride.*] And I the son of a strong farmer [*with a sudden qualm*], God rest his soul, could have bought up the whole of your old house a while since, from the butt of his tail-pocket, and not have missed the weight of it gone.

MICHAEL. [*Impressed.*] If it 's not stealing, it 's maybe something big.

CHRISTY. [*Flattered.*] Aye; it 's maybe something big.

JIMMY. He 's a wicked-looking young fellow. Maybe he followed after a young woman on a lonesome night.

CHRISTY. [*Shocked.*] Oh, the saints forbid, mister; I was all times a decent lad.

PHILLY. [*Turning on Jimmy.*] You 're a silly man, Jimmy Farrell. He said his father was a farmer a while since, and there 's himself now in a poor state. Maybe the land was grabbed from him, and he did what any decent man would do.

MICHAEL. [*To Christy, mysteriously.*] Was it bailiffs?

CHRISTY. The divil a one.

MICHAEL. Agents?

CHRISTY. The divil a one.

MICHAEL. Landlords?

CHRISTY. [*Peevishly.*] Ah, not at all, I 'm saying. You 'd see the like of them stories on any little paper of a Munster town. But I 'm not calling to mind any person, gentle, simple, judge or jury, did the like of me.

[*They all draw nearer with delighted curiosity.*

PHILLY. Well, that lad 's a puzzle-the-world.

JIMMY. He 'd beat Dan Davies's circus, or the holy missioners making sermons on the villainy of man. Try him again, Philly.

PHILLY. Did you strike golden guineas out of solder, young fellow, or shilling coins itself?

CHRISTY. I did not, mister, not sixpence nor a farthing coin.

JIMMY. Did you marry three wives maybe? I 'm told there 's a sprinkling have done that among the holy Luthers of the preaching north.

CHRISTY. [*Shyly.*] I never married with one, let alone with a couple or three.

PHILLY. Maybe he went fighting for the Boers, the like of the man beyond, was judged to be hanged, quartered, and drawn. Were you off east, young fellow, fighting bloody wars for Kruger and the freedom of the Boers?

CHRISTY. I never left my own parish till Tuesday was a week.

PEGEEN. [*Coming from counter.*] He's done nothing, so. [*To Christy.*] If you didn't commit murder or a bad, nasty thing; or false coining, or robbery, or butchery, or the like of them, there isn't anything that would be worth your troubling for to run from now. You did nothing at all.

CHRISTY. [*His feelings hurt.*] That's an unkindly thing to be saying to a poor orphaned traveller, has a prison behind him, and hanging before, and hell's gap gaping below.

PEGEEN. [*With a sign to the men to be quiet.*] You're only saying it. You did nothing at all. A soft lad the like of you wouldn't slit the wind pipe of a screeching sow.

CHRISTY. [*Offended.*] You're not speaking the truth.

PEGEEN. [*In mock rage.*] Not speaking the truth, is it? Would you have me knock the head of you with the butt of the broom?

CHRISTY. [*Twisting round on her with a sharp cry of horror.*] Don't strike me. I killed my poor father, Tuesday was a week, for doing the like of that.

PEGEEN. [*With blank amazement.*] Is it killed your father?

CHRISTY. [*Subsiding.*] With the help of God I did, surely, and that the Holy Immaculate Mother may intercede for his soul.

PHILLY. [*Retreating with Jimmy.*] There's a daring fellow.

JIMMY. Oh, glory be to God!

MICHAEL. [*With great respect.*] That was a hanging crime, mister honey. You should have had good reason for doing the like of that.

CHRISTY. [*In a very reasonable tone.*] He was a dirty man, God forgive him, and he getting old and crusty, the way I couldn't put up with him at all.

PEGEEN. And you shot him dead?

CHRISTY. [*Shaking his head.*] I never used weapons. I've no licence, and I'm a law-fearing man.

MICHAEL. It was with a hilted knife maybe? I'm told, in the big world, it's bloody knives they use.

CHRISTY. [*Loudly, scandalized.*] Do you take me for a slaughter-boy?

PEGEEN. You never hanged him, the way Jimmy Farrell hanged his dog from the licence, and had it screeching and wriggling three hours at the butt of a string, and himself swearing it was a dead dog, and the peelers swearing it had life?

CHRISTY. I did not, then. I just riz the loy and let fall the edge of it on the ridge of his skull, and he went down at my feet like an empty sack, and never let a grunt or groan from him at all.

MICHAEL. [*Making a sign to Pegeen to fill Christy's glass.*] And what way weren't you hanged, mister? Did you bury him then?

CHRISTY. [*Considering.*] Aye. I buried him then. Wasn't I digging spuds in the field?

MICHAEL. And the peelers never followed after you the eleven days that you 're out?

CHRISTY. [*Shaking his head.*] Never a one of them, and I walking forward facing hog, dog, or divil on the highway of the road.

PHILLY. [*Nodding wisely.*] It 's only with a common week-day kind of a murderer them lads would be trusting their carcass, and that man should be a great terror when his temper 's roused.

MICHAEL. He should then. [*To Christy.*] And where was it, mister honey, that you did the deed?

CHRISTY. [*Looking at him with suspicion.*] Oh, a distant place, master of the house, a windy corner of high, distant hills.

PHILLY. [*Nodding with approval.*] He 's a close man, and he 's right, surely.

PEGEEN. That 'd be a lad with the sense of Solomon to have for a pot-boy, Michael James, if it 's the truth you 're seeking one at all.

PHILLY. The peelers is fearing him, and if you 'd that lad in the house there isn't one of them would come smelling around if the dogs itself were lapping poteen from the dung-pit of the yard.

JIMMY. Bravery's a treasure in a lonesome place, and a lad would kill his father, I 'm thinking, would face a foxy divil with a pitchpike on the flags of hell.

PEGEEN. It 's the truth they 're saying, and if I 'd that lad in the house, I wouldn't be fearing the loosèd khaki cut-throats, or the walking dead.

CHRISTY. [*Swelling with surprise and triumph.*] Well, glory be to God!

MICHAEL. [*With deference.*] Would you think well to stop here and be pot-boy, mister honey, if we gave you good wages, and didn't destroy you with the weight of work.

SHAWN. [*Coming forward uneasily.*] That 'd be a queer kind to bring into a decent, quiet household with the like of Pegeen Mike.

PEGEEN. [*Very sharply.*] Will you whisht? Who 's speaking to you?

SHAWN. [*Retreating.*] A bloody-handed murderer the like of . . .

PEGEEN. [*Snapping at him.*] Whisht, I am saying; we 'll take no fooling from your like at all. [*To Christy, with a honeyed voice.*] And you, young fellow, you 'd have a right to stop, I 'm thinking, for we 'd do our all and utmost to content your needs.

CHRISTY. [*Overcome with wonder.*] And I 'd be safe this place from the searching law?

MICHAEL. You would, surely. If they 're not fearing you, itself, the peelers in this place is decent, drouthy poor fellows, wouldn't touch a cur dog and not give warning in the dead of night.

PEGEEN. [*Very kindly and persuasively.*] Let you stop a short while anyhow. Aren't you destroyed walking with your feet in bleeding blisters, and your whole skin needing washing like a Wicklow sheep.

CHRISTY. [*Looking round with satisfaction.*] It 's a nice room, and if it 's not humbugging me you are, I 'm thinking that I 'll surely stay.

JIMMY. [*Jumps up.*] Now, by the grace of God, herself will be safe this night, with a man killed his father holding danger from the door, and let you come on, Michael James, or they 'll have the best stuff drunk at the wake.

MICHAEL. [*Going to the door with men.*] And begging your pardon, mister, what name will we call you, for we 'd like to know?

CHRISTY. Christopher Mahon.

MICHAEL. Well, God bless you, Christy, and a good rest till we meet again when the sun 'll be rising to the noon of day.

CHRISTY. God bless you all.

MEN. God bless you.

[*They go out, except Shawn, who lingers at the door.*

SHAWN. [*To Pegeen.*] Are you wanting me to stop along with you and keep you from harm?

PEGEEN. [*Gruffly.*] Didn't you say you were fearing Father Reilly?

SHAWN. There 'd be no harm staying now, I 'm thinking, and himself in it too.

PEGEEN. You wouldn't stay when there was need for you, and let you step off nimble this time when there 's none.

SHAWN. Didn't I say it was Father Reilly . . .

PEGEEN. Go on, then, to Father Reilly [*in a jeering tone*], and let him put you in the holy brotherhoods, and leave that lad to me.

SHAWN. If I meet the Widow Quin . . .

PEGEEN. Go on, I 'm saying, and don't be waking this place with your noise. [*She hustles him out and bolts door.*] That lad would wear the spirits from the saints of peace. [*Bustles about, then takes off her apron and pins it up in the window as a blind, Christy watching her timidly. Then she comes to him and speaks with bland good humour.*] Let you stretch out now by the fire, young fellow. You should be destroyed travelling.

CHRISTY. [*Shyly again, drawing off his boots.*] I 'm tired surely, walking wild eleven days, and waking fearful in the night.

[*He holds up one of his feet, feeling his blisters, and looking at them with compassion.*

PEGEEN. [*Standing beside him, watching him with delight.*] You

should have had great people in your family, I'm
thinking, with the little, small feet you have, and
you with a kind of a quality name, the like of what
you'd find on the great powers and potentates of France
and Spain.

CHRISTY. [*With pride.*] We were great, surely, with wide
and windy acres of rich Munster land.

PEGEEN. Wasn't I telling you, and you a fine, handsome
young fellow with a noble brow?

CHRISTY. [*With a flush of delighted surprise.*] Is it me?

PEGEEN. Aye.   Did you never hear that from the young
girls where you come from in the west or south?

CHRISTY. [*With venom.*] I did not, then.   Oh, they're
bloody liars in the naked parish where I grew a man.

PEGEEN. If they are itself, you've heard it these days, I'm
thinking, and you walking the world telling out your
story to young girls or old.

CHRISTY. I've told my story no place till this night, Pegeen
Mike, and it's foolish I was here, maybe, to be talking
free; but you're decent people, I'm thinking, and
yourself a kindly woman, the way I wasn't fearing you
at all.

PEGEEN. [*Filling a sack with straw.*] You've said the like of
that, maybe, in every cot and cabin where you've met a
young girl on your way.

CHRISTY. [*Going over to her, gradually raising his voice.*] I've
said it nowhere till this night, I'm telling you; for I've
seen none the like of you the eleven long days I am walking
the world, looking over a low ditch or a high ditch on my
north or south, into stony, scattered fields, or scribes of
bog, where you'd see young, limber girls, and fine, prancing
women making laughter with the men.

PEGEEN. If you weren't destroyed travelling, you'd have as
much talk and streeleen, I'm thinking, as Owen Roe
O'Sullivan or the poets of the Dingle Bay; and I've heard
all times it's the poets are your like—fine, fiery fellows
with great rages when their temper's roused.

CHRISTY. [*Drawing a little nearer to her.*] You've a power

of rings, God bless you, and would there be any offence if I was asking are you single now?

PEGEEN. What would I want wedding so young?

CHRISTY. [*With relief.*] We 're alike so.

PEGEEN. [*She puts sack on settle and beats it up.*] I never killed my father. I 'd be afeard to do that, except I was the like of yourself with blind rages tearing me within, for I 'm thinking you should have had great tussling when the end was come.

CHRISTY. [*Expanding with delight at the first confidential talk he has ever had with a woman.*] We had not then. It was a hard woman was come over the hill; and if he was always a crusty kind, when he 'd a hard woman setting him on, not the divil himself or his four fathers could put up with him at all.

PEGEEN. [*With curiosity.*] And isn't it a great wonder that one wasn't fearing you?

CHRISTY. [*Very confidentially.*] Up to the day I killed my father, there wasn't a person in Ireland knew the kind I was, and I there drinking, waking, eating, sleeping, a quiet, simple poor fellow with no man giving me heed.

PEGEEN. [*Getting a quilt out of cupboard and putting it on the sack.*] It was the girls were giving you heed, maybe, and I 'm thinking it 's most conceit you 'd have to be gaming with their like.

CHRISTY. [*Shaking his head, with simplicity.*] Not the girls itself, and I won't tell you a lie. There wasn't any one heeding me in that place saving only the dumb beasts of the field. [*He sits down at fire.*

PEGEEN. [*With disappointment.*] And I thinking you should have been living the like of a king of Norway or the eastern world.

[*She comes and sits beside him after placing bread and mug of milk on the table.*

CHRISTY. [*Laughing piteously.*] The like of a king, is it? And I after toiling, moiling, digging, dodging from the dawn till dusk; with never a sight of joy or sport saving only when I 'd be abroad in the dark night poaching rabbits on hills, for I was a divil to poach, God forgive me [*very naïvely*], and I near got six months for going with a dung fork and stabbing a fish.

PEGEEN. And it 's that you 'd call sport, is it, to be abroad in the darkness with yourself alone?

CHRISTY. I did, God help me, and there I 'd be as happy as the sunshine of St Martin's Day, watching the light passing the north or the patches of fog, till I 'd hear a rabbit starting to screech and I 'd go running in the furze.   Then, when I 'd my full share, I 'd come walking down where you 'd see the ducks and geese stretched sleeping on the highway of the road, and before I 'd pass the dunghill, I 'd hear himself snoring out—a loud, lonesome snore he 'd be making all times, the while he was sleeping; and he a man 'd be raging all times, the while he was waking, like a gaudy officer you 'd hear cursing and damning and swearing oaths.

PEGEEN. Providence and Mercy, spare us all!

CHRISTY. It 's that you 'd say surely if you seen him and he after drinking for weeks, rising up in the red dawn, or before it maybe, and going out into the yard as naked as an ash-tree in the moon of May, and shying clods against the visage of the stars till he 'd put the fear of death into the banbhs and the screeching sows.

PEGEEN. I 'd be well-nigh afeard of that lad myself, I 'm thinking.   And there was no one in it but the two of you alone?

CHRISTY. The divil a one, though he 'd sons and daughters walking all great states and territories of the world, and not a one of them, to this day, but would say their seven curses on him, and they rousing up to let a cough or sneeze, maybe, in the deadness of the night.

PEGEEN. [*Nodding her head.*] Well, you should have been a queer lot.   I never cursed my father the like of that, though I 'm twenty and more years of age.

CHRISTY. Then you 'd have cursed mine, I 'm telling you, and he a man never gave peace to any, saving when he 'd get two months or three, or be locked in the asylums for battering peelers or assaulting men [*with depression*], the way it was a bitter life he led me till I did up a Tuesday and halve his skull.

PEGEEN. [*Putting her hand on his shoulder.*] Well, you 'll have peace in this place, Christy Mahon, and none to trouble you, and it 's near time a fine lad like you should have your good share of the earth.

CHRISTY. It 's time surely, and I a seemly fellow with great strength in me and bravery of . . . [*Someone knocks.*

CHRISTY. [*Clinging to Pegeen.*] Oh, glory! it 's late for knocking, and this last while I 'm in terror of the peelers, and the walking dead. [*Knocking again.*

PEGEEN. Who 's there?

VOICE. [*Outside.*] Me.

PEGEEN. Who 's me?

VOICE. The Widow Quin.

PEGEEN. [*Jumping up and giving him the bread and milk.*] Go on now with your supper, and let on to be sleepy, for if she found you were such a warrant to talk, she 'd be stringing gabble till the dawn of day.

[*He takes bread and sits shyly with his back to the door.*

PEGEEN. [*Opening door, with temper.*] What ails you, or what is it you 're wanting at this hour of the night?

WIDOW QUIN. [*Coming in a step and peering at Christy.*] I 'm after meeting Shawn Keogh and Father Reilly below, who told me of your curiosity man, and they fearing by this time he was maybe roaring, romping on your hands with drink.

PEGEEN. [*Pointing to Christy.*] Look now is he roaring, and he stretched out drowsy with his supper and his mug of milk. Walk down and tell that to Father Reilly and to Shaneen Keogh.

WIDOW QUIN. [*Coming forward.*] I 'll not see them again, for I 've their word to lead that lad forward for to lodge with me.

PEGEEN. [*In blank amazement.*] This night is it?

WIDOW QUIN. [*Going over.*] This night. 'It isn't fitting,' says the priesteen, 'to have his likeness lodging with an orphaned girl.' [*To Christy.*] God save you, mister!

CHRISTY. [*Shyly.*] God save you kindly!

WIDOW QUIN. [*Looking at him with half amused curiosity.*] Well, aren't you a little smiling fellow? It should have been great and bitter torments did rouse your spirits to a deed of blood.

CHRISTY. [*Doubtfully.*] It should, maybe.

WIDOW QUIN. It's more than 'maybe' I'm saying, and it'd soften my heart to see you sitting so simple with your cup and cake, and you fitter to be saying your catechism than slaying your da.

PEGEEN. [*At counter, washing glasses.*] There's talking when any'd see he's fit to be holding his head high with the wonders of the world. Walk on from this, for I'll not have him tormented, and he destroyed travelling since Tuesday was a week.

WIDOW QUIN. [*Peaceably.*] We'll be walking surely when his supper's done, and you'll find we're great company, young fellow, when it's of the like of you and me you'd hear the penny poets singing in an August Fair.

CHRISTY. [*Innocently.*] Did you kill your father?

PEGEEN. [*Contemptuously.*] She did not. She hit himself with a worn pick, and the rusted poison did corrode his blood the way he never overed it, and died after. That was a sneaky kind of murder did win small glory with the boys itself. [*She crosses to Christy's left.*

WIDOW QUIN. [*With good humour.*] If it didn't, maybe all knows a widow woman has buried her children and destroyed her man is a wiser comrade for a young lad than a girl, the like of you, who'd go helter-skeltering after any man would let you a wink upon the road.

PEGEEN. [*Breaking out into wild rage.*] And you'll say that, Widow Quin, and you gasping with the rage you had racing the hill beyond to look on his face.

WIDOW QUIN. [*Laughing derisively.*] Me, is it? Well, Father Reilly has cuteness to divide you now. [*She pulls Christy up.*] There's great temptation in a man did slay his da, and we'd best be going, young fellow; so rise up and come with me.

PEGEEN. [*Seizing his arm.*] He'll not stir. He's pot-boy in this place, and I'll not have him stolen off and kidnapped while himself's abroad.

WIDOW QUIN. It'd be a crazy pot-boy 'd lodge him in the shebeen where he works by day, so you'd have a right to come on, young fellow, till you see my little houseen, a perch off on the rising hill.

PEGEEN. Wait till morning, Christy Mahon. Wait till you lay eyes on her leaky thatch is growing more pasture for her buck goat than her square of fields, and she without a tramp itself to keep in order her place at all.

WIDOW QUIN. When you see me contriving in my little gardens, Christy Mahon, you'll swear the Lord God formed me to be living lone, and that there isn't my match in Mayo for thatching, or mowing, or shearing a sheep.

PEGEEN. [*With noisy scorn.*] It's true the Lord God formed you to contrive indeed. Doesn't the world know you reared a black ram at your own breast, so that the Lord Bishop of Connaught felt the elements of a Christian, and he eating it after in a kidney stew? Doesn't the world know you've been seen shaving the foxy skipper from France for a threepenny-bit and a sop of grass tobacco would wring the liver from a mountain goat you'd meet leaping the hills?

WIDOW QUIN. [*With amusement.*] Do you hear her now, young fellow? Do you hear the way she'll be rating at your own self when a week is by?

PEGEEN. [*To Christy.*] Don't heed her. Tell her to go on into her pigsty and not plague us here.

WIDOW QUIN. I'm going; but he'll come with me.

PEGEEN. [*Shaking him.*] Are you dumb, young fellow?

CHRISTY. [*Timidly to Widow Quin.*] God increase you; but I'm pot-boy in this place, and it's here I liefer stay.

PEGEEN. [*Triumphantly.*] Now you have heard him, and go on from this.

WIDOW QUIN. [*Looking round the room.*] It's lonesome this hour crossing the hill, and if he won't come along with me, I'd have a right maybe to stop this night with yourselves.

Let me stretch out on the settle, Pegeen Mike; and himself can lie by the hearth.

PEGEEN. [*Short and fiercely.*] Faith, I won't. Quit off or I will send you now.

WIDOW QUIN. [*Gathering her shawl up.*] Well, it 's a terror to be aged a score. [*To Christy.*] God bless you now, young fellow, and let you be wary, or there 's right torment will await you here if you go romancing with her like, and she waiting only, as they bade me say, on a sheepskin parchment to be wed with Shawn Keogh of Killakeen.

CHRISTY. [*Going to Pegeen as she bolts door.*] What 's that she 's after saying?

PEGEEN. Lies and blather, you 've no call to mind. Well, isn't Shawn Keogh an impudent fellow to send up spying on me? Wait till I lay hands on him. Let him wait, I 'm saying.

CHRISTY. And you 're not wedding him at all?

PEGEEN. I wouldn't wed him if a bishop came walking for to join us here.

CHRISTY. That God in glory may be thanked for that.

PEGEEN. There 's your bed now. I 've put a quilt upon you I 'm after quilting a while since with my own two hands, and you 'd best stretch out now for your sleep, and may God give you a good rest till I call you in the morning when the cocks will crow.

CHRISTY. [*As she goes to inner room.*] May God and Mary and St Patrick bless you and reward you for your kindly talk. [*She shuts the door behind her. He settles his bed slowly, feeling the quilt with immense satisfaction.*] Well, it 's a clean bed and soft with it, and it 's great luck and company I 've won me in the end of time—two fine women fighting for the likes of me—till I 'm thinking this night wasn't I a foolish fellow not to kill my father in the years gone by.

CURTAIN

Act II

*Scene as before. Brilliant morning light. Christy, looking
bright and cheerful, is cleaning a girl's boots.*

CHRISTY. [*To himself, counting jugs on dresser.*] Half a
hundred beyond. Ten there. A score that above.
Eighty jugs. Six cups and a broken one. Two plates.
A power of glasses. Bottles, a schoolmaster 'd be hard set
to count, and enough in them, I 'm thinking, to drunken
all the wealth and wisdom of the county Clare. [*He puts
down the boot carefully.*] There 's her boots now, nice and
decent for her evening use, and isn't it grand brushes she
has? [*He puts them down and goes by degrees to the looking-
glass.*] Well, this 'd be a fine place to be my whole life
talking out with swearing Christians, in place of my old
dogs and cat; and I stalking around, smoking my pipe and
drinking my fill, and never a day's work but drawing a cork
an odd time, or wiping a glass, or rinsing out a shiny
tumbler for a decent man. [*He takes the looking-glass from
the wall and puts it on the back of a chair; then sits down in
front of it and begins washing his face.*] Didn't I know
rightly, I was handsome, though it was the divil's own
mirror we had beyond, would twist a squint across an
angel's brow; and I 'll be growing fine from this day, the
way I 'll have a soft lovely skin on me and won't be the
like of the clumsy young fellows do be ploughing all times
in the earth and dung. [*He starts.*] Is she coming again?
[*He looks out.*] Stranger girls. God help me, where 'll
I hide myself away and my long neck naked to the world?
[*He looks out.*] I 'd best go to the room maybe till I 'm
dressed again.

> [*He gathers up his coat and the looking-glass, and runs
> into the inner room. The door is pushed open, and
> Susan Brady looks in, and knocks on door.*

SUSAN. There 's nobody in it.   [*Knocks again.*

NELLY. [*Pushing her in and following her, with Honor Blake and Sara Tansey.*] It 'd be early for them both to be out walking the hill.

SUSAN. I 'm thinking Shawn Keogh was making game of us, and there 's no such man in it at all.

HONOR. [*Pointing to straw and quilt.*] Look at that.   He 's been sleeping there in the night.   Well, it 'll be a hard case if he 's gone off now, the way we 'll never set our eyes on a man killed his father, and we after rising early and destroying ourselves running fast on the hill.

NELLY. Are you thinking them 's his boots?

SARA. [*Taking them up.*] If they are, there should be his father's track on them.   Did you never read in the papers the way murdered men do bleed and drip?

SUSAN. Is that blood there, Sara Tansey?

SARA. [*Smelling it.*] That 's bog water, I 'm thinking; but it 's his own they are, surely, for I never seen the like of them for whitey mud, and red mud, and turf on them, and the fine sands of the sea.   That man 's been walking, I 'm telling you.

> [*She goes down right, putting on one of his boots.*

SUSAN. [*Going to window.*] Maybe he 's stolen off to Belmullet with the boots of Michael James, and you 'd have a right so to follow after him, Sara Tansey, and you the one yoked the ass-cart and drove ten miles to set your eyes on the man bit the yellow lady's nostril on the northern shore.   [*She looks out.*

SARA. [*Running to window, with one boot on.*] Don't be talking, and we fooled to-day. [*Putting on the other boot.*] There 's a pair do fit me well and I 'll be keeping them for walking to the priest, when you 'd be ashamed this place, going up winter and summer with nothing worth while to confess at all.

HONOR. [*Who has been listening at door.*] Whisht! there 's someone inside the room. [*She pushes door a chink open.*] It 's a man.

> [*Sara kicks off boots and puts them where they were. They all stand in a line looking through chink.*

SARA. I'll call him. Mister! Mister! [*He puts in his head.*] Is Pegeen within?

CHRISTY. [*Coming in as meek as a mouse, with the looking-glass held behind his back.*] She's above on the cnuceen, seeking the nanny goats, the way she'd have a sup of goats' milk for to colour my tea.

SARA. And asking your pardon, is it you's the man killed his father?

CHRISTY. [*Sidling toward the nail where the glass was hanging.*] I am, God help me!

SARA. [*Taking eggs she has brought.*] Then my thousand welcomes to you, and I've run up with a brace of duck's eggs for your food to-day. Pegeen's ducks is no use, but these are the real rich sort. Hold out your hand and you'll see it's no lie I'm telling you.

CHRISTY. [*Coming forward shyly, and holding out his left hand.*] They're a great and weighty size.

SUSAN. And I run up with a pat of butter, for it'd be a poor thing to have you eating your spuds dry, and you after running a great way since you did destroy your da.

CHRISTY. Thank you kindly.

HONOR. And I brought you a little cut of a cake, for you should have a thin stomach on you, and you that length walking the world.

NELLY. And I brought you a little laying pullet—boiled and all she is—was crushed at the fall of night by the curate's car. Feel the fat of the breast, mister.

CHRISTY. It's bursting, surely.

[*He feels it with the back of his hand, in which he holds the presents.*

SARA. Will you pinch it? Is your right hand too sacred for to use at all? [*She slips round behind him.*] It's a glass he has. Well, I never seen to this day a man with a looking-glass held to his back. Them that kills their fathers is a vain lot surely.   [*Girls giggle.*

CHRISTY. [*Smiling innocently and piling presents on glass.*] I'm very thankful to you all to-day. . . .

WIDOW QUIN. [*Coming in quickly, at door.*] Sara Tansey,

Susan Brady, Honor Blake! What in glory has you here at this hour of day?

GIRLS. [*Giggling.*] That's the man killed his father.

WIDOW QUIN. [*Coming to them.*] I know well it's the man; and I'm after putting him down in the sports below for racing, leaping, pitching, and the Lord knows what.

SARA. [*Exuberantly.*] That's right, Widow Quin. I'll bet my dowry that he'll lick the world.

WIDOW QUIN. If you will, you'd have a right to have him fresh and nourished in place of nursing a feast. [*Taking presents.*] Are you fasting or fed, young fellow?

CHRISTY. Fasting, if you please.

WIDOW QUIN. [*Loudly.*] Well, you're the lot. Stir up now and give him his breakfast. [*To Christy.*] Come here to me [*she puts him on bench beside her while the girls make tea and get his breakfast*], and let you tell us your story before Pegeen will come, in place of grinning your ears off like the moon of May.

CHRISTY. [*Beginning to be pleased.*] It's a long story; you'd be destroyed listening.

WIDOW QUIN. Don't be letting on to be shy, a fine, gamy, treacherous lad the like of you. Was it in your house beyond you cracked his skull?

CHRISTY. [*Shy but flattered.*] It was not. We were digging spuds in his cold, sloping, stony, divil's patch of a field.

WIDOW QUIN. And you went asking money of him, or making talk of getting a wife would drive him from his farm?

CHRISTY. I did not, then; but there I was, digging and digging, and 'You squinting idiot,' says he, 'let you walk down now and tell the priest you'll wed the Widow Casey in a score of days.'

WIDOW QUIN. And what kind was she?

CHRISTY. [*With horror.*] A walking terror from beyond the hills, and she two score and five years, and two hundred-weights and five pounds in the weighing scales, with a limping leg on her, and a blinded eye, and she a woman of noted misbehaviour with the old and young.

GIRLS. [*Clustering round him, serving him.*] Glory be.

WIDOW QUIN. And what did he want driving you to wed with her? [*She takes a bit of the chicken.*

CHRISTY. [*Eating with growing satisfaction.*] He was letting on I was wanting a protector from the harshness of the world, and he without a thought the whole while but how he'd have her hut to live in and her gold to drink.

WIDOW QUIN. There's maybe worse than a dry hearth and a widow woman and your glass at night. So you hit him then?

CHRISTY. [*Getting almost excited.*] I did not. 'I won't wed her,' says I, 'when all know she did suckle me for six weeks when I came into the world, and she a hag this day with a tongue on her has the crows and seabirds scattered, the way they wouldn't cast a shadow on her garden with the dread of her curse.'

WIDOW QUIN. [*Teasingly.*] That one should be right company.

SARA. [*Eagerly.*] Don't mind her. Did you kill him then?

CHRISTY. 'She's too good for the like of you,' says he, 'and go on now or I'll flatten you out like a crawling beast has passed under a dray.' 'You will not if I can help it,' says I. 'Go on,' says he, 'or I'll have the divil making garters of your limbs to-night.' 'You will not if I can help it,' says I. [*He sits up brandishing his mug.*

SARA. You were right surely.

CHRISTY. [*Impressively.*] With that the sun came out between the cloud and the hill, and it shining green in my face. 'God have mercy on your soul,' says he, lifting a scythe. 'Or on your own,' says I, raising the loy.

SUSAN. That's a grand story.

HONOR. He tells it lovely.

CHRISTY. [*Flattered and confident, waving bone.*] He gave a drive with the scythe, and I gave a lep to the east. Then I turned around with my back to the north, and I hit a blow on the ridge of his skull, laid him stretched out, and he split to the knob of his gullet. [*He raises the chicken bone to his Adam's apple.*

GIRLS. [*Together.*] Well, you 're a marvel!   Oh, God bless you!   You 're the lad, surely!

SUSAN. I 'm thinking the Lord God sent him this road to make a second husband to the Widow Quin, and she with a great yearning to be wedded, though all dread her here. Lift him on her knee, Sara Tansey.

WIDOW QUIN. Don't tease him.

SARA. [*Going over to dresser and counter very quickly and getting two glasses and porter.*] You 're heroes, surely, and let you drink a supeen with your arms linked like the outlandish lovers in the sailor's song. [*She links their arms and gives them the glasses.*] There now.   Drink a health to the wonders of the western world, the pirates, preachers, poteen-makers, with the jobbing jockies; parching peelers, and the juries fill their stomachs selling judgments of the English law.   [*Brandishing the bottle.*

WIDOW QUIN. That 's a right toast, Sara Tansey.   Now, Christy.

> [*They drink with their arms linked, he drinking with his left hand, she with her right.   As they are drinking, Pegeen Mike comes in with a milk-can and stands aghast.   They all spring away from Christy.   He goes down left.   Widow Quin remains seated.*

PEGEEN. [*Angrily to Sara.*] What is it you 're wanting?

SARA. [*Twisting her apron.*] An ounce of tobacco.

PEGEEN. Have you tuppence?

SARA. I 've forgotten my purse.

PEGEEN. Then you 'd best be getting it and not be fooling us here. [*To the Widow Quin, with more elaborate scorn.*] And what is it you 're wanting, Widow Quin?

WIDOW QUIN. [*Insolently.*] A penn'orth of starch.

PEGEEN. [*Breaking out.*] And you without a white shift or a shirt in your whole family since the drying of the flood. I 've no starch for the like of you, and let you walk on now to Killamuck.

WIDOW QUIN. [*Turning to Christy, as she goes out with the girls.*] Well, you 're mighty huffy this day, Pegeen Mike, and you, young fellow, let you not forget the sports and racing when the noon is by. [*They go out.*

PEGEEN. [*Imperiously.*] Fling out that rubbish and put them cups away. [*Christy tidies away in great haste.*] Shove in the bench by the wall. [*He does so.*] And hang that glass on the nail. What disturbed it at all?

CHRISTY. [*Very meekly.*] I was making myself decent only, and this a fine country for young lovely girls.

PEGEEN. [*Sharply.*] Whisht your talking of girls.

[*Goes to counter on right.*

CHRISTY. Wouldn't any wish to be decent in a place . . .

PEGEEN. Whisht, I 'm saying.

CHRISTY. [*Looks at her face for a moment with great misgivings, then as a last effort takes up a loy, and goes towards her, with feigned assurance.*] It was with a loy the like of that I killed my father.

PEGEEN. [*Still sharply.*] You 've told me that story six times since the dawn of day.

CHRISTY. [*Reproachfully.*] It 's a queer thing you wouldn't care to be hearing it and them girls after walking four miles to be listening to me now.

PEGEEN. [*Turning round astonished.*] Four miles?

CHRISTY. [*Apologetically.*] Didn't himself say there were only bona fides living in the place?

PEGEEN. It 's bona fides by the road they are, but that lot came over the river lepping the stones. It 's not three perches when you go like that, and I was down this morning looking on the papers the post-boy does have in his bag. [*With meaning and emphasis.*] For there was great news this day, Christopher Mahon.

[*She goes into room on left.*

CHRISTY. [*Suspiciously.*] Is it news of my murder?

PEGEEN. [*Inside.*] Murder, indeed.

CHRISTY. [*Loudly.*] A murdered da?

PEGEEN. [*Coming in again and crossing right.*] There was not, but a story filled half a page of the hanging of a man. Ah, that should be a fearful end, young fellow, and it worst of all for a man destroyed his da; for the like of him would get small mercies, and when it 's dead he is they 'd put him in a narrow grave, with cheap sacking wrapping him round, and pour down quicklime on his head, the way you 'd see a woman pouring any frish-frash from a cup.

CHRISTY. [*Very miserably.*] Oh, God help me. Are you thinking I 'm safe? You were saying at the fall of night I was shut of jeopardy and I here with yourselves.

PEGEEN. [*Severely.*] You 'll be shut of jeopardy no place if you go talking with a pack of wild girls the like of them do be walking abroad with the peelers, talking whispers at the fall of night.

CHRISTY. [*With terror.*] And you 're thinking they 'd tell?

PEGEEN. [*With mock sympathy.*] Who knows, God help you?

CHRISTY. [*Loudly.*] What joy would they have to bring hanging to the likes of me?

PEGEEN. It 's queer joys they have, and who knows the thing they 'd do, if it 'd make the green stones cry itself to think of you swaying and swiggling at the butt of a rope, and you with a fine, stout neck, God bless you! the way you 'd be a half an hour, in great anguish, getting your death.

CHRISTY. [*Getting his boots and putting them on.*] If there 's that terror of them, it 'd be best, maybe, I went on wandering like Esau or Cain and Abel on the sides of Neifin or the Erris plain.

PEGEEN. [*Beginning to play with him.*] It would, maybe, for I 've heard the circuit judges this place is a heartless crew.

CHRISTY. [*Bitterly.*] It 's more than judges this place is a heartless crew. [*Looking up at her.*] And isn't it a poor thing to be starting again, and I a lonesome fellow will be looking out on women and girls the way the needy fallen spirits do be looking on the Lord?

PEGEEN. What call have you to be that lonesome when there 's poor girls walking Mayo in their thousands now?

CHRISTY. [*Grimly.*] It 's well you know what call I have. It 's well you know it 's a lonesome thing to be passing small towns with the lights shining sideways when the night is down, or going in strange places with a dog noising before you and a dog noising behind, or drawn to the cities where you 'd hear a voice kissing and talking deep love in every shadow of the ditch, and you passing on with an empty, hungry stomach failing from your heart.

PEGEEN. I 'm thinking you 're an odd man, Christy Mahon. The oddest walking fellow I ever set my eyes on to this hour to-day.

CHRISTY. What would any be but odd men and they living lonesome in the world?

PEGEEN. I 'm not odd, and I 'm my whole life with my father only.

CHRISTY. [*With infinite admiration.*] How would a lovely, handsome woman the like of you be lonesome when all men should be thronging around to hear the sweetness of your voice, and the little infant children should be pestering your steps, I 'm thinking, and you walking the roads.

PEGEEN. I 'm hard set to know what way a coaxing fellow the like of yourself should be lonesome either.

CHRISTY. Coaxing?

PEGEEN. Would you have me think a man never talked with the girls would have the words you 've spoken to-day? It 's only letting on you are to be lonesome, the way you 'd get around me now.

CHRISTY. I wish to God I was letting on; but I was lonesome all times, and born lonesome, I 'm thinking, as the moon of dawn. [*Going to door.*

PEGEEN. [*Puzzled by his talk.*] Well, it 's a story I 'm not understanding at all why you 'd be worse than another, Christy Mahon, and you a fine lad with the great savagery to destroy your da.

CHRISTY. It 's little I 'm understanding myself, saving only that my heart 's scalded this day, and I going off stretching out the earth between us, the way I 'll not be waking near you another dawn of the year till the two of us do arise to hope or judgment with the saints of God, and now I 'd best be going with my wattle in my hand, for hanging is a poor thing [*turning to go*], and it 's little welcome only is left me in this house to-day.

PEGEEN. [*Sharply.*] Christy. [*He turns round.*] Come here
to me. [*He goes towards her.*] Lay down that switch and
throw some sods on the fire.   You're pot-boy in this
place, and I'll not have you mitch off from us now.

CHRISTY. You were saying I'd be hanged if I stay.

PEGEEN. [*Quite kindly at last.*] I'm after going down and
reading the fearful crimes of Ireland for two weeks or
three, and there wasn't a word of your murder. [*Getting
up and going over to the counter.*] They've likely not
found the body.   You're safe so with ourselves.

CHRISTY. [*Astonished, slowly.*] It's making game of me you
were [*following her with fearful joy*], and I can stay so,
working at your side, and I not lonesome from this mortal
day.

PEGEEN. What's to hinder you staying, except the widow
woman or the young girls would inveigle you off?

CHRISTY. [*With rapture.*] And I'll have your words from
this day filling my ears, and that look is come upon you
meeting my two eyes, and I watching you loafing around
in the warm sun, or rinsing your ankles when the night is
come.

PEGEEN. [*Kindly, but a little embarrassed.*] I'm thinking
you'll be a loyal young lad to have working around, and if
you vexed me a while since with your leaguing with the
girls, I wouldn't give a thraneen for a lad hadn't a mighty
spirit in him and a gamy heart.

[*Shawn Keogh runs in carrying a cleeve on his back,
followed by the Widow Quin.*

SHAWN. [*To Pegeen.*] I was passing below, and I seen your
mountainy sheep eating cabbages in Jimmy's field.   Run
up or they'll be bursting surely.

PEGEEN. Oh, God mend them!

[*She puts a shawl over her head and runs out.*

CHRISTY. [*Looking from one to the other.   Still in high spirits.*]
I'd best go to her aid maybe.   I'm handy with ewes.

WIDOW QUIN. [*Closing the door.*] She can do that much, and
there is Shaneen has long speeches for to tell you now.

[*She sits down with an amused smile.*

SHAWN. [*Taking something from his pocket and offering it to Christy.*] Do you see that, mister?

CHRISTY. [*Looking at it.*] The half of a ticket to the Western States!

SHAWN. [*Trembling with anxiety.*] I 'll give it to you and my new hat [*pulling it out of hamper*]; and my breeches with the double seat [*pulling it out*]; and my new coat is woven from the blackest shearings for three miles around [*giving him the coat*]; I 'll give you the whole of them, and my blessing, and the blessing of Father Reilly itself, maybe, if you 'll quit from this and leave us in the peace we had till last night at the fall of dark.

CHRISTY. [*With a new arrogance.*] And for what is it you 're wanting to get shut of me?

SHAWN. [*Looking to the Widow for help.*] I 'm a poor scholar with middling faculties to coin a lie, so I 'll tell you the truth, Christy Mahon. I 'm wedding with Pegeen beyond, and I don't think well of having a clever fearless man the like of you dwelling in her house.

CHRISTY. [*Almost pugnaciously.*] And you 'd be using bribery for to banish me?

SHAWN. [*In an imploring voice.*] Let you not take it badly, mister honey; isn't beyond the best place for you, where you 'll have golden chains and shiny coats and you riding upon hunters with the ladies of the land.

[*He makes an eager sign to the Widow Quin to come to help him.*

WIDOW QUIN. [*Coming over.*] It 's true for him, and you 'd best quit off and not have that poor girl setting her mind on you, for there 's Shaneen thinks she wouldn't suit you, though all is saying that she 'll wed you now. [*Christy beams with delight.*

SHAWN. [*In terrified earnest.*] She wouldn't suit you, and she with the divil's own temper the way you 'd be strangling one another in a score of days. [*He makes the movement of strangling with his hands.*] It 's the like of me only that she 's fit for; a quiet simple fellow wouldn't raise a hand upon her if she scratched itself.

WIDOW QUIN. [*Putting Shawn's hat on Christy.*] Fit them clothes on you anyhow, young fellow, and he 'd maybe loan them to you for the sports. [*Pushing him towards inner door.*] Fit them on and you can give your answer when you have them tried.

CHRISTY. [*Beaming, delighted with the clothes.*] I will then. I 'd like herself to see me in them tweeds and hat.

[*He goes into room and shuts the door.*

SHAWN. [*In great anxiety.*] He 'd like herself to see them. He 'll not leave us, Widow Quin. He 's a score of divils in him the way it 's well-nigh certain he will wed Pegeen.

WIDOW QUIN. [*Jeeringly.*] It 's true all girls are fond of courage and do hate the like of you.

SHAWN. [*Walking about in desperation.*] Oh, Widow Quin, what 'll I be doing now? I 'd inform again him, but he 'd burst from Kilmainham and he 'd be sure and certain to destroy me. If I wasn't so God-fearing, I 'd near have courage to come behind him and run a pike into his side. Oh, it 's a hard case to be an orphan and not to have your father that you 're used to, and you 'd easy kill and make yourself a hero in the sight of all. [*Coming up to her.*] Oh, Widow Quin, will you find me some contrivance when I 've promised you a ewe?

WIDOW QUIN. A ewe 's a small thing, but what would you give me if I did wed him and did save you so?

SHAWN. [*With astonishment.*] You?

WIDOW QUIN. Aye. Would you give me the red cow you have and the mountainy ram, and the right of way across your rye path, and a load of dung at Michaelmas, and turbary upon the western hill?

SHAWN. [*Radiant with hope.*] I would, surely, and I 'd give you the wedding-ring I have, and the loan of a new suit, the way you 'd have him decent on the wedding-day. I 'd give you two kids for your dinner, and a gallon of poteen, and I 'd call the piper on the long car to your wedding from Crossmolina or from Ballina. I 'd give you . . .

WIDOW QUIN. That 'll do, so, and let you whisht, for he 's coming now again.

[*Christy comes in very natty in the new clothes. Widow Quin goes to him admiringly.*

WIDOW QUIN. If you seen yourself now, I 'm thinking you 'd be too proud to speak to at all, and it 'd be a pity surely to have your like sailing from Mayo to the western world.

CHRISTY. [*As proud as a peacock.*] I 'm not going. If this is a poor place itself, I 'll make myself contented to be lodging here.

[*Widow Quin makes a sign to Shawn to leave them.*

SHAWN. Well, I 'm going measuring the racecourse while the tide is low, so I 'll leave you the garments and my blessing for the sports to-day. God bless you!

[*He wriggles out.*

WIDOW QUIN. [*Admiring Christy.*] Well, you 're mighty spruce, young fellow. Sit down now while you 're quiet till you talk with me.

CHRISTY. [*Swaggering.*] I 'm going abroad on the hillside for to seek Pegeen.

WIDOW QUIN. You 'll have time and plenty for to seek Pegeen, and you heard me saying at the fall of night the two of us should be great company.

CHRISTY. From this out I 'll have no want of company when all sorts is bringing me their food and clothing [*he swaggers to the door, tightening his belt*], the way they 'd set their eyes upon a gallant orphan cleft his father with one blow to the breeches belt. [*He opens door, then staggers back.*] Saints of Glory! Holy angels from the throne of light!

WIDOW QUIN. [*Going over.*] What ails you?

CHRISTY. It 's the walking spirit of my murdered da!

WIDOW QUIN. [*Looking out.*] Is it that tramper?

CHRISTY. [*Wildly.*] Where 'll I hide my poor body from that ghost of hell?

[*The door is pushed open, and old Mahon appears on threshold. Christy darts in behind door.*

WIDOW QUIN. [*In great amazement.*] God save you, my poor man.

MAHON. [*Gruffly.*] Did you see a young lad passing this way in the early morning or the fall of night?

WIDOW QUIN. You 're a queer kind to walk in not saluting at all.

MAHON. Did you see the young lad?

WIDOW QUIN. [*Stiffly.*] What kind was he?

MAHON. An ugly young streeler with a murderous gob on him, and a little switch in his hand. I met a tramper seen him coming this way at the fall of night.

WIDOW QUIN. There 's harvest hundreds do be passing these days for the Sligo boat. For what is it you 're wanting him, my poor man?

MAHON. I want to destroy him for breaking the head on me with the clout of a loy. [*He takes off a big hat, and shows his head in a muss of bandages and plaster, with some pride.*] It was he did that, and amn't I a great wonder to think I 've traced him ten days with that rent in my crown?

WIDOW QUIN. [*Taking his head in both hands and examining it with extreme delight.*] That was a great blow. And who hit you? A robber maybe?

MAHON. It was my own son hit me, and he the divil a robber, or anything else, but a dirty, stuttering lout.

WIDOW QUIN. [*Letting go his skull and wiping her hands in her apron.*] You 'd best be wary of a mortified scalp, I think they call it, lepping around with that wound in the splendour of the sun. It was a bad blow, surely, and you should have vexed him fearful to make him strike that gash in his da.

MAHON. Is it me?

WIDOW QUIN. [*Amusing herself.*] Aye. And isn't it a great shame when the old and hardened do torment the young?

MAHON. [*Raging.*] Torment him is it? And I after holding out with the patience of a martyred saint till there 's nothing but destruction on, and I 'm driven out in my old age with none to aid me.

WIDOW QUIN. [*Greatly amused.*] It's a sacred wonder the way that wickedness will spoil a man.

MAHON. My wickedness, is it? Amn't I after saying it is himself has me destroyed, and he a lier on walls, a talker of folly, a man you'd see stretched the half of the day in the brown ferns with his belly to the sun.

WIDOW QUIN. Not working at all?

MAHON. The divil a work, or if he did itself, you'd see him raising up a haystack like the stalk of a rush, or driving our last cow till he broke her leg at the hip, and when he wasn't at that he'd be fooling over little birds he had— finches and felts—or making mugs at his own self in the bit of a glass we had hung on the wall.

WIDOW QUIN. [*Looking at Christy.*] What way was he so foolish? It was running wild after the girls maybe?

MAHON. [*With a shout of derision.*] Running wild, is it? If he seen a red petticoat coming swinging over the hill, he'd be off to hide in the sticks, and you'd see him shooting out his sheep's eyes between the little twigs and the leaves, and his two ears rising like a hare looking out through a gap. Girls, indeed!

WIDOW QUIN. It was drink maybe?

MAHON. And he a poor fellow would get drunk on the smell of a pint. He'd a queer rotten stomach, I'm telling you, and when I gave him three pulls from my pipe a while since, he was taken with contortions till I had to send him in the ass-cart to the females' nurse.

WIDOW QUIN. [*Clasping her hands.*] Well, I never, till this day, heard tell of a man the like of that!

MAHON. I'd take a mighty oath you didn't, surely, and wasn't he the laughing joke of every female woman where four baronies meet, the way the girls would stop their weeding if they seen him coming the road to let a roar at him, and call him the loony of Mahon's?

WIDOW QUIN. I'd give the world and all to see the like of him. What kind was he?

MAHON. A small, low fellow.

WIDOW QUIN. And dark?

MAHON. Dark and dirty.

WIDOW QUIN. [*Considering*]. I 'm thinking I seen him.

MAHON. [*Eagerly.*] An ugly young blackguard.

WIDOW QUIN. A hideous, fearful villain, and the spit of you.

MAHON. What way is he fled?

WIDOW QUIN. Gone over the hills to catch a coasting steamer to the north or south.

MAHON. Could I pull up on him now?

WIDOW QUIN. If you 'll cross the sands below where the tide is out, you 'll be in it as soon as himself, for he had to go round ten miles by the top of the bay. [*She points to the door.*] Strike down by the head beyond and then follow on the roadway to the north and east.

[*Mahon goes abruptly.*

WIDOW QUIN. [*Shouting after him.*] Let you give him a good vengeance when you come up with him, but don't put yourself in the power of the law, for it 'd be a poor thing to see a judge in his black cap reading out his sentence on a civil warrior the like of you. [*She swings the door to and looks at Christy, who is cowering in terror, for a moment, then she bursts into a laugh.*] Well, you 're the walking Playboy of the Western World, and that 's the poor man you had divided to his breeches belt.

CHRISTY. [*Looking out; then, to her.*] What 'll Pegeen say when she hears that story?   What 'll she be saying to me now?

WIDOW QUIN. She 'll knock the head of you, I 'm thinking, and drive you from the door.   God help her to be taking you for a wonder, and you a little schemer making up a story you destroyed your da.

CHRISTY. [*Turning to the door, nearly speechless with rage, half to himself.*] To be letting on he was dead, and coming back to his life, and following after me like an old weasel tracing a rat, and coming in here laying desolation between my own self and the fine women of Ireland, and he a kind of carcass that you 'd fling upon the sea. . . .

WIDOW QUIN. [*More soberly.*] There 's talking for a man's one only son.

CHRISTY. [*Breaking out.*] His one son, is it? May I meet him with one tooth and it aching, and one eye to be seeing seven and seventy divils in the twists of the road, and one old timber leg on him to limp into the scalding grave. [*Looking out.*] There he is now crossing the strands, and that the Lord God would send a high wave to wash him from the world.

WIDOW QUIN. [*Scandalized.*] Have you no shame? [*Putting her hand on his shoulder and turning him round.*] What ails you? Near crying, is it?

CHRISTY. [*In despair and grief.*] Amn't I after seeing the love-light of the star of knowledge shining from her brow, and hearing words would put you thinking on the holy Brigid speaking to the infant saints, and now she 'll be turning again, and speaking hard words to me, like an old woman with a spavindy ass she 'd have, urging on a hill.

WIDOW QUIN. There 's poetry talk for a girl you 'd see itching and scratching, and she with a stale stink of poteen on her from selling in the shop.

CHRISTY. [*Impatiently.*] It 's her like is fitted to be handling merchandise in the heavens above, and what 'll I be doing now, I ask you, and I a kind of wonder was jilted by the heavens when a day was by.

[*There is a distant noise of girls' voices. Widow Quin looks from window and comes to him, hurriedly.*

WIDOW QUIN. You 'll be doing like myself, I 'm thinking, when I did destroy my man, for I 'm above many 's the day, odd times in great spirits, abroad in the sunshine, darning a stocking or stitching a shift; and odd times again looking out on the schooners, hookers, trawlers is sailing the sea, and I thinking on the gallant hairy fellows are drifting beyond, and myself long years living alone.

CHRISTY. [*Interested.*] You 're like me, so.

WIDOW QUIN. I am your like, and it 's for that I 'm taking a fancy to you, and I with my little houseen above where there 'd be myself to tend you, and none to ask were you a murderer or what at all.

CHRISTY. And what would I be doing if I left Pegeen?

WIDOW QUIN. I 've nice jobs you could be doing—gathering shells to make a whitewash for our hut within, building up a little goose-house, or stretching a new skin on an old curagh I have, and if my hut is far from all sides, it 's there you 'll meet the wisest old men, I tell you, at the corner of my wheel, and it 's there yourself and me will have great times whispering and hugging. . . .

VOICES. [*Outside, calling far away.*] Christy! Christy Mahon! Christy!

CHRISTY. Is it Pegeen Mike?

WIDOW QUIN. It 's the young girls, I 'm thinking, coming to bring you to the sports below, and what is it you 'll have me to tell them now?

CHRISTY. Aid me for to win Pegeen. It 's herself only that I 'm seeking now. [*Widow Quin gets up and goes to window.*] Aid me for to win her, and I 'll be asking God to stretch a hand to you in the hour of death, and lead you short cuts through the Meadows of Ease, and up the floor of heaven to the Footstool of the Virgin's Son.

WIDOW QUIN. There 's praying!

VOICES. [*Nearer.*] Christy! Christy Mahon!

CHRISTY. [*With agitation.*] They 're coming. Will you swear to aid and save me, for the love of Christ?

WIDOW QUIN. [*Looks at him for a moment.*] If I aid you, will you swear to give me a right of way I want, and a mountainy ram, and a load of dung at Michaelmas, the time that you 'll be master here?

CHRISTY. I will, by the elements and stars of night.

WIDOW QUIN. Then we 'll not say a word of the old fellow, the way Pegeen won't know your story till the end of time.

CHRISTY. And if he chances to return again?

WIDOW QUIN. We 'll swear he 's a maniac and not your da. I could take an oath I seen him raving on the sands to-day.

[*Girls run in.*

SUSAN. Come on to the sports below. Pegeen says you 're to come.

SARA TANSEY. The lepping 's beginning, and we 've a

jockey's suit to fit upon you for the mule race on the sands below.

HONOR. Come on, will you?

CHRISTY. I will then if Pegeen 's beyond.

SARA. She 's in the boreen making game of Shaneen Keogh.

CHRISTY. Then I 'll be going to her now.

[*He runs out, followed by the girls.*

WIDOW QUIN. Well, if the worst comes in the end of all, it 'll be great game to see there 's none to pity him but a widow woman, the like of me, has buried her children and destroyed her man. [*She goes out.*

CURTAIN

Act III

Scene as before.   Later in the day.   Jimmy comes in, slightly drunk.

JIMMY. [*Calls.*] Pegeen! [*Crosses to inner door.*] Pegeen Mike! [*Comes back again into the room.*] Pegeen! [*Philly comes in in the same state.—To Philly.*] Did you see herself?

PHILLY. I did not; but I sent Shawn Keogh with the ass-cart for to bear him home. [*Trying cupboards, which are locked.*] Well, isn't he a nasty man to get into such staggers at a morning wake; and isn't herself the divil's daughter for locking, and she so fussy after that young gaffer, you might take your death with drouth and none to heed you?

JIMMY. It 's little wonder she 'd be fussy, and he after bringing bankrupt ruin on the roulette man, and the trick-o'-the-loop man, and breaking the nose of the cockshot-man, and winning all in the sports below, racing, lepping, dancing, and the Lord knows what! He 's right luck, I 'm telling you.

PHILLY. If he has, he 'll be rightly hobbled yet, and he not able to say ten words without making a brag of the way he killed his father, and the great blow he hit with the loy.

JIMMY. A man can't hang by his own informing, and his father should be rotten by now.

[*Old Mahon passes window slowly.*

PHILLY. Supposing a man 's digging spuds in that field with a long spade, and supposing he flings up the two halves of that skull, what 'll be said then in the papers and the courts of law?

JIMMY. They 'd say it was an old Dane, maybe, was drowned in the flood. [*Old Mahon comes in and sits down near door listening.*] Did you never hear tell of the skulls they have in the city of Dublin, ranged out like blue jugs in a cabin of Connaught?

PHILLY. And you believe that?

JIMMY. [*Pugnaciously.*] Didn't a lad see them and he after coming from harvesting in the Liverpool boat? 'They have them there,' says he, 'making a show of the great people there was one time walking the world. White skulls and black skulls and yellow skulls, and some with full teeth, and some haven't only but one.'

PHILLY. It was no lie, maybe, for when I was a young lad there was a graveyard beyond the house with the remnants of a man who had thighs as long as your arm. He was a horrid man, I'm telling you, and there was many a fine Sunday I'd put him together for fun, and he with shiny bones, you wouldn't meet the like of these days in the cities of the world.

MAHON. [*Getting up.*] You wouldn't, is it? Lay your eyes on that skull, and tell me where and when there was another the like of it, is splintered only from the blow of a loy.

PHILLY. Glory be to God! And who hit you at all?

MAHON. [*Triumphantly.*] It was my own son hit me. Would you believe that?

JIMMY. Well, there's wonders hidden in the heart of man!

PHILLY. [*Suspiciously.*] And what way was it done?

MAHON. [*Wandering about the room.*] I'm after walking hundreds and long scores of miles, winning clean beds and the fill of my belly four times in the day, and I doing nothing but telling stories of that naked truth. [*He comes to them a little aggressively.*] Give me a supeen and I'll tell you now.

> [*Widow Quin comes in and stands aghast behind him. He is facing Jimmy and Philly, who are on the left.*

JIMMY. Ask herself beyond. She's the stuff hidden in her shawl.

WIDOW QUIN. [*Coming to Mahon quickly.*] You here, is it? You didn't go far at all?

MAHON. I seen the coasting steamer passing, and I got a drouth upon me and a cramping leg, so I said: 'The divil go along with him,' and turned again. [*Looking under her*

shawl.] And let you give me a supeen, for I 'm destroyed
travelling since Tuesday was a week.

WIDOW QUIN. [*Getting a glass, in a cajoling tone.*] Sit down
then by the fire and take your ease for a space.   You 've
a right to be destroyed indeed, with your walking, and
fighting, and facing the sun. [*Giving him poteen from a stone
jar she has brought in.*] There now is a drink for you, and
may it be to your happiness and length of life.

MAHON. [*Taking glass greedily, and sitting down by fire.*]
God increase you!

WIDOW QUIN. [*Taking men to the right stealthily.*] Do you
know what?   That man 's raving from his wound to-day,
for I met him a while since telling a rambling tale of a
tinker had him destroyed.   Then he heard of Christy's
deed, and he up and says it was his son had cracked his
skull.   Oh, isn't madness a fright, for he 'll go killing
someone yet, and he thinking it 's the man has struck
him so?

JIMMY. [*Entirely convinced.*] It 's a fright surely.   I knew a
party was kicked in the head by a red mare, and he went
killing horses a great while, till he eat the insides of a clock
and died after.

PHILLY. [*With suspicion.*] Did he see Christy?

WIDOW QUIN. He didn't. [*With a warning gesture.*] Let
you not be putting him in mind of him, or you 'll be likely
summoned if there 's murder done. [*Looking round at
Mahon.*] Whisht!   He 's listening.   Wait now till you
hear me taking him easy and unravelling all. [*She goes to
Mahon.*] And what way are you feeling, mister?   Are
you in contentment now?

MAHON. [*Slightly emotional from his drink.*] I 'm poorly
only, for it 's a hard story the way I 'm left to-day, when it
was I did tend him from his hour of birth, and he a dunce
never reached his second book, the way he 'd come from
school, many 's the day, with his legs lamed under him,
and he blackened with his beatings like a tinker's ass.   It 's
a hard story, I 'm saying, the way some do have their next
and nighest raising up a hand of murder on them, and

some is lonesome getting their death with lamentation in the dead of night.

WIDOW QUIN. [*Not knowing what to say.*] To hear you talking so quiet, who'd know you were the same fellow we seen pass to-day?

MAHON. I'm the same surely. The wrack and ruin of threescore years; and it's a terror to live that length, I tell you, and to have your sons going to the dogs against you, and you wore out scolding them, and skelping them, and God knows what.

PHILLY. [*To Jimmy.*] He's not raving. [*To Widow Quin.*] Will you ask him what kind was his son?

WIDOW QUIN. [*To Mahon, with a peculiar look.*] Was your son that hit you a lad of one year and a score maybe, a great hand at racing and lepping and licking the world?

MAHON. [*Turning on her with a roar of rage.*] Didn't you hear me say he was the fool of men, the way from this out he'll know the orphan's lot, with old and young making game of him, and they swearing, raging, kicking at him like a mangy cur.

[*A great burst of cheering outside, some way off.*

MAHON. [*Putting his hands to his ears.*] What in the name of God do they want roaring below?

WIDOW QUIN. [*With the shade of a smile.*] They're cheering a young lad, the champion Playboy of the Western World. [*More cheering.*

MAHON. [*Going to window.*] It'd split my heart to hear them, and I with pulses in my brain-pan for a week gone by. Is it racing they are?

JIMMY. [*Looking from door.*] It is, then. They are mounting him for the mule race will be run upon the sands. That's the playboy on the winkered mule.

MAHON. [*Puzzled.*] That lad, is it? If you said it was a fool he was, I'd have laid a mighty oath he was the likeness of my wandering son. [*Uneasily, putting his hand to his head.*] Faith, I'm thinking I'll go walking for to view the race.

WIDOW QUIN. [*Stopping him, sharply.*] You will not

You 'd best take the road to Belmullet, and not be dilly-dallying in this place where there isn't a spot you could sleep.

PHILLY. [*Coming forward.*] Don't mind her. Mount there on the bench and you 'll have a view of the whole. They 're hurrying before the tide will rise, and it 'd be near over if you went down the pathway through the crags below.

MAHON. [*Mounts on bench, Widow Quin beside him.*] That 's a right view again the edge of the sea. They 're coming now from the point. He 's leading. Who is he at all?

WIDOW QUIN. He 's the champion of the world, I tell you, and there isn't a ha'p'orth isn't falling lucky to his hands to-day.

PHILLY. [*Looking out, interested in the race.*] Look at that. They 're pressing him now.

JIMMY. He 'll win it yet.

PHILLY. Take your time, Jimmy Farrell. It 's too soon to say.

WIDOW QUIN. [*Shouting.*] Watch him taking the gate. There 's riding.

JIMMY. [*Cheering.*] More power to the young lad!

MAHON. He 's passing the third.

JIMMY. He 'll lick them yet.

WIDOW QUIN. He 'd lick them if he was running races with a score itself.

MAHON. Look at the mule he has, kicking the stars.

WIDOW QUIN. There was a lep! [*Catching hold of Mahon in her excitement.*] He 's fallen? He 's mounted again! Faith, he 's passing them all!

JIMMY. Look at him skelping her!

PHILLY. And the mountain girls hooshing him on!

JIMMY. It 's the last turn! The post 's cleared for them now!

MAHON. Look at the narrow place. He 'll be into the bogs! [*With a yell.*] Good rider! He 's through it again!

JIMMY. He 's neck and neck!

MAHON. Good boy to him! Flames, but he 's in!

[*Great cheering, in which all join.*

MAHON. [*With hesitation.*] What's that? They're raising him up. They're coming this way. [*With a roar of rage and astonishment.*] It's Christy, by the stars of God! I'd know his way of spitting and he astride the moon.

[*He jumps down and makes a run for the door, but Widow Quin catches him and pulls him back.*

WIDOW QUIN. Stay quiet, will you? That's not your son. [*To Jimmy.*] Stop him, or you'll get a month for the abetting of manslaughter and be fined as well.

JIMMY. I'll hold him.

MAHON. [*Struggling.*] Let me out! Let me out, the lot of you, till I have my vengeance on his head to-day.

WIDOW QUIN. [*Shaking him, vehemently.*] That's not your son. That's a man is going to make a marriage with the daughter of this house, a place with fine trade, with a licence, and with poteen too.

MAHON. [*Amazed.*] That man marrying a decent and a moneyed girl! Is it mad yous are? Is it in a crazy-house for females that I'm landed now?

WIDOW QUIN. It's mad yourself is with the blow upon your head. That lad is the wonder of the western world.

MAHON. I see it's my son.

WIDOW QUIN. You seen that you're mad. [*Cheering outside.*] Do you hear them cheering him in the zigzags of the road? Aren't you after saying that your son's a fool, and how would they be cheering a true idiot born?

MAHON. [*Getting distressed.*] It's maybe out of reason that that man's himself. [*Cheering again.*] There's none surely will go cheering him. Oh, I'm raving with a madness that would fright the world! [*He sits down with his hand to his head.*] There was one time I seen ten scarlet divils letting on they'd cork my spirit in a gallon can; and one time I seen rats as big as badgers sucking the lifeblood from the butt of my lug; but I never till this day confused that dribbling idiot with a likely man. I'm destroyed surely.

WIDOW QUIN. And who'd wonder when it's your brain-pan that is gaping now?

MAHON. Then the blight of the sacred drouth upon myself and him, for I never went mad to this day, and I not three weeks with the Limerick girls drinking myself silly and parlatic from the dusk to dawn. [*To Widow Quin, suddenly.*] Is my visage astray?

WIDOW QUIN. It is, then. You 're a sniggering maniac, a child could see.

MAHON. [*Getting up more cheerfully.*] Then I 'd best be going to the union beyond, and there 'll be a welcome before me, I tell you [*with great pride*], and I a terrible and fearful case, the way that there I was one time, screeching in a straightened waistcoat, with seven doctors writing out my sayings in a printed book. Would you believe that?

WIDOW QUIN. If you 're a wonder itself, you 'd best be hasty, for them lads caught a maniac one time and pelted the poor creature till he ran out, raving and foaming, and was drowned in the sea.

MAHON. [*With philosophy.*] It 's true mankind is the divil when your head 's astray. Let me out now and I 'll slip down the boreen, and not see them so.

WIDOW QUIN. [*Showing him out.*] That 's it. Run to the right, and not a one will see. [*He runs off.*

PHILLY. [*Wisely.*] You 're at some gaming, Widow Quin; but I 'll walk after him and give him his dinner and a time to rest, and I 'll see then if he 's raving or as sane as you.

WIDOW QUIN. [*Annoyed.*] If you go near that lad, let you be wary of your head, I 'm saying. Didn't you hear him telling he was crazed at times?

PHILLY. I heard him telling a power; and I 'm thinking we 'll have right sport before night will fall. [*He goes out.*

JIMMY. Well, Philly 's a conceited and foolish man. How could that madman have his senses and his brain-pan slit? I 'll go after them and see him turn on Philly now.

[*He goes; Widow Quin hides poteen behind counter. Then hubbub outside.*

VOICES. There you are! Good jumper! Grand lepper!

Darlint boy! He's the racer! Bear him on, will you!
[Christy comes in, in jockey's dress, with Pegeen Mike, Sara, and other girls and men.

PEGEEN. *[To crowd.]* Go on now, and don't destroy him, and he drenching with sweat. Go along, I'm saying, and have your tug-of-warring till he's dried his skin.

CROWD. Here's his prizes! A bagpipes! A fiddle was played by a poet in the years gone by! A flat and three-thorned blackthorn would lick the scholars out of Dublin town!

CHRISTY. *[Taking prizes from the men.]* Thank you kindly, the lot of you. But you'd say it was little only I did this day if you'd seen me a while since striking my one single blow.

TOWN CRIER. *[Outside ringing a bell.]* Take notice, last event of this day! Tug-of-warring on the green below! Come on, the lot of you! Great achievements for all Mayo men!

PEGEEN. Go on and leave him for to rest and dry. Go on, I tell you, for he'll do no more.
[She hustles crowd out; Widow Quin following them.

MEN. *[Going.]* Come on, then. Good luck for the while!

PEGEEN. *[Radiantly, wiping his face with her shawl.]* Well, you're the lad, and you'll have great times from this out when you could win that wealth of prizes, and you sweating in the heat of noon!

CHRISTY. *[Looking at her with delight.]* I'll have great times if I win the crowning prize I'm seeking now, and that's your promise that you'll wed me in a fortnight, when our banns is called.

PEGEEN. *[Backing away from him.]* You've right daring to go ask me that, when all knows you'll be starting to some girl in your own townland, when your father's rotten in four months, or five.

CHRISTY. *[Indignantly.]* Starting from you, is it? *[He follows her.]* I will not, then, and when the airs is warming, in four months or five, it's then yourself and me should be pacing Neifin in the dews of night, the times sweet smells do be rising, and you 'd see a little, shiny new moon, maybe sinking on the hills.

PEGEEN. [*Looking at him playfully.*] And it 's that kind of a poacher's love you 'd make, Christy Mahon, on the sides of Neifin, when the night is down?

CHRISTY. It 's little you 'll think if my love 's a poacher's, or an earl's itself, when you 'll feel my two hands stretched around you, and I squeezing kisses on your puckered lips, till I 'd feel a kind of pity for the Lord God is all ages sitting lonesome in His golden chair.

PEGEEN. That 'll be right fun, Christy Mahon, and any girl would walk her heart out before she 'd meet a young man was your like for eloquence, or talk at all.

CHRISTY. [*Encouraged.*] Let you wait, to hear me talking, till we 're astray in Erris, when Good Friday 's by, drinking a sup from a well, and making mighty kisses with our wetted mouths, or gaming in a gap of sunshine, with yourself stretched back unto your necklace, in the flowers of the earth.

PEGEEN. [*In a low voice, moved by his tone.*] I 'd be nice so, is it?

CHRISTY. [*With rapture.*] If the mitred bishops seen you that time, they 'd be the like of the holy prophets, I 'm thinking, do be straining the bars of paradise to lay eyes on the Lady Helen of Troy, and she abroad, pacing back and forward, with a nosegay in her golden shawl.

PEGEEN. [*With real tenderness.*] And what is it I have, Christy Mahon, to make me fitting entertainment for the like of you, that has such poet's talking, and such bravery of heart.

CHRISTY. [*In a low voice.*] Isn't there the light of seven heavens in your heart alone, the way you 'll be an angel's lamp to me from this out, and I abroad in the darkness, spearing salmons in the Owen or the Carrowmore?

PEGEEN. If I was your wife I 'd be along with you those nights, Christy Mahon, the way you 'd see I was a great hand at coaxing bailiffs, or coining funny nicknames for the stars of night.

CHRISTY. You, is it? Taking your death in the hailstones, or in the fogs of dawn.

PEGEEN. Yourself and me would shelter easy in a narrow bush [*with a qualm of dread*]; but we're only talking, maybe, for this would be a poor, thatched place to hold a fine lad is the like of you.

CHRISTY. [*Putting his arm round her.*] If I wasn't a good Christian, it's on my naked knees I'd be saying my prayers and paters to every jackstraw you have roofing your head, and every stony pebble is paving the laneway to your door.

PEGEEN. [*Radiantly.*] If that's the truth I'll be burning candles from this out to the miracles of God that have brought you from the south to-day, and I with my gowns bought ready, the way that I can wed you, and not wait at all.

CHRISTY. It's miracles, and that's the truth. Me there toiling a long while, and walking a long while, not knowing at all I was drawing all times nearer to this holy day.

PEGEEN. And myself, a girl, was tempted often to go sailing the seas till I'd marry a Jew-man, with ten kegs of gold, and I not knowing at all there was the like of you drawing nearer, like the stars of God.

CHRISTY. And to think I'm long years hearing women talking that talk, to all bloody fools, and this the first time I've heard the like of your voice talking sweetly for my own delight.

PEGEEN. And to think it's me is talking sweetly, Christy Mahon, and I the fright of seven townlands for my biting tongue. Well, the heart's a wonder; and, I'm thinking, there won't be our like in Mayo, for gallant lovers, from this hour to-day. [*Drunken singing is heard outside.*] There's my father coming from the wake, and when he's had his sleep we'll tell him, for he's peaceful then.

[*They separate.*

MICHAEL. [*Singing outside.*]

The jailer and the turnkey
They quickly ran us down,

And brought us back as prisoners
Once more to Cavan town.

[*He comes in supported by Shawn.*

There we lay bewailing
All in a prison bound. . . .

[*He sees Christy.   Goes and shakes him drunkenly by the
hand, while Pegeen and Shawn talk on the left.*

MICHAEL. [*To Christy.*] The blessing of God and the holy
angels on your head, young fellow.   I hear tell you 're
after winning all in the sports below; and wasn't it a shame
I didn't bear you along with me to Kate Cassidy's wake, a
fine, stout lad, the like of you, for you 'd never see the
match of it for flows of drink, the way when we sunk her
bones at noonday in her narrow grave, there were five
men, aye, and six men, stretched out retching speechless
on the holy stones.

CHRISTY. [*Uneasily, watching Pegeen.*] Is that the truth?

MICHAEL. It is, then; and aren't you a louty schemer to
go burying your poor father unbeknownst when you 'd
a right to throw him on the crupper of a Kerry mule and
drive him westwards, like holy Joseph in the days gone by,
the way we could have given him a decent burial, and not
have him rotting beyond, and not a Christian drinking a
smart drop to the glory of his soul?

CHRISTY. [*Gruffly.*] It 's well enough he 's lying, for the
likes of him.

MICHAEL. [*Slapping him on the back.*] Well, aren't you a
hardened slayer?   It 'll be a poor thing for the household man where you go sniffing for a female wife; and
[*pointing to Shawn*] look beyond at that shy and decent
Christian I have chosen for my daughter's hand, and I
after getting the gilded dispensation this day for to wed
them now.

CHRISTY. And you 'll be wedding them this day, is it?

MICHAEL. [*Drawing himself up.*] Aye.   Are you thinking,
if I 'm drunk itself, I 'd leave my daughter living single
with a little frisky rascal is the like of you?

PEGEEN. [*Breaking away from Shawn.*] Is it the truth the dispensation 's come?

MICHAEL. [*Triumphantly.*] Father Reilly 's after reading it in gallous Latin, and 'It 's come in the nick of time,' says he; 'so I 'll wed them in a hurry, dreading that young gaffer who 'd capsize the stars.'

PEGEEN. [*Fiercely.*] He 's missed his nick of time, for it 's that lad, Christy Mahon, that I 'm wedding now.

MICHAEL. [*Loudly, with horror.*] You 'd be making him a son to me, and he wet and crusted with his father's blood?

PEGEEN. Aye. Wouldn't it be a bitter thing for a girl to go marrying the like of Shaneen, and he a middling kind of a scarecrow, with no savagery or fine words in him at all?

MICHAEL. [*Gasping and sinking on a chair.*] Oh, aren't you a heathen daughter to go shaking the fat of my heart, and I swamped and drownded with the weight of drink? Would you have them turning on me the way that I 'd be roaring to the dawn of day with the wind upon my heart? Have you not a word to aid me, Shaneen? Are you not jealous at all?

SHAWN. [*In great misery.*] I'd be afeard to be jealous of a man did slay his da.

PEGEEN. Well, it 'd be a poor thing to go marrying your like. I 'm seeing there 's a world of peril for an orphan girl, and isn't it a great blessing I didn't wed you before himself came walking from the west or south?

SHAWN. It 's a queer story you 'd go picking a dirty tramp up from the highways of the world.

PEGEEN. [*Playfully.*] And you think you 're a likely beau to go straying along with the shiny Sundays of the opening year, when it 's sooner on a bullock's liver you 'd put a poor girl thinking than on the lily or the rose?

SHAWN. And have you no mind of my weight of passion, and the holy dispensation, and the drift of heifers I 'm giving, and the golden ring?

PEGEEN. I 'm thinking you 're too fine for the like of me, Shawn Keogh of Killakeen, and let you go off till you 'd find a radiant lady with droves of bullocks on the plains

of Meath, and herself bedizened in the diamond jewelleries
of Pharaoh's ma.   That 'd be your match, Shaneen.   So
God save you now!   [*She retreats behind Christy.*

SHAWN. Won't you hear me telling you . . . ?

CHRISTY. [*With ferocity.*] Take yourself from this, young
fellow, or I 'll maybe add a murder to my deeds to-day.

MICHAEL. [*Springing up with a shriek.*] Murder is it?   Is
it mad yous are?   Would you go making murder in this
place, and it piled with poteen for our drink to-night?
Go on to the foreshore if it 's fighting you want, where
the rising tide will wash all traces from the memory of man.
                            [*Pushing Shawn towards Christy.*

SHAWN. [*Shaking himself free, and getting behind Michael.*]
I 'll not fight him, Michael James.   I 'd liefer live a
bachelor, simmering in passions to the end of time, than
face a lepping savage the like of him has descended from
the Lord knows where.   Strike him yourself, Michael
James, or you 'll lose my drift of heifers and my blue bull
from Sneem.

MICHAEL. Is it me fight him, when it 's father-slaying he 's
bred to now?   [*Pushing Shawn.*] Go on, you fool, and
fight him now.

SHAWN. [*Coming forward a little.*] Will I strike him with
my hand?

MICHAEL. Take the loy is on your western side.

SHAWN. I 'd be afeard of the gallows if I struck with that.

CHRISTY. [*Taking up the loy.*] Then I 'll make you face
the gallows or quit off from this.
                            [*Shawn flies out of the door.*

CHRISTY. Well, fine weather be after him [*going to Michael,
coaxingly*], and I 'm thinking you wouldn't wish to have
that quaking blackguard in your house at all.   Let you
give us your blessing and hear her swear her faith to me,
for I 'm mounted on the spring-tide of the stars of luck,
the way it 'll be good for any to have me in the house.

PEGEEN. [*At the other side of Michael.*] Bless us now, for I
swear to God I 'll wed him, and I 'll not renege.

MICHAEL. [*Standing up in the centre, holding on to both of them.*] It 's the will of God, I 'm thinking, that all should win an easy or a cruel end, and it 's the will of God that all should rear up lengthy families for the nurture of the earth. What 's a single man, I ask you, eating a bit in one house and drinking a sup in another, and he with no place of his own, like an old braying jackass strayed upon the rocks? [*To Christy.*] It 's many would be in dread to bring your like into their house for to end them, maybe, with a sudden end; but I 'm a decent man of Ireland, and I liefer face the grave untimely and I seeing a score of grandsons growing up little gallant swearers by the name of God, than go peopling my bedside with puny weeds the like of what you 'd breed, I 'm thinking, out of Shaneen Keogh. [*He joins their hands.*] A daring fellow is the jewel of the world, and a man did split his father's middle with a single clout should have the bravery of ten, so may God and Mary and St Patrick bless you, and increase you from this mortal day.

CHRISTY *and* PEGEEN. Amen, O Lord!

> [*Hubbub outside. Old Mahon rushes in, followed by all the crowd, and Widow Quin. He makes a rush at Christy, knocks him down, and begins to beat him.*

PEGEEN. [*Dragging back his arm.*] Stop that, will you? Who are you at all?

MAHON. His father, God forgive me!

PEGEEN. [*Drawing back.*] Is it rose from the dead?

MAHON. Do you think I look so easy quenched with the tap of a loy? [*Beats Christy again.*

PEGEEN. [*Glaring at Christy.*] And it 's lies you told, letting on you had him slitted, and you nothing at all.

CHRISTY. [*Catching Mahon's stick.*] He 's not my father. He 's a raving maniac would scare the world. [*Pointing to Widow Quin.*] Herself knows it is true.

CROWD. You 're fooling, Pegeen! The Widow Quin seen him this day, and you likely knew! You 're a liar!

CHRISTY. [*Dumbfounded.*] It 's himself was a liar, lying stretched out with an open head on him, letting on he was dead.

MAHON. Weren't you off racing the hills before I got my breath with the start I had seeing you turn on me at all?

PEGEEN. And to think of the coaxing glory we had given him, and he after doing nothing but hitting a soft blow and chasing northward in a sweat of fear. Quit off from this.

CHRISTY. [*Piteously.*] You 've seen my doings this day, and let you save me from the old man; for why would you be in such a scorch of haste to spur me to destruction now?

PEGEEN. It 's there your treachery is spurring me, till I 'm hard set to think you 're the one I 'm after lacing in my heart-strings half an hour gone by. [*To Mahon.*] Take him on from this, for I think bad the world should see me raging for a Munster liar, and the fool of men.

MAHON. Rise up now to retribution, and come on with me.

CROWD. [*Jeeringly.*] There 's the playboy! There 's the lad thought he 'd rule the roost in Mayo! Slate him now, mister.

CHRISTY. [*Getting up in shy terror.*] What is it drives you to torment me here, when I 'd asked the thunders of the might of God to blast me if I ever did hurt to any saving only that one single blow.

MAHON. [*Loudly.*] If you didn't, you 're a poor good-for-nothing, and isn't it by the like of you the sins of the whole world are committed?

CHRISTY. [*Raising his hands.*] In the name of the Almighty God . . .

MAHON. Leave troubling the Lord God. Would you have Him sending down droughts, and fevers, and the old hen and the cholera morbus?

CHRISTY. [*To Widow Quin.*] Will you come between us and protect me now?

WIDOW QUIN. I 've tried a lot, God help me, and my share is done.

CHRISTY. [*Looking round in desperation.*] And I must go back into my torment is it, or run off like a vagabond straying through the unions with the dust of August making mudstains in the gullet of my throat; or the winds of March blowing on me till I 'd take an oath I felt them making whistles of my ribs within?

SARA. Ask Pegeen to aid you. Her like does often change.

CHRISTY. I will not, then, for there 's torment in the splendour of her like, and she a girl any moon of midnight would take pride to meet, facing southwards on the heaths of Keel. But what did I want crawling forward to scorch my understanding at her flaming brow?

PEGEEN. [*To Mahon, vehemently, fearing she will break into tears.*] Take him on from this or I 'll set the young lads to destroy him here.

MAHON. [*Going to him, shaking his stick.*] Come on now if you wouldn't have the company to see you skelped.

PEGEEN. [*Half laughing, through her tears.*] That 's it, now the world will see him pandied, and he an ugly liar was playing off the hero, and the fright of men.

CHRISTY. [*To Mahon, very sharply.*] Leave me go!

CROWD. That 's it. Now, Christy. If them two set fighting, it will lick the world.

MAHON. [*Making a grab at Christy.*] Come here to me.

CHRISTY. [*More threateningly.*] Leave me go, I 'm saying.

MAHON. I will, maybe, when your legs is limping, and your back is blue.

CROWD. Keep it up, the two of you. I 'll back the old one. Now the playboy.

CHRISTY. [*In low and intense voice.*] Shut your yelling, for if you 're after making a mighty man of me this day by the power of a lie, you 're setting me now to think if it 's a poor thing to be lonesome it 's worse, maybe, go mixing with the fools of earth.

[*Mahon makes a movement towards him.*

CHRISTY. [*Almost shouting.*] Keep off . . . lest I do show a blow unto the lot of you would set the guardian angels winking in the clouds above.

[*He swings round with a sudden rapid movement and picks up a loy.*

CROWD. [*Half frightened, half amused.*] He 's going mad! Mind yourselves! Run from the idiot!

CHRISTY. If I am an idiot, I 'm after hearing my voice this day saying words would raise the top-knot on a poet in a merchant's town. I 've won your racing, and your lepping, and . . .

MAHON. Shut your gullet and come on with me.

CHRISTY. I 'm going, but I 'll stretch you first.

[*He runs at old Mahon with the loy, chases him out of the door, followed by crowd and Widow Quin. There is a great noise outside, then a yell, and dead silence for a moment. Christy comes in, half dazed, and goes to fire.*]

WIDOW QUIN. [*Coming in hurriedly, and going to him.*] They 're turning again you. Come on, or you 'll be hanged, indeed.

CHRISTY. I 'm thinking, from this out, Pegeen 'll be giving me praises, the same as in the hours gone by.

WIDOW QUIN. [*Impatiently.*] Come by the back door. I 'd think bad to have you stifled on the gallows tree.

CHRISTY. [*Indignantly.*] I will not, then. What good 'd be my lifetime if I left Pegeen?

WIDOW QUIN. Come on, and you 'll be no worse than you were last night; and you with a double murder this time to be telling to the girls.

CHRISTY. I 'll not leave Pegeen Mike.

WIDOW QUIN. [*Impatiently.*] Isn't there the match of her in every parish public, from Binghamstown unto the plain of Meath? Come on, I tell you, and I 'll find you finer sweethearts at each waning moon.

CHRISTY. It 's Pegeen I 'm seeking only, and what 'd I care if you brought me a drift of chosen females, standing in their shifts itself, maybe, from this place to the eastern world?

SARA. [*Runs in, pulling off one of her petticoats.*] They 're going to hang him. [*Holding out petticoat and shawl.*] Fit these upon him, and let him run off to the east.

WIDOW QUIN. He 's raving now; but we 'll fit them on him, and I 'll take him in the ferry to the Achill boat.

CHRISTY. [*Struggling feebly.*] Leave me go, will you? when

I 'm thinking of my luck to-day, for she will wed me surely, and I a proven hero in the end of all.

> [*They try to fasten petticoat round him.*

WIDOW QUIN. Take his left hand and we 'll pull him now. Come on, young fellow.

CHRISTY. [*Suddenly starting up.*] You 'll be taking me from her? You 're jealous, is it, of her wedding me? Go on from this.

> [*He snatches up a stool, and threatens them with it.*

WIDOW QUIN. [*Going.*] It 's in the madhouse they should put him, not in jail, at all. We 'll go by the back door to call the doctor, and we 'll save him so.

> [*She goes out, with Sara, through inner room. Men crowd in the doorway. Christy sits down again by the fire.*

MICHAEL. [*In a terrified whisper.*] Is the old lad killed surely?

PHILLY. I 'm after feeling the last gasps quitting his heart.

> [*They peer in at Christy.*

MICHAEL. [*With a rope.*] Look at the way he is. Twist a hangman's knot on it, and slip it over his head, while he 's not minding at all.

PHILLY. Let you take it, Shaneen. You 're the soberest of all that 's here.

SHAWN. Is it me to go near him, and he the wickedest and worst with me? Let you take it, Pegeen Mike.

PEGEEN. Come on, so.

> [*She goes forward with the others, and they drop the double hitch over his head.*

CHRISTY. What ails you?

SHAWN. [*Triumphantly, as they pull the rope tight on his arms.*] Come on to the peelers, till they stretch you now.

CHRISTY. Me!

MICHAEL. If we took pity on you the Lord God would, maybe, bring us ruin from the law to-day, so you 'd best come easy, for hanging is an easy and a speedy end.

CHRISTY. I 'll not stir. [*To Pegeen.*] And what is it you 'll say to me, and I after doing it this time in the face of all?

PEGEEN. I 'll say, a strange man is a marvel, with his mighty talk; but what 's a squabble in your back yard, and the blow of a loy, have taught me that there 's a great gap between a gallous story and a dirty deed. [*To men.*] Take him on from this, or the lot of us will be likely put on trial for his deed to-day.

CHRISTY. [*With horror in his voice.*] And it 's yourself will send me off, to have a horny-fingered hangman hitching slip-knots at the butt of my ear.

MEN. [*Pulling rope.*] Come on, will you?

[*He is pulled down on the floor.*

CHRISTY. [*Twisting his legs round the table.*] Cut the rope, Pegeen, and I 'll quit the lot of you, and live from this out, like the madman of Keel, eating muck and green weeds on the faces of the cliffs.

PEGEEN. And leave us to hang, is it, for a saucy liar, the like of you? [*To men.*] Take him on, out from this.

SHAWN. Pull a twist on his neck, and squeeze him so.

PHILLY. Twist yourself. Sure he cannot hurt you, if you keep your distance from his teeth alone.

SHAWN. I 'm afeard of him. [*To Pegeen.*] Lift a lighted sod, will you, and scorch his leg.

PEGEEN. [*Blowing the fire with a bellows.*] Leave go now, young fellow, or I 'll scorch your shins.

CHRISTY. You 're blowing for to torture me. [*His voice rising and growing stronger.*] That 's your kind, is it? Then let the lot of you be wary, for, if I 've to face the gallows, I 'll have a gay march down, I tell you, and shed the blood of some of you before I die.

SHAWN. [*In terror.*] Keep a good hold, Philly. Be wary, for the love of God. For I 'm thinking he would liefest wreak his pains on me.

CHRISTY. [*Almost gaily.*] If I do lay my hands on you, it 's the way you 'll be at the fall of night, hanging as a scarecrow for the fowls of hell. Ah, you 'll have a gallous jaunt, I 'm saying, coaching out through limbo with my father's ghost.

SHAWN. [*To Pegeen.*] Make haste, will you? Oh, isn't

he a holy terror, and isn't it true for Father Reilly, that
all drink's a curse that has the lot of you so shaky and
uncertain now?

CHRISTY. If I can wring a neck among you, I 'll have a
royal judgment looking on the trembling jury in the courts
of law.   And won't there be crying out in Mayo the day
I 'm stretched upon the rope, with ladies in their silks and
satins snivelling in their lacy kerchiefs, and they rhyming
songs and ballads on the terror of my fate?

    [*He squirms round on the floor and bites Shawn's leg.*

SHAWN. [*Shrieking.*] My leg 's bit on me.   He 's the like of
a mad dog, I 'm thinking, the way that I will surely die.

CHRISTY. [*Delighted with himself.*] You will, then, the way
you can shake out hell's flags of welcome for my coming
in two weeks or three, for I 'm thinking Satan hasn't many
have killed their da in Kerry, and in Mayo too.

    [*Old Mahon comes in behind on all fours and looks on
       unnoticed.*

MEN. [*To Pegeen.*] Bring the sod, will you?

PEGEEN. [*Coming over.*] God help him so. [*Burns his leg.*

CHRISTY. [*Kicking and screaming.*] Oh, glory be to God!

    [*He kicks loose from the table, and they all drag him
       towards the door.*

JIMMY. [*Seeing old Mahon.*] Will you look what 's come in?

    [*They all drop Christy and run left.*

CHRISTY. [*Scrambling on his knees face to face with old
Mahon.*] Are you coming to be killed a third time, or
what ails you now?

MAHON. For what is it they have you tied?

CHRISTY. They 're taking me to the peelers to have me
hanged for slaying you.

MICHAEL. [*Apologetically.*] It is the will of God that all
should guard their little cabins from the treachery of law,
and what would my daughter be doing if I was ruined or
was hanged itself?

MAHON. [*Grimly, loosening Christy.*] It 's little I care if you
put a bag on her back, and went picking cockles till the
hour of death; but my son and myself will be going our

own way, and we 'll have great times from this out telling stories of the villainy of Mayo, and the fools is here. [*To Christy, who is freed.*] Come on now.

CHRISTY. Go with you, is it? I will then, like a gallant captain with his heathen slave. Go on now and I 'll see you from this day stewing my oatmeal and washing my spuds, for I 'm master of all fights from now. [*Pushing Mahon.*] Go on, I 'm saying.

MAHON. Is it me?

CHRISTY. Not a word out of you. Go on from this.

MAHON. [*Walking out and looking back at Christy over his shoulder.*] Glory be to God! [*With a broad smile.*] I am crazy again.   [*Goes.*

CHRISTY. Ten thousand blessings upon all that 's here, for you 've turned me a likely gaffer in the end of all, the way I 'll go romancing through a romping lifetime from this hour to the dawning of the Judgment Day. [*He goes out.*

MICHAEL. By the will of God, we 'll have peace now for our drinks. Will you draw the porter, Pegeen?

SHAWN. [*Going up to her.*] It 's a miracle Father Reilly can wed us in the end of all, and we 'll have none to trouble us when his vicious bite is healed.

PEGEEN. [*Hitting him a box on the ear.*] Quit my sight. [*Putting her shawl over her head and breaking out into wild lamentations.*] Oh, my grief, I 've lost him surely. I 've lost the only Playboy of the Western World.

CURTAIN

DEIRDRE OF THE SORROWS

PERSONS IN THE PLAY

LAVARCHAM, Deirdre's nurse
OLD WOMAN, Lavarcham's servant
OWEN, Conchubor's attendant and spy
CONCHUBOR, High King of Ulster
FERGUS, Conchubor's friend
DEIRDRE
NAISI, Deirdre's lover
AINNLE, Naisi's brother
ARDAN, Naisi's brother
TWO SOLDIERS

SCENE. *Act I, Lavarcham's house in Slieve Fuadh. Act II, Alban. Early morning in the beginning of winter. Outide the tent of Deirdre and Naisi. Act III, Tent below Emain Macha*

DEIRDRE OF THE SORROWS

ACT I

*Lavarcham's house on Slieve Fuadh. There is a door to inner
room on the left, and a door to open air on the right. Window
at back and a frame with a half-finished piece of tapestry.
There are also a large press and heavy oak chest near the back
wall. The place is neat and clean but bare. Lavarcham,
woman of fifty, is working at tapestry frame. Old Woman
comes in from left.*

OLD WOMAN. She hasn't come yet, is it, and it falling to the
night?

LAVARCHAM. She has not. . . . [*Concealing her anxiety.*]
It's dark with the clouds are coming from the west and
south, but it isn't later than the common.

OLD WOMAN. It's later, surely, and I hear tell the Sons of
Usna, Naisi and his brothers, are above chasing hares for
two days or three, and the same awhile since when the
moon was full.

LAVARCHAM. [*More anxiously.*] The gods send they don't
set eyes on her—[*with a sign of helplessness*] yet if they do
itself, it wasn't my wish brought them or could send them
away.

OLD WOMAN. [*Reprovingly.*] If it wasn't you'd do well to
keep a check on her, and she turning a woman that was
meant to be a queen.

LAVARCHAM. Who'd check her like was made to have her
pleasure only, the way if there were no warnings told about
her you'd see troubles coming when an old king is taking
her, and she without a thought but for her beauty and to
be straying the hills.

OLD WOMAN. The gods help the lot of us. . . . Shouldn't

she be well pleased getting the like of Conchubor, and he middling settled in his years itself? I don't know what he wanted putting her this wild place to be breaking her in, or putting myself to be roasting her supper and she with no patience for her food at all. [*She looks out.*

LAVARCHAM. Is she coming from the glen?

OLD WOMAN. She is not. But whisht—there's two men leaving the furze—[*crying out*] it's Conchubor and Fergus along with him. Conchubor 'll be in a blue stew this night and herself abroad.

LAVARCHAM. [*Settling room hastily.*] Are they close by?

OLD WOMAN. Crossing the stream, and there's herself on the hillside with a load of twigs. Will I run out and put her in order before they 'll set eyes on her at all?

LAVARCHAM. You will not. Would you have him see you, and he a man would be jealous of a hawk would fly between her and the rising sun. [*She looks out.*] Go up to the hearth and be as busy as if you hadn't seen them at all.

OLD WOMAN. [*Sitting down to polish vessel.*] There 'll be trouble this night, for he should be in his tempers from the way he 's stepping out, and he swinging his hands.

LAVARCHAM. [*Wearied with the whole matter.*] It 'd be best of all, maybe, if he got in tempers with herself, and made an end quickly, for I 'm in a poor way between the pair of them. [*Going back to tapestry frame.*] There they are now at the door. [*Conchubor and Fergus come in.*

CONCHUBOR *and* FERGUS. The gods save you.

LAVARCHAM. [*Getting up and curtsying.*] The gods save and keep you kindly, and stand between you and all harm for ever.

CONCHUBOR. [*Looking round.*] Where is Deirdre?

LAVARCHAM. [*Trying to speak with indifference.*] Abroad upon Slieve Fuadh. She does be all times straying around picking flowers or nuts, or sticks itself; but so long as she 's gathering new life I 've a right not to heed her, I 'm thinking, and she taking her will.

[*Fergus talks to Old Woman.*

CONCHUBOR. [*Stiffly.*] A night with thunder coming is no night to be abroad.

LAVARCHAM. [*More uneasily.*] She 's used to every track and pathway, and the lightning itself wouldn't let down its flame to singe the beauty of her like.

FERGUS. [*Cheerfully.*] She 's right, Conchubor, and let you sit down and take your ease [*he takes a wallet from under his cloak*], and I 'll count out what we 've brought, and put it in the presses within.

[*He goes into the inner room with the Old Woman.*

CONCHUBOR. [*Sitting down and looking about.*] Where are the mats and hangings and the silver skillets I sent up for Deirdre?

LAVARCHAM. The mats and hangings are in this press, Conchubor. She wouldn't wish to be soiling them, she said, running out and in with mud and grasses on her feet, and it raining since the night of Samhain. The silver skillets and the golden cups we have beyond locked in the chest.

CONCHUBOR. Bring them out and use them from this day.

LAVARCHAM. We 'll do it, Conchubor.

CONCHUBOR. [*Getting up and going to frame.*] Is this hers?

LAVARCHAM. [*Pleased to speak of it.*] It is, Conchubor. All say there isn't her match at fancying figures and throwing purple upon crimson, and she edging them all times with her greens and gold.

CONCHUBOR. [*A little uneasily.*] Is she keeping wise and busy since I passed before, and growing ready for her life in Emain?

LAVARCHAM. [*Dryly.*] That is a question will give small pleasure to yourself or me. [*Making up her mind to speak out.*] If it 's the truth I 'll tell you, she 's growing too wise to marry a big king and she a score only. Let you not be taking it bad, Conchubor, but you 'll get little good seeing her this night, for with all my talking it 's wilfuller she 's growing these two months or three.

CONCHUBOR. [*Severely, but relieved things are no worse.*] Isn't it a poor thing you 're doing so little to school her to meet what is to come?

LAVARCHAM. I 'm after serving you two score of years, and
I 'll tell you this night, Conchubor, she 's little call to mind
an old woman when she has the birds to school her, and
the pools in the rivers where she goes bathing in the sun.
I 'll tell you if you seen her that time, with her white
skin, and her red lips, and the blue water and the ferns
about her, you 'd know, maybe, and you greedy itself, it
wasn't for your like she was born at all.

CONCHUBOR. It 's little I heed for what she was born; she 'll
be my comrade, surely.   [*He examines her workbox.*

LAVARCHAM. [*Sinking into sadness again.*] I 'm in dread so
they were right saying she 'd bring destruction on the world,
for it 's a poor thing when you see a settled man putting
the love he has for a young child, and the love he has for
a full woman, on a girl the like of her; and it 's a poor
thing, Conchubor, to see a High King, the way you are
this day, prying after her needles and numbering her lines
of thread.

CONCHUBOR. [*Getting up.*] Let you not be talking too far
and you old itself. [*Walks across room and back.*] Does she
know the troubles are foretold?

LAVARCHAM. [*In the tone of the earlier talk.*] I 'm after
telling her one time and another, but I 'd do as well speaking to a lamb of ten weeks and it racing the hills. . . . It 's
not the dread of death or troubles that would tame her like.

CONCHUBOR. [*He looks out.*] She 's coming now, and let you
walk in and keep Fergus till I speak with her a while.

LAVARCHAM. [*Going left.*] If I 'm after vexing you itself,
it 'd be best you weren't taking her hasty or scolding her
at all.

CONCHUBOR. [*Very stiffly.*] I 've no call to. I 'm well
pleased she 's light and airy.

LAVARCHAM. [*Offended at his tone.*] Well pleased is it?
[*With a snort of irony.*] It 's a queer thing the way the
likes of me do be telling the truth, and the wise are lying
all times.

[*She goes into room on left.   Conchubor arranges himself
before a mirror for a moment, then goes a little to the*

*left and waits. Deirdre comes in poorly dressed,
with a little bag and a bundle of twigs in her arms.
She is astonished for a moment when she sees Conchubor; then she makes a curtsy to him, and goes to
the hearth without any embarrassment.*

CONCHUBOR. The gods save you, Deirdre. I have come up
bringing you rings and jewels from Emain Macha.

DEIRDRE. The gods save you.

CONCHUBOR. What have you brought from the hills?

DEIRDRE. [*Quite self-possessed.*] A bag of nuts, and twigs
for our fires at the dawn of day.

CONCHUBOR. [*Showing annoyance in spite of himself.*] And
it's that way you're picking up the manners will fit you
to be Queen of Ulster?

DEIRDRE. [*Made a little defiant by his tone.*] I have no wish
to be a queen.

CONCHUBOR. [*Almost sneeringly.*] You'd wish to be dressing
in your duns and grey, and you herding your geese or
driving your calves to their shed—like the common lot
scattered in the glens.

DEIRDRE. [*Very defiant.*] I would not, Conchubor. [*She
goes to tapestry and begins to work.*] A girl born the way
I'm born is more likely to wish for a mate who'd be her
likeness. . . . A man with his hair like the raven, maybe,
and his skin like the snow and his lips like blood spilt on it.

CONCHUBOR. [*Sees his mistake, and after a moment takes a
flattering tone, looking at her work.*] Whatever you wish,
there's no queen but would be well pleased to have your
skill at choosing colours and making pictures on the cloth.
[*Looking closely.*] What is it you're figuring?

DEIRDRE. [*Deliberately.*] Three young men and they chasing in the green gap of a wood.

CONCHUBOR. [*Now almost pleading.*] It's soon you'll have
dogs with silver chains to be chasing in the woods of Emain,
for I have white hounds rearing up for you, and grey
horses, that I've chosen from the finest in Ulster and
Britain and Gaul.

DEIRDRE. [*Unmoved as before.*] I've heard tell, in Ulster

and Britain and Gaul, Naisi and his brothers have no match
and they chasing in the woods.

CONCHUBOR. [*Very gravely.*] Isn't it a strange thing you 'd
be talking of Naisi and his brothers, or figuring them either,
when you know the things that are foretold about themselves and you? Yet you 've little knowledge, and I 'd
do wrong taking it bad when it 'll be my share from this
out to keep you in the way you 'll have little call to trouble
for knowledge, or its want either.

DEIRDRE. Yourself should be wise, surely.

CONCHUBOR. The like of me has a store of knowledge that 's
a weight and terror. It 's for that we do choose out the
like of yourself that are young and glad only. . . . I 'm
thinking you are gay and lively each day in the year?

DEIRDRE. I don't know if that 's true, Conchubor. There
are lonesome days and bad nights in this place like another.

CONCHUBOR. You should have as few sad days, I 'm thinking, as I have glad and good ones.

DEIRDRE. What is it has you that way ever coming this
place, when you 'd hear the old woman saying a good
child 's as happy as a king?

CONCHUBOR. How would I be happy seeing age coming on
me each year, when the dry leaves are blowing back and
forward at the gate of Emain? And yet this last while
I 'm saying out, when I see the furze breaking and the
daws sitting two and two on ash-trees by the duns of Emain,
Deirdre 's a year nearer her full age when she 'll be my
mate and comrade, and then I 'm glad surely.

DEIRDRE. [*Almost to herself.*] I will not be your mate in
Emain.

CONCHUBOR. [*Not heeding her.*] It 's there you 'll be proud
and happy and you 'll learn that, if young men are great
hunters, yet it 's with the like of myself you 'll find a
knowledge of what is priceless in your own like. What
we all need is a place is safe and splendid, and it 's that
you 'll get in Emain in two days or three.

DEIRDRE. [*Aghast.*] Two days!

CONCHUBOR. I have the rooms ready, and in a little while

you 'll be brought down there, to be my queen and queen of the five parts of Ireland.

DEIRDRE. [*Standing up frightened and pleading.*] I 'd liefer stay this place, Conchubor. . . . Leave me this place, where I 'm well used to the tracks and pathways and the people of the glens. . . . It 's for this life I 'm born, surely.

CONCHUBOR. You 'll be happier and greater with myself in Emain. It is I will be your comrade and will stand between you and the great troubles are foretold.

DEIRDRE. I will not be your queen in Emain when it 's my pleasure to be having my freedom on the edges of the hills.

CONCHUBOR. It 's my wish to have you quickly; I 'm sick and weary thinking of the day you 'll be brought down to me, and seeing you walking into my big, empty halls. I 've made all sure to have you, and yet all said there 's a fear in the back of my mind I 'd miss you and have great troubles in the end . It 's for that, Deirdre, I 'm praying that you 'll come quickly; and you may take the word of a man has no lies, you 'll not find, with any other, the like of what I 'm bringing you in wildness and confusion in my own mind.

DEIRDRE. I cannot go, Conchubor.

CONCHUBOR. [*Taking a triumphant tone.*] It is my pleasure to have you, and I a man is waiting a long while on the throne of Ulster. Wouldn't you liefer be my comrade, growing up the like of Emer and Maeve, than to be in this place and you a child always?

DEIRDRE. You don't know me and you 'd have little joy taking me, Conchubor. . . . I 'm a long while watching the days getting a great speed passing me by. I 'm too long taking my will, and it 's that way I 'll be living always.

CONCHUBOR. [*Dryly.*] Call Fergus to come with me. This is your last night upon Slieve Fuadh.

DEIRDRE. [*Now pleadingly.*] Leave me a short space longer, Conchubor. Isn't it a poor thing I should be hastened away, when all these troubles are foretold? Leave me a year, Conchubor; it isn't much I 'm asking.

CONCHUBOR. It 's much to have me twoscore and two weeks waiting for your voice in Emain, and you in this place growing lonesome and shy. I 'm a ripe man and in great love, and yet, Deirdre, I 'm the King of Ulster. [*He gets up.*] I 'll call Fergus, and we 'll make Emain ready in the morning.　　　　　　　　　[*He goes towards door on left.*

DEIRDRE. [*Clinging to him.*] Do not call him, Conchubor. . . . Promise me a year of quiet. . . . It 's one year I 'm asking only.

CONCHUBOR. You 'd be asking a year next year, and the years that follow. [*Calling.*] Fergus! Fergus! [*To Deirdre.*] Young girls are slow always; it is their lovers that must say the word. [*Calling.*] Fergus!

　　[*Deirdre springs away from him as Fergus comes in with Lavarcham and the Old Woman.*

CONCHUBOR. [*To Fergus.*] There is a storm coming, and we 'd best be going to our people when the night is young.

FERGUS. [*Cheerfully.*] The gods shield you, Deirdre. [*To Conchubor.*] We 're late already, and it 's no work the High King to be slipping on stepping-stones and hilly pathways when the floods are rising with the rain.

　　　　　　　　[*He helps Conchubor into his cloak.*

CONCHUBOR. [*Glad that he has made his decision—to Lavarcham.*] Keep your rules a few days longer, and you 'll be brought down to Emain, you and Deirdre with you.

LAVARCHAM. [*Obediently.*] Your rules are kept always.

CONCHUBOR. The gods shield you.

　　　[*He goes out with Fergus. Old Woman bolts door.*

LAVARCHAM. [*Looking at Deirdre, who has covered her face.*] Wasn't I saying you 'd do it? You 've brought your marriage a sight nearer not heeding those are wiser than yourself.

DEIRDRE. [*With agitation.*] It wasn't I did it. Will you take me from this place, Lavarcham, and keep me safe in the hills?

LAVARCHAM. He 'd have us tracked in the half of a day, and then you 'd be his queen in spite of you, and I and mine would be destroyed for ever.

DEIRDRE. [*Terrified with the reality that is before her.*] Are there none can go against Conchubor?

LAVARCHAM. Maeve of Connaught only, and those that are her like.

DEIRDRE. Would Fergus go against him?

LAVARCHAM. He would, maybe, and his temper roused.

DEIRDRE. [*In a lower voice with sudden excitement.*] Would Naisi and his brothers?

LAVARCHAM. [*Impatiently.*] Let you not be dwelling on Naisi and his brothers. . . . In the end of all there is none can go against Conchubor, and it 's folly that we 're talking, for if any went against Conchubor it 's sorrows he 'd earn and the shortening of his day of life.

[*She turns away, and Deirdre stands up stiff with excitement and goes and looks out of the window.*

DEIRDRE. Are the stepping-stones flooding, Lavarcham? Will the night be stormy in the hills?

LAVARCHAM. [*Looking at her curiously.*] The stepping-stones are flooding, surely, and the night will be the worst, I 'm thinking, we 've seen these years gone by.

DEIRDRE. [*Tearing open the press and pulling out clothes and tapestries.*] Lay these mats and hangings by the windows, and at the tables for our feet, and take out the skillets of silver, and the golden cups we have, and our two flasks of wine.

LAVARCHAM. What ails you?

DEIRDRE. [*Gathering up a dress.*] Lay them out quickly, Lavarcham, we 've no call dawdling this night. Lay them out quickly; I 'm going into the room to put on the rich dresses and jewels have been sent from Emain.

LAVARCHAM. Putting on dresses at this hour, and it dark and drenching with the weight of rain! Are you away in your head!

DEIRDRE. [*Gathering her things together with an outburst of excitement.*] I will dress like Emer in Dundealgan, or Maeve in her house in Connaught. If Conchubor 'll make me a queen, I 'll have the right of a queen who is a master, taking her own choice and making a stir to the edges of the seas. . . . Lay out your mats and hangings where I can stand this night and look about me. Lay out the skins of the rams of Connaught and of the goats of the west. I will not be a child or plaything; I 'll put on my robes that are the richest, for I will not be brought down to Emain as Cuchulain brings his horse to the yoke, or Conall Cearneach puts his shield upon his arm; and maybe from this day I will turn the men of Ireland like a wind blowing on the heath.

> [*She goes into room. Lavarcham and Old Woman look at each other, then the Old Woman goes over, looks in at Deirdre through chink of the door, and then closes it carefully.*

OLD WOMAN. [*In a frightened whisper.*] She 's thrown off the rags she had about her, and there she is in her skin; she 's putting her hair in shiny twists. Is she raving, Lavercham, or has she a good right turning to a queen like Maeve?

LAVARCHAM. [*Putting up hanging very anxiously.*] It 's more than raving 's in her mind, or I 'm the more astray; and yet she 's as good a right as another, maybe, having her pleasure, though she 'd spoil the world.

OLD WOMAN. [*Helping her.*] Be quick before she 'll come back. . . . Who 'd have thought we 'd run before her, and she so quiet till to-night. Will the High King get the better of her, Lavarcham? If I was Conchubor, I wouldn't marry with her like at all.

LAVARCHAM. Hang that by the window. That should please her, surely. When all 's said, it 's her like will be the master till the end of time.

OLD WOMAN. [*At the window.*] There 's a mountain of blackness in the sky, and the greatest rain falling has been these long years on the earth. The gods help Conchubor. He 'll be a sorry man this night, reaching his dun, and he with all his spirits, thinking to himself he 'll be putting his arms around her in two days or three.

LAVARCHAM. It 's more than Conchubor 'll be sick and sorry, I 'm thinking, before this story is told to the end.

> [*Loud knocking on door at the right.*

LAVARCHAM. [*Startled.*] Who is that?

NAISI. [*Outside.*] Naisi, and his brothers.

LAVARCHAM. We are lonely women. What is it you 're
wanting in the blackness of the night?

NAISI. We met a young girl in the woods who told us
we might shelter this place if the rivers rose on the pathways and the floods gathered from the butt of the hills.

> [*Old Woman clasps her hands in horror.*

LAVARCHAM. [*With great alarm.*] You cannot come in. ....
There is no one let in here, and no young girl with us.

NAISI. Let us in from the great storm. Let us in and we will
go further when the cloud will rise.

LAVARCHAM. Go round east to the shed and you 'll have
shelter. You cannot come in.

NAISI. [*Knocking loudly.*] Open the door or we will burst it.

> [*The door is shaken.*

OLD WOMAN. [*In a timid whisper.*] Let them in, and keep
Deirdre in her room to-night.

AINNLE *and* ARDAN. [*Outside.*] Open! Open!

LAVARCHAM. [*To Old Woman.*] Go in and keep her.

OLD WOMAN. I couldn't keep her. I 've no hold on her.
Go in yourself and I will free the door.

LAVARCHAM. I must stay and turn them out. [*She pulls her
hair and cloak over her face.*] Go in and keep her.

OLD WOMAN. The gods help us.

> [*She runs into the inner room.*

VOICES. Open!

LAVARCHAM. [*Opening the door.*] Come in then and ill-luck
if you 'll have it so.

> [*Naisi and Ainnle and Ardan come in and look round with
> astonishment.*

NAISI. It 's a rich man has this place, and no herd at all.

LAVARCHAM. [*Sitting down with her head half covered.*] It
is not, and you 'd best be going quickly.

NAISI. [*Hilariously, shaking rain from his clothes.*] When
we 've had the pick of luck finding princely comfort in the
darkness of the night! Some rich man of Ulster should
come here and he chasing in the woods. May we drink?

[*He takes up flask.*] Whose wine is this that we may drink his health?

LAVARCHAM. It's no one's that you've call to know.

NAISI. Your own health then and length of life.

[*Pouring out wine for the three.   They drink.*

LAVARCHAM. [*Very crossly.*] You're great boys taking a welcome where it isn't given, and asking questions where you've no call to. . . . If you'd a quiet place settled up to be playing yourself, maybe, with a gentle queen, what'd you think of young men prying around and carrying tales? When I was a bit of a girl the big men of Ulster had better manners, and they the like of your three selves, in the top folly of youth. That'll be a story to tell out in Tara that Naisi is a tippler and stealer, and Ainnle the drawer of a stranger's cork.

NAISI. [*Quite cheerfully, sitting down beside her.*] At your age you should know there are nights when a king like Conchubor would spit upon his arm ring, and queens will stick their tongues out at the rising moon. We're that way this night, and it's not wine we're asking only. Where is the young girl told us we might shelter here?

LAVARCHAM. Asking me you'd be? . . . We're decent people, and I wouldn't put you tracking a young girl, not if you gave me the gold clasp you have hanging on your coat.

NAISI. [*Giving it to her.*] Where is she?

LAVARCHAM. [*In confidential whisper, putting her hand on his arm.*] Let you walk back into the hills and turn up by the second cnuceen where there are three together. You'll see a path running on the rocks and then you'll hear the dogs barking in the houses, and their noise will guide you till you come to a bit of cabin at the foot of an ash-tree. It's there there is a young and flighty girl that I'm thinking is the one you've seen.

NAISI. [*Hilariously.*] Here's health, then, to herself and you!

ARDAN. Here's to the years when you were young as she!

AINNLE. [*In a frightened whisper.*] Naisi!

[*Naisi looks up and Ainnle beckons to him.   He goes over and Ainnle points to something on the golden mug he holds in his hand.*

NAISI. [*Looking at it in astonishment.*] This is the High King's . . . I see his mark on the rim.   Does Conchubor come lodging here?

LAVARCHAM. [*Jumping up with extreme annoyance.*] Who says it's Conchubor's?   How dare young fools the like of you [*speaking with vehement insolence*] come prying around, running the world into troubles for some slip of a girl?   What brings you this place straying from Emain? [*Very bitterly.*] Though you think, maybe, young men can do their fill of foolery and there is none to blame them.

NAISI. [*Very soberly.*] Is the rain easing?

ARDAN. The clouds are breaking. . . . I can see Orion in the gap of the glen.

NAISI. [*Still cheerfully.*] Open the door and we'll go forward to the little cabin between the ash-tree and the rocks. Lift the bolt and pull it.

[*Deirdre comes in on left royally dressed and very beautiful. She stands for a moment, and then as the door opens she calls softly.*

DEIRDRE. Naisi!   Do not leave me, Naisi.   I am Deirdre of the Sorrows.

NAISI. [*Transfixed with amazement.*] And it is you who go around in the woods making the thrushes bear a grudge against the heavens for the sweetness of your voice singing.

DEIRDRE. It is with me you've spoken surely. [*To Lavarcham and Old Woman.*] Take Ainnle and Ardan, these two princes, into the little hut where we eat, and serve them with what is best and sweetest.   I have many things for Naisi only.

LAVARCHAM. [*Overawed by her tone.*] I will do it, and I ask their pardon.   I have fooled them here.

DEIRDRE. [*To Ainnle and Arden.*] Do not take it badly that I am asking you to walk into our hut for a little.   You will have a supper that is cooked by the cook of Conchubor, and Lavarcham will tell you stories of Maeve and Nessa and Rogh.

AINNLE. We 'll ask Lavarcham to tell us stories of yourself, and with that we 'll be well pleased to be doing your wish.

[*They all go out except Deirdre and Naisi.*

DEIRDRE. [*Sitting in the high chair in the centre.*] Come to this stool, Naisi. [*Pointing to the stool.*] If it 's low itself the High King would sooner be on it this night than on the throne of Emain Macha.

NAISI. [*Sitting down.*] You are Fedlimid's daughter that Conchubor has walled up from all the men of Ulster.

DEIRDRE. Do many know what is foretold, that Deirdre will be the ruin of the Sons of Usna, and have a little grave by herself, and a story will be told for ever?

NAISI. It 's a long while men have been talking of Deirdre, the child who had all gifts, and the beauty that has no equal; there are many know it, and there are kings would give a great price to be in my place this night and you grown to a queen.

DEIRDRE. It isn't many I 'd call, Naisi. . . . I was in the woods at the full moon and I heard a voice singing. Then I gathered up my skirts, and I ran on a little path I have to the verge of a rock, and I saw you pass by underneath, in your crimson cloak, singing a song, and you standing out beyond your brothers are called the Flower of Ireland.

NAISI. It 's for that you called us in the dusk?

DEIRDRE. [*In a low voice.*] Since that, Naisi, I have been one time the like of a ewe looking for a lamb that had been taken away from her, and one time seeing new gold on the stars, and a new face on the moon, and all times dreading Emain.

NAISI. [*Pulling himself together and beginning to draw back a little.*] Yet it should be a lonesome thing to be in this place and you born for great company.

DEIRDRE. [*Softly.*] This night I have the best company in the whole world.

NAISI. [*Still a little formally.*] It is I who have the best company, for when you 're queen in Emain you will have none to be your match or fellow.

DEIRDRE. I will not be queen in Emain.

NAISI. Conchubor has made an oath you will, surely.

DEIRDRE. It 's for that maybe I 'm called Deirdre, the girl of many sorrows . . . for it 's a sweet life you and I could have, Naisi. . . . It should be a sweet thing to have what is best and richest, if it 's for a short space only.

NAISI. [*Very distressed.*] And we 've a short space only to be triumphant and brave.

DEIRDRE. You must not go, Naisi, and leave me to the High King, a man is ageing in his dun, with his crowds round him, and his silver and gold. [*More quickly.*] I will not live to be shut up in Emain, and wouldn't we do well paying, Naisi, with silence and a near death? [*She stands up and walks away from him.*] I 'm a long while in the woods with my own self, and I 'm in little dread of death, and it earned with riches would make the sun red with envy, and he going up the heavens; and the moon pale and lonesome, and she wasting away. [*She comes to him and puts her hands on his shoulders.*] Isn't it a small thing is foretold about the ruin of ourselves, Naisi, when all men have age coming and great ruin in the end?

NAISI. Yet it 's a poor thing it 's I should bring you to a tale of blood and broken bodies, and the filth of the grave. . . . Wouldn't we do well to wait, Deirdre, and I each twilight meeting you on the sides of the hills?

DEIRDRE. [*Despondently.*] His messengers are coming.

NAISI. Messengers are coming?

DEIRDRE. To-morrow morning or the next, surely.

NAISI. Then we 'll go away. It isn't I will give your like to Conchubor, not if the grave was dug to be my lodging when a week was by. [*He looks out.*] The stars are out, Deirdre, and let you come with me quickly, for it is the stars will be our lamps many nights and we abroad in Alban, and taking our journeys among the little islands in the sea. There has never been the like of the joy we 'll have, Deirdre, you and I, having our fill of love at the evening and the morning till the sun is high.

DEIRDRE. And yet I 'm in dread leaving this place, where I have lived always. Won't I be lonesome and I thinking on the little hills beyond, and the apple-trees, do be budding in the springtime by the post of the door? [*A little shaken by what has passed.*] Won't I be in great dread to bring you to destruction, Naisi, and you so happy and young?

NAISI. Are you thinking I'd go on living after this night, Deirdre, and you with Conchubor in Emain? Are you thinking I'd go out after hares when I've had your lips in my sight?

[*Lavarcham comes in as they cling to each other.*

LAVARCHAM. Are you raving, Deirdre? Are you choosing this night to destroy the world?

DEIRDRE. [*Very deliberately.*] It's Conchubor has chosen this night calling me to Emain. [*To Naisi.*] Bring in Ainnle and Ardan, and take me from this place, where I'm in dread from this out of the footsteps of a hare passing.

[*He goes.*

DEIRDRE. [*Clinging to Lavarcham.*] Do not take it bad I'm going, Lavarcham. It's you have been a good friend and given me great freedom and joy, and I living on Slieve Fuadh; and maybe you'll be well pleased one day saying you have nursed Deirdre.

LAVARCHAM. [*Moved.*] It isn't I'll be well pleased and I far away from you. Isn't it a hard thing you're doing, but who can help it? Birds go mating in the spring of the year, and ewes at the leaves falling, but a young girl must have her lover in all the course of the sun and moon.

DEIRDRE. Will you go to Emain in the morning?

LAVARCHAM. I will not. I'll go to Brandon in the south; and in the course of a piece, maybe, I'll be sailing back and forward on the seas to be looking on your face and the little ways you have that none can equal.

[*Naisi comes back with Ainnle and Ardan and Old Woman.*

DEIRDRE. [*Taking Naisi's hand.*] My two brothers, I am going with Naisi to Alban and the north to face the troubles are foretold. Will you take word to Conchubor in Emain?

AINNLE. We will go with you.

ARDAN. We will be your servants and your huntsmen, Deirdre.

DEIRDRE. It isn't one brother only of you three is brave and courteous. Will you wed us, Lavarcham? You have the words and customs.

LAVARCHAM. I will not, then. What would I want meddling in the ruin you will earn?

NAISI. Let Ainnle wed us. . . . He has been with wise men and he knows their ways.

AINNLE. [*Joining their hands.*] By the sun and moon and the whole earth, I wed Deirdre to Naisi. [*He steps back and holds up his hands.*] May the air bless you, and water and the wind, the sea, and all the hours of the sun and moon.

CURTAIN

Act II

Alban. Early morning in the beginning of winter. A wood outside the tent of Deirdre and Naisi. Lavarcham comes in muffled in a cloak.

LAVARCHAM. [*Calling.*] Deirdre. . . . Deirdre. . . .

DEIRDRE. [*Coming from tent.*] My welcome, Lavarcham. . . . Whose curagh is rowing from Ulster? I saw the oars through the tops of the trees, and I thought it was you were coming towards us.

LAVARCHAM. I came in the shower was before dawn.

DEIRDRE. And who is coming?

LAVARCHAM. [*Mournfully.*] Let you not be startled or taking it bad, Deirdre. It's Fergus bringing messages of peace from Conchubor to take Naisi and his brother back to Emain. [*Sitting down.*

DEIRDRE. [*Lightly.*] Naisi and his brothers are well pleased with this place; and what would take them back to Conchubor in Ulster?

LAVARCHAM. Their like would go any place where they'd see death standing. [*With more agitation.*] I'm in dread Conchubor wants to have yourself and to kill Naisi, and that that'll be the ruin of the Sons of Usna. I'm silly, maybe, to be dreading the like, but those have a great love for yourself have a right to be in dread always.

DEIRDRE. [*More anxiously.*] Emain should be no safe place for myself and Naisi. And isn't it a hard thing they'll leave us no peace, Lavarcham, and we so quiet in the woods?

LAVARCHAM. [*Impressively.*] It's a hard thing, surely; but let you take my word and swear Naisi, by the earth, and the sun over it, and the four quarters of the moon, he'll not go back to Emain—for good faith or bad faith—the time Conchubor's keeping the high throne of Ireland. . . . It's that would save you, surely.

DEIRDRE. [*Without hope.*] There 's little power in oaths to stop what 's coming, and little power in what I 'd do, Lavarcham, to change the story of Conchubor and Naisi and the things old men foretold.

LAVARCHAM. [*Aggressively.*] Was there little power in what you did the night you dressed in your finery and ran Naisi off along with you, in spite of Conchubor and the big nobles did dread the blackness of your luck? It was power enough you had that night to bring distress and anguish; and now I 'm pointing you a way to save Naisi, you 'll not stir stick or straw to aid me.

DEIRDRE. [*A little haughtily.*] Let you not raise your voice against me, Lavarcham, if you have will itself to guard Naisi.

LAVARCHAM. [*Breaking out in anger.*] Naisi is it? I didn't care if the crows were stripping his thigh-bones at the dawn of day. It 's to stop your own despair and wailing, and you waking up in a cold bed, without the man you have your heart on, I am raging now. [*Starting up with temper.*] Yet there is more men than Naisi in it; and maybe I was a big fool thinking his dangers, and this day, would fill you up with dread.

DEIRDRE. [*Sharply.*] Let you end; such talking is a fool's only, when it 's well you know if a thing harmed Naisi it isn't I would live after him. [*With distress.*] It 's well you know it 's this day I 'm dreading seven years, and I fine nights watching the heifers walking to the haggard with long shadows on the grass; [*with emotion*] or the time I 've been stretched in the sunshine, when I 've heard Ainnle and Ardan stepping lightly, and they saying: 'Was there ever the like of Deirdre for a happy and sleepy queen?'

LAVARCHAM. [*Not fully pacified.*] And yet you 'll go, and welcome is it, if Naisi chooses?

DEIRDRE. I 've dread going or staying, Lavarcham. It 's lonesome this place, having happiness like ours, till I 'm asking each day will this day match yesterday, and will to-morrow take a good place beside the same day in the year that 's gone, and wondering all times is it a game worth playing, living on until you 're dried and old, and our joy is gone for ever.

LAVARCHAM. If it 's that ails you, I tell you there 's little hurt getting old, though young girls and poets do be storming at the shapes of age. [*Passionately.*] There 's little hurt getting old, saving when you 're looking back, the way I 'm looking this day, and seeing the young you have a love for breaking up their hearts with folly. [*Going to Deirdre.*] Take my word and stop Naisi, and the day 'll come you 'll have more joy having the senses of an old woman and you with your little grandsons shrieking round you, than I 'd have this night putting on the red mouth and the white arms you have, to go walking lonesome by-ways with a gamy king.

DEIRDRE. It 's little joy of a young woman, or an old woman, I 'll have from this day, surely. But what use is in our talking when there 's Naisi on the foreshore, and Fergus with him?

LAVARCHAM. [*Despairingly.*] I 'm late so with my warnings, for Fergus 'd talk the moon over to take a new path in the sky. [*With reproach.*] You 'll not stop him this day, and isn't it a strange story you were a plague and torment, since you were that height, to those did hang their life-times on your voice. [*Overcome with trouble; gathering her cloak about her.*] Don't think bad of my crying. I 'm not the like of many and I 'd see a score of naked corpses and not heed them at all, but I 'm destroyed seeing yourself in your hour of joy when the end is coming surely.

[*Owen comes in quickly, rather ragged, bows to Deirdre.*

OWEN. [*To Lavarcham.*] Fergus's men are calling you. You were seen on the path, and he and Naisi want you for their talk below.

LAVARCHAM. [*Looking at him with dislike.*] Yourself 's an ill-lucky thing to meet a morning is the like of this. Yet if you are a spy itself I 'll go and give my word that 's wanting surely.   [*Goes out.*

OWEN. [*To Deirdre.*] So I 've found you alone, and I after waiting three weeks getting ague and asthma in the chill of the bogs, till I saw Naisi caught with Fergus.

DEIRDRE. I've heard news of Fergus; what brought you from Ulster?

OWEN. [*Who has been searching, finds a loaf and sits down eating greedily, and cutting it with a large knife.*] The full moon, I'm thinking, and it squeezing the crack in my skull. Was there ever a man crossed nine waves after a fool's wife and he not away in his head?

DEIRDRE. [*Absently.*] It should be a long time since you left Emain, where there's civility in speech with queens.

OWEN. It's a long while, surely. It's three weeks I am losing my manners beside the Saxon bull-frogs at the head of the bog. Three weeks is a long space, and yet you're seven years spancelled with Naisi and the pair.

DEIRDRE. [*Beginning to fold up her silks and jewels.*] Three weeks of your days might be long, surely, yet seven years are a short space for the like of Naisi and myself.

OWEN. [*Derisively.*] If they're a short space there aren't many the like of you. Wasn't there a queen in Tara had to walk out every morning till she'd meet a stranger and see the flame of courtship leaping up within his eye? Tell me now [*leaning towards her*], are you well pleased that length with the same man snorting next you at the dawn of day?

DEIRDRE. [*Very quietly.*] Am I well pleased seven years seeing the same sun throwing light across the branches at the dawn of day? It's a heart-break to the wise that it.'s for a short space we have the same things only. [*With contempt.*] Yet the earth itself is a silly place, maybe, when a man's a fool and talker.

OWEN. [*Sharply.*] Well, go, take your choice. Stay here and rot with Naisi or go to Conchubor in Emain. Conchubor's a wrinkled fool with a swelling belly on him, and eyes falling downward from his shining crown; Naisi should be stale and weary. Yet there are many roads, Deirdre, and I tell you I'd liefer be bleaching in a bog-hole than living on without a touch of kindness from your eyes and voice.　　It 's a poor thing to be so lonesome you 'd squeeze kisses on a cur dog's nose.

DEIRDRE.　Are there no women like yourself could be your friends in Emain?

OWEN. [*Vehemently.*] There are none like you, Deirdre. It 's for that I 'm asking are you going back this night with Fergus?

DEIRDRE.　I will go where Naisi chooses.

OWEN. [*With a burst of rage.*] It 's Naisi, Naisi, is it? Then I tell you, you 'll have great sport one day seeing Naisi getting a harshness in his two sheep's eyes, and he looking on yourself.　　Would you credit it, my father used to be in the broom and heather kissing Lavarcham, with a little bird chirping out above their heads, and now she 'd scare a raven from a carcass on a hill. [*With a sad cry that brings dignity into his voice.*] Queens get old, Deirdre, with their white and long arms going from them, and their backs hooping.　　I tell you it 's a poor thing to see a queen's nose reaching down to scrape her chin.

DEIRDRE. [*Looking out, a little uneasy.*] Naisi and Fergus are coming on the path.

OWEN.　I 'll go so, for if I had you seven years I 'd be jealous of the midges and the dust is in the air. [*Muffles himself in his cloak; with a sort of warning in his voice.*] I 'll give you a riddle, Deirdre: Why isn't my father as ugly and old as Conchubor?　You 've no answer? . . . It 's because Naisi killed him. [*With curious expression.*] Think of that and you awake at night, hearing Naisi snoring, or the night you hear strange stories of the things I 'm doing in Alban or in Ulster either.

　　[*He goes out, and in a moment Naisi and Fergus come in on the other side.*

NAISI. [*Gaily.*] Fergus has brought messages of peace from Conchubor.

DEIRDRE. [*Greeting Fergus.*] He is welcome. Let you rest, Fergus, you should be hot and thirsty after mounting the rocks.

FERGUS.　It 's a sunny nook you 've found in Alban; yet any

man would be well pleased mounting higher rocks to fetch yourself and Naisi back to Emain.

DEIRDRE. [*With keenness.*] They 've answered? They would go?

FERGUS. [*Benignly.*] They have not, but when I was a young man we 'd have given a lifetime to be in Ireland a score of weeks; and to this day the old men have nothing so heavy as knowing it 's in a short while they 'll lose the high skies are over Ireland, and the lonesome mornings with birds crying on the bogs. Let you come this day, for there 's no place but Ireland where the Gael can have peace always.

NAISI. [*Gruffly.*] It 's true, surely. Yet we 're better this place while Conchubor 's in Emain Macha.

FERGUS. [*Giving him parchments.*] There are your sureties and Conchubor's seal. [*To Deirdre.*] I am your surety with Conchubor. You 'll not be young always, and it 's time you were making yourselves ready for the years will come, building up a homely dun beside the seas of Ireland, and getting in your children from the princes' wives. It 's little joy wandering till age is on you and your youth is gone away, so you 'd best come this night, for you 'd have great pleasure putting out your foot and saying: 'I am in Ireland, surely.'

DEIRDRE. It isn't pleasure I 'd have while Conchubor is king in Emain.

FERGUS. [*Almost annoyed.*] Would you doubt the seals of Conal Cearneach and the kings of Meath? [*He gets parchments from his cloak and gives them to Naisi. More gently.*] It 's easy being fearful and you alone in the woods, yet it would be a poor thing if a timid woman [*taunting her a little*] could turn away the Sons of Usna from the life of kings. Let you be thinking on the years to come, Deirdre, and the way you 'd have a right to see Naisi a high and white-haired justice beside some king of Emain. Wouldn't it be a poor story if a queen the like of you should have no thought but to be scraping up her hours dallying in the sunshine with the sons of kings?

DEIRDRE. [*Turning away a little haughtily.*] I leave the choice to Naisi. [*Turning back towards Fergus.*] Yet you 'd do well, Fergus, to go on your own way, for the sake of your own years, so you 'll not be saying till your hour of death, maybe, it was yourself brought Naisi and his brothers to a grave was scooped by treachery. [*Goes into tent.*

FERGUS. It is a poor thing to see a queen so lonesome and afraid. [*He watches till he is sure Deirdre cannot hear him.*] Listen now to what I 'm saying. You 'd do well to come back to men and women are your match and comrades, and not be lingering until the day that you 'll grow weary, and hurt Deirdre showing her the hardness will grow up within your eyes. . . . You 're here years and plenty to know it 's truth I 'm saying.

[*Deirdre comes out of tent with a horn of wine, she catches the beginning of Naisi's speech and stops with stony wonder.*

NAISI. [*Very thoughtfully.*] I 'll not tell you a lie. There have been days a while past when I 've been throwing a line for salmon or watching for the run of hares, that I 've a dread upon me a day 'd come I 'd weary of her voice [*very slowly*], and Deirdre 'd see I 'd wearied.

FERGUS. [*Sympathetic but triumphant.*] I knew it, Naisi. . . . And take my word, Deirdre 's seen your dread and she 'll have no peace from this out in the woods.

NAISI. [*With confidence.*] She 's not seen it. . . . Deirdre 's no thought of getting old or wearied; it 's that puts wonder in her ways, and she with spirits would keep bravery and laughter in a town with plague.

[*Deirdre drops the horn of wine and crouches down where she is.*

FERGUS. That humour 'll leave her. But we 've no call going too far, with one word borrowing another. Will you come this night to Emain Macha?

NAISI. I 'll not go, Fergus. I 've had dreams of getting old and weary, and losing my delight in Deirdre; but my dreams were dreams only. What are Conchubor's seals and all your talk of Emain and the fools of Meath beside one evening in Glen Masain? We 'll stay this place till our lives and time are worn out. It 's that word you may take in your curagh to Conchubor in Emain.

FERGUS. [*Gathering up his parchments.*] And you won't go, surely?

NAISI. I will not. . . . I 've had dread, I tell you, dread winter and summer, and the autumn and the springtime, even when there 's a bird in every bush making his own stir till the fall of night; but this talk 's brought me ease, and I see we 're as happy as the leaves on the young trees, and we 'll be so ever and always, though we 'd live the age of the eagle and the salmon and the crow of Britain.

FERGUS. [*With anger.*] Where are your brothers? My message is for them also.

NAISI. You 'll see them above chasing otters by the stream.

FERGUS. [*Bitterly.*] It isn't much I was mistaken, thinking you were hunters only.

[*He goes, Naisi turns towards tent, and sees Deirdre crouching down with her cloak round her face. Deirdre comes out.*

NAISI. You 've heard my words to Fergus? [*She does not answer. A pause. He puts his arm around her.*] Leave troubling, and we 'll go this night to Glen da Ruadh, where the salmon will be running with the tide.

[*Crosses and sits down.*

DEIRDRE. [*In a very low voice.*] With the tide in a little while we will be journeying again, or it is our own blood maybe will be running away. [*She turns and clings to him.*] The dawn and evening are a little while, the winter and the summer pass quickly, and what way would you and I, Naisi, have joy for ever?

NAISI. We 'll have the joy is highest till our age is come, for it isn't Fergus's talk of great deeds could take us back to Emain.

DEIRDRE. It isn't to great deeds you 're going but to near troubles, and the shortening of your days the time that they are bright and sunny; and isn't it a poor thing that I, Deirdre, could not hold you away?

NAISI. I 've said we 'd stay in Alban always.

DEIRDRE. There 's no place to stay always. . . . It 's a long time we 've had, pressing the lips together, going up and down, resting in our arms, Naisi, waking with the smell of June in the tops of the grasses, and listening to the birds in the branches that are highest. . . . It 's a long time we 've had, but the end has come, surely.

NAISI. Would you have us go to Emain, though if any ask the reason we do not know it, and we journeying as the thrushes come from the north, or young birds fly out on a dark sea?

DEIRDRE. There 's reason all times for an end that 's come. And I 'm well pleased, Naisi, we 're going forward in the winter the time the sun has a low place, and the moon has her mastery in a dark sky, for it 's you and I are well lodged our last day, where there is a light behind the clear trees, and the berries on the thorns are a red wall.

NAISI. If our time in this place is ended, come away without Ainnle and Ardan to the woods of the east, for it 's right to be away from all people when two lovers have their love only. Come away and we 'll be safe always.

DEIRDRE. [Broken-hearted.] There 's no safe place, Naisi, on the ridge of the world. . . . And it 's in the quiet woods I 've seen them digging our grave, throwing out the clay on leaves are bright and withered.

NAISI. [Still more eagerly.] Come away, Deirdre, and it 's little we 'll think of safety or the grave beyond it, and we resting in a little corner between the daytime and the long night.

DEIRDRE. [Clearly and gravely.] It 's this hour we 're between the daytime and a night where there is sleep for ever, and isn't it a better thing to be following on to a near death, than to be bending the head down, and dragging with the feet, and seeing one day a blight showing upon love where it is sweet and tender?

NAISI. [His voice broken with distraction.] If a near death is coming what will be my trouble losing the earth and the stars over it, and you, Deirdre, are their flame and bright crown? Come away into the safety of the woods.

DEIRDRE. [*Shaking her head slowly.*] There are as many
ways to wither love as there are stars in a night of Samhain;
but there is no way to keep life, or love with it, a short
space only. . . . It 's for that there 's nothing lonesome
like a love is watching out the time most lovers do be
sleeping. . . . It 's for that we 're setting out for Emain
Macha when the tide turns on the sand.

NAISI. [*Giving in.*] You 're right, maybe. It should be a
poor thing to see great lovers and they sleepy and old.

DEIRDRE. [*With a more tender intensity.*] We 're seven
years without roughness or growing weary; seven years
so sweet and shining, the gods would be hard set to give
us seven days the like of them. It 's for that we 're going
to Emain, where there 'll be a rest for ever, or a place for
forgetting, in great crowds and they making a stir.

NAISI. [*Very softly.*] We 'll go, surely, in place of keeping
a watch on a love had no match and it wasting away.
[*They cling to each other for a moment, then Naisi looks up.*]
There are Fergus and Lavarcham and my two brothers.

[*Deirdre goes. Naisi sits with his head bowed. Owen
runs in stealthily, comes behind Naisi, and seizes him
round the arms. Naisi shakes him off and whips
out his sword.*

OWEN. [*Screaming with derisive laughter and showing his
empty hands.*] Ah, Naisi, wasn't it well I didn't kill you
that time? There was a fright you got! I 've been
watching Fergus above—don't be frightened—and I 've
come down to see him getting the cold shoulder, and going
off alone.

[*Fergus and others come in. They are all subdued like
men at a queen's wake.*

NAISI. [*Putting up his sword.*] There he is. [*Goes to Fergus.*]
We are going back when the tide turns, I and Deirdre
with yourself.

ALL. Going back!

AINNLE. And you 'll end your life with Deirdre, though she
has no match for keeping spirits in a little company is far
away by itself?

ARDAN. It's seven years myself and Ainnle have been servants and bachelors for yourself and Deirdre. Why will you take her back to Conchubor?

NAISI. I have done what Deirdre wishes and has chosen.

FERGUS. You've made a choice wise men will be glad of in the five ends of Ireland.

OWEN. Wise men is it, and they going back to Conchubor? I could stop them only Naisi put in his sword among my father's ribs, and when a man's done that he'll not credit your oath. Going to Conchubor! I could tell of plots and tricks, and spies were well paid for their play. [*He throws up a bag of gold.*] Are you paid, Fergus?

[*He scatters gold pieces over Fergus.*

FERGUS. He is raving. . . . Seize him.

OWEN. [*Flying between them.*] You won't. Let the lot of you be off to Emain, but I'll be off before you. . . . Dead men, dead men! Men who'll die for Deirdre's beauty; I'll be before you in the grave!

[*Runs out with his knife in his hand. They all run after him except Lavarcham, who looks out and then clasps her hands. Deirdre comes out to her in a dark cloak.*

DEIRDRE. What has happened?

LAVARCHAM. It's Owen's gone raging mad, and he's after splitting his gullet beyond at the butt of the stone. There was ill luck this day in his eye. And he knew a power if he'd said it all.

[*Naisi comes back quickly, followed by the others.*

AINNLE. [*Coming in very excited.*] That man knew plots of Conchubor's. We'll not go to Emain, where Conchubor may love her and have hatred for yourself.

FERGUS. Would you mind a fool and raver?

AINNLE. It's many times there's more sense in madmen than the wise. We will not obey Conchubor.

NAISI. I and Deirdre have chosen; we will go back with Fergus.

ARDAN. We will not go back. We will burn your curaghs by the sea.

FERGUS. My sons and I will guard them.

AINNLE. We will blow the horn of Usna and our friends will come to aid us.

NAISI. It is my friends will come.

AINNLE. Your friends will bind your hands, and you out of your wits.

[*Deirdre comes forward quickly and comes between Ainnle and Naisi.*

DEIRDRE. [*In a low voice.*] For seven years the Sons of Usna have not raised their voices in a quarrel.

AINNLE. We will not take you to Emain.

ARDAN. It is Conchubor has broken our peace.

AINNLE. [*To Deirdre.*] Stop Naisi going. What way would we live if Conchubor should take you from us?

DEIRDRE. There is no one could take me from you. I have chosen to go back with Fergus. Will you quarrel with me, Ainnle, though I have been your queen these seven years in Alban?

AINNLE. [*Subsiding suddenly.*] Naisi has no call to take you.

ARDAN. Why are you going?

DEIRDRE. [*To both of them and the others.*] It is my wish. . . . It may be I will not have Naisi growing an old man in Alban with an old woman at his side, and young girls pointing out and saying: 'That is Deirdre and Naisi had great beauty in their youth.' It may be we do well putting a sharp end to the day is brave and glorious, as our fathers put a sharp end to the days of the kings of Ireland; or that I 'm wishing to set my foot on Slieve Fuadh, where I was running one time and leaping the streams [*to Lavarcham*], and that I 'd be well pleased to see our little apple-trees, Lavarcham, behind our cabin on the hill; or that I 've learned, Fergus, it 's a lonesome thing to be away from Ireland always.

AINNLE. [*Giving in.*] There is no place but will be lonesome to us from this out, and we thinking on our seven years in Alban.

DEIRDRE. [*To Naisi.*] It 's in this place we 'd be lonesome in the end. . . . Take down Fergus to the sea. He has been a guest had a hard welcome and he bringing messages of peace.

FERGUS. We will make your curagh ready and it fitted for the voyage of a king.　　　　　*[He goes with Naisi.*

DEIRDRE. Take your spears, Ainnle and Ardan, and go down before me, and take your horse-boys to be carrying my cloaks are on the threshold.

AINNLE. [*Obeying.*] It 's with a poor heart we 'll carry your things this day we have carried merrily so often, and we hungry and cold.　　　*[They gather up things and go out.*

DEIRDRE. [*To Lavarcham.*] Go you, too, Lavarcham. You are old, and I will follow quickly.

LAVARCHAM. I 'm old, surely, and the hopes I had my pride in are broken and torn.

　　　　　[She goes out with a look of awe at Deirdre.

DEIRDRE. [*Clasping her hands.*] Woods of Cuan, woods of Cuan, dear country of the east!　It 's seven years we 've had a life was joy only, and this day we 're going west, this day we 're facing death, maybe, and death should be a poor, untidy thing, though it 's a queen that dies.

　　　　　　　　[She goes out slowly.

CURTAIN

ACT III

Tent below Emain, with shabby skins and benches.   There is an opening at each side and at back, the latter closed.   Old Woman comes in with food and fruits and arranges them on table.   Conchubor comes in on right.

CONCHUBOR. [*Sharply.*] Has no one come with news for me?

OLD WOMAN. I 've seen no one at all, Conchubor.

CONCHUBOR. [*Watches her working for a moment, then makes sure opening at back is closed.*] Go up then to Emain, you 're not wanting here. [*A noise heard left.*]   Who is that?

OLD WOMAN. [*Going left.*] It 's Lavarcham coming again. She 's a great wonder for jogging back and forward through the world, and I made certain she 'd be off to meet them; but she 's coming alone, Conchubor, my dear child Deirdre isn't with her at all.

CONCHUBOR. Go up so and leave us.

OLD WOMAN. [*Pleadingly.*] I 'd be well pleased to set my eyes on Deirdre if she 's coming this night, as we 're told.

CONCHUBOR. [*Impatiently.*] It 's not long till you 'll see her. But I 've matters with Lavarcham, and let you go now, I 'm saying.

[*He shows her out right, Lavarcham comes in on the left.*

LAVARCHAM. [*Looking round her with suspicion.*] This is a queer place to find you, and it 's a queer place to be lodging Naisi and his brothers, and Deirdre with them, and the lot of us tired out with the long way we have been walking.

CONCHUBOR. You 've come along with them the whole journey?

LAVARCHAM. I have, then, though I 've no call now to be wandering that length to a wedding or a burial, or the two together. [*She sits down wearily.*] It 's a poor thing the way me and you is getting old, Conchubor, and I 'm thinking you yourself have no call to be loitering this place getting your death, maybe, in the cold of night.

CONCHUBOR. I 'm waiting only to know is Fergus stopped in the north.

LAVARCHAM. [*More sharply.*] He 's stopped, surely, and that 's a trick hås me thinking you have it in mind to bring trouble this night on Emain and Ireland and the big world 's east beyond them. [*She goes to him.*] And yet you 'd do well to be going to your dun, and not putting shame on her meeting the High King, and she seamed and sweaty and in great disorder from the dust of many roads. [*Laughing derisively.*] Ah, Conchubor, my lad, beauty goes quickly in the woods, and you 'd let a great gasp, I tell you, if you set your eyes this night on Deirdre.

CONCHUBOR. [*Fiercely.*] It 's little I care if she 's white and worn, for it 's I did rear her from a child. I should have a good right to meet and see her always.

LAVARCHAM. A good right is it? Haven't the blind a good right to be seeing, and the lame to be dancing, and the dummies singing tunes? It 's that right you have to be looking for gaiety on Deirdre's lips. [*Coaxingly.*] Come on to your dun, I 'm saying, and leave her quiet for one night itself.

CONCHUBOR. [*With sudden anger.*] I 'll not go, when it 's long enough I am above in my dun stretching east and west without a comrade, and I more needy, maybe, than the thieves of Meath. . . . You think I 'm old and wise, but I tell you the wise know the old must die, and they 'll leave no chance for a thing slipping from them they 've set their blood to win.

LAVARCHAM. [*Nodding her head.*] If you 're old and wise, it 's I 'm the same, Conchubor, and I 'm telling you you 'll not have her though you 're ready to destroy mankind and skin the gods to win her. There 's things a king can't have, Conchubor, and if you go rampaging this night you 'll be apt to win nothing but death for many, and a sloppy face of trouble on your own self before the day will come.

CONCHUBOR. It 's too much talk you have. [*Goes right.*]

Where is Owen?   Did you see him no place and you coming the road?

LAVARCHAM. I seen him surely.   He went spying on Naisi, and now the worms is spying on his own inside.

CONCHUBOR. [*Exultingly.*] Naisi killed him?

LAVARCHAM. He did not, then.   It was Owen destroyed himself running mad because of Deirdre.   Fools and kings and scholars are all one in a story with her like, and Owen thought he 'd be a great man, being the first corpse in the game you 'll play this night in Emain.

CONCHUBOR. It 's yourself should be the first corpse, but my other messengers are coming, men from the clans that hated Usna.

LAVARCHAM. [*Drawing back hopelessly.*] Then the gods have pity on us all!   [*Men with weapons come in.*

CONCHUBOR. [*To soldiers.*] Are Ainnle and Ardan separate from Naisi?

MEN. They are, Conchubor.   We 've got them off, saying they were needed to make ready Deirdre's house.

CONCHUBOR. And Naisi and Deirdre are coming?

SOLDIER. Naisi 's coming, surely, and a woman with him is putting out the glory of the moon is rising and the sun is going down.

CONCHUBOR. [*Looking at Lavarcham.*] That 's your story that she 's seamed and ugly?

SOLDIER. I have more news. [*Pointing to Lavarcham.*] When that woman heard you were bringing Naisi this place, she sent a horse-boy to call Fergus from the north.

CONCHUBOR. [*To Lavarcham.*] It 's for that you 've been playing your tricks, but what you 've won is a nearer death for Naisi. [*To soldiers.*] Go up and call my fighters, and take that woman up to Emain.

LAVARCHAM. I 'd liefer stay this place.   I 've done my best, but if a bad end is coming, surely it would be a good thing maybe I was here to tend her.

CONCHUBOR. [*Fiercely.*] Take her to Emain; it 's too many tricks she 's tried this day already.   [*A soldier goes to her.*

LAVARCHAM. Don't touch me. [*She puts her cloak round her*

and catches Conchubor's arm.] I thought to stay your hand with my stories till Fergus would come to be beside them, the way I 'd save yourself, Conchubor, and Naisi and Emain Macha; but I 'll walk up now into your halls, and I 'll say [*with a gesture*] it 's here nettles will be growing and beyond thistles and docks. I 'll go into your high chambers, where you 've been figuring yourself stretching out your neck for the kisses of a queen of women; and I 'll say it 's here there 'll be deer stirring and goats scratching, and sheep waking and coughing when there is a great wind from the north. [*Shaking herself loose. Conchubor makes a sign to soldiers.*] I 'm going, surely. In a short space I 'll be sitting up with many listening to the flames crackling, and the beams breaking, and I looking on the great blaze will be the end of Emain.   [*She goes out.*

CONCHUBOR. [*Looking out.*] I see two people in the trees; it should be Naisi and Deirdre. [*To soldier.*] Let you tell them they 'll lodge here to-night.

> [*Conchubor goes out right. Naisi and Deirdre come in on left, very weary.*

NAISI. [*To soldiers.*] Is it this place he 's made ready for myself and Deirdre?

SOLDIER. The Red Branch House is being aired and swept and you 'll be called there when a space is by; till then you 'll find fruits and drink on this table, and so the gods be with you.   [*Goes out right.*

NAISI. [*Looking round.*] It 's a strange place he 's put us camping and we come back as his friends.

DEIRDRE. He 's likely making up a welcome for us, having curtains shaken out and rich rooms put in order; and it 's right he 'd have great state to meet us, and you his sister's son.

NAISI. [*Gloomily.*] It 's little we want with state or rich rooms or curtains, when we 're used to the ferns only and cold streams and they making a stir.

DEIRDRE. [*Roaming round room.*] We want what is our right in Emain [*looking at hangings*], and though he 's riches in store for us it 's a shabby, ragged place he 's put us waiting, with frayed rugs and skins are eaten by the moths.

NAISI. [*A little impatiently.*] There are few would worry over skins and moths on this first night that we 've come back to Emain.

DEIRDRE. [*Brightly.*] You should be well pleased it 's for that I 'd worry all times, when it 's I have kept your tent these seven years as tidy as a bee-hive or a linnet's nest. If Conchubor 'd a queen like me in Emain he 'd not have stretched these rags to meet us. [*She pulls hanging, and it opens.*] There 's new earth on the ground and a trench dug. . . . It 's a grave, Naisi, that is wide and deep.

NAISI. [*Goes over and pulls back curtain showing grave.*] And that 'll be our home in Emain. . . . He 's dug it wisely at the butt of a hill, with fallen trees to hide it. He 'll want to have us killed and buried before Fergus comes.

DEIRDRE. Take me away. . . . Take me to hide in the rocks, for the night is coming quickly.

NAISI. [*Pulling himself together.*] I will not leave my brothers.

DEIRDRE. [*Vehemently.*] It 's of us two he 's jealous. Come away to the places where we 're used to have our company. . . . Wouldn't it be a good thing to lie hid in the high ferns together? [*She pulls him left.*] I hear strange words in the trees.

NAISI. It should be the strange fighters of Conchubor. I saw them passing as we come.

DEIRDRE. [*Pulling him towards the right.*] Come to this side. Listen, Naisi!

NAISI. There are more of them. . . . We are shut in, and I have not Ainnle and Ardan to stand near me. Isn't it a hard thing that we three who have conquered many may not die together?

DEIRDRE. [*Sinking down.*] And isn't it a hard thing that you and I are this place by our opened grave; though none have lived had happiness like ours those days in Alban that went by so quick.

NAISI. It 's a hard thing, surely, we 've lost those days for ever; and yet it 's a good thing, maybe, that all goes quick, for when I 'm in that grave it 's soon a day 'll come you 'll be too wearied to be crying out, and that day 'll bring you ease.

DEIRDRE. I 'll not be here to know if that is true.

NAISI. It 's our three selves he 'll kill to-night, and then in two months or three you 'll see him walking down for courtship with yourself.

DEIRDRE. I 'll not be here.

NAISI. [*Hard.*] You 'd best keep him off, maybe, and then, when the time comes, make your way to some place west in Donegal, and it 's there you 'll get used to stretching out lonesome at the fall of night, and waking lonesome for the day.

DEIRDRE. Let you not be saying things are worse than death.

NAISI. [*A little recklessly.*] I 've one word left. If a day comes in the west that the larks are cocking their crests on the edge of the clouds, and the cuckoos making a stir, and there 's a man you 'd fancy, let you not be thinking that day I 'd be well pleased you 'd go on keening always.

DEIRDRE. [*Turning to look at him.*] And if it was I that died, Naisi, would you take another woman to fill up my place?

NAISI. [*Very mournfully.*] It 's little I know, saving only that it 's a hard and bitter thing leaving the earth, and a worse and harder thing leaving yourself alone and desolate to be making lamentation on its face always.

DEIRDRE. I 'll die when you do, Naisi. I 'd not have come from Alban but I knew I 'd be along with you in Emain, and you living or dead. . . . Yet this night it 's strange and distant talk you 're making only.

NAISI. There 's nothing, surely, the like of a new grave of open earth for putting a great space between two friends that love.

DEIRDRE. If there isn't, it 's that grave when it 's closed

will make us one for ever, and we two lovers have had great space without weariness or growing old or any sadness of the mind.

CONCHUBOR. [*Coming in on right.*] I 'd bid you welcome, Naisi.

NAISI. [*Standing up.*] You 're welcome, Conchubor, I 'm well pleased you 've come.

CONCHUBOR. [*Blandly.*] Let you not think bad of this place where I 've put you till other rooms are readied.

NAISI. [*Breaking out.*] We know the room you 've readied. We know what stirred you to send your seals and Fergus into Alban and stop him in the north [*opening curtain and pointing to the grave*], and dig that grave before us. Now I ask what brought you here?

CONCHUBOR. I 've come to look on Deirdre.

NAISI. Look on her. You 're a knacky fancier, and it 's well you chose the one you 'd lure from Alban. Look on her, I tell you, and when you 've looked I 've got ten fingers will squeeze your mottled goose neck, though you 're king itself.

DEIRDRE. [*Coming between them.*] Hush, Naisi! Maybe Conchubor 'll make peace. . . . Do not mind him, Conchubor; he has cause to rage.

CONCHUBOR. It 's little I heed his raging, when a call would bring my fighters from the trees. . . . But what do you say, Deirdre?

DEIRDRE. I 'll say so near that grave we seem three lonesome people, and by a new-made grave there 's no man will keep brooding on a woman's lips, or on the man he hates. It 's not long till your own grave will be dug in Emain, and you 'd go down to it more easy if you 'd let call Ainnle and Ardan, the way we 'd have a supper all together, and fill that grave, and you 'll be well pleased from this out, having four new friends the like of us in Emain.

CONCHUBOR. [*Looking at her for a moment.*] That 's the first friendly word I 've heard you speaking, Deirdre. A game the like of yours should be the proper thing for softening the heart and putting sweetness in the tongue; and yet this night when I hear you I 've small blame left for Naisi that he stole you off from Ulster.

DEIRDRE. [*To Naisi.*] Now, Naisi, answer gently, and we 'll be friends to-night.

NAISI. [*Doggedly.*] I have no call but to be friendly. I 'll answer what you will.

DEIRDRE. [*Taking Naisi's hand.*] Then you 'll call Conchubor your friend and king, the man who reared me up upon Slieve Fuadh.

[*As Conchubor is going to clasp Naisi's hand cries are heard behind.*

CONCHUBOR. What noise is that?

AINNLE. [*Behind.*] Naisi. . . . Naisi. . . . Come to us; we are betrayed and broken.

NAISI. It 's Ainnle crying out in a battle.

CONCHUBOR. I was near won this night, but death 's between us now. [*He goes out.*

DEIRDRE. [*Clinging to Naisi.*] There is no battle. . . . Do not leave me, Naisi.

NAISI. I must go to them.

DEIRDRE. [*Beseechingly.*] Do not leave me, Naisi. Let us creep up in the darkness behind the grave. If there 's a battle, maybe the strange fighters will be destroyed, when Ainnle and Ardan are against them. [*Cries heard.*

NAISI. [*Wildly.*] I hear Ardan crying out. Do not hold me from my brothers.

DEIRDRE. Do not leave me, Naisi. Do not leave me broken and alone.

NAISI. I cannot leave my brothers when it is I who have defied the king.

DEIRDRE. I will go with you.

NAISI. You cannot come. Do not hold me from the fight. [*He throws her aside almost roughly.*

DEIRDRE. [*With restraint.*] Go to your brothers. For seven years you have been kindly, but the hardness of death has come between us.

NAISI. [*Looking at her aghast.*] And you 'll have me meet death with a hard word from your lips in my ear?

DEIRDRE. We 've had a dream, but this night has waked us surely.   In a little while we 've lived too long, Naisi, and isn't it a poor thing we should miss the safety of the grave, and we trampling its edge?

AINNLE. [*Behind.*] Naisi, Naisi, we are attacked and ruined!

DEIRDRE. Let you go where they are calling. [*She looks at him for an instant coldly.*] Have you no shame loitering and talking, and a cruel death facing Ainnle and Ardan in the woods?

NAISI. [*Frantic.*] They 'll not get a death that 's cruel, and they with men alone.   It 's women that have loved are cruel only; and if I went on living from this day I 'd be putting a curse on the lot of them I 'd meet walking in the east or west, putting a curse on the sun that gave them beauty, and on the madder and the stonecrop put red upon their cloaks.

DEIRDRE. [*Bitterly.*] I 'm well pleased there 's no one in this place to make a story that Naisi was a laughing-stock the night he died.

NAISI. There 'd not be many 'd make a story, for that mockery is in your eyes this night will spot the face of Emain with a plague of pitted graves.   [*He goes out.*

CONCHUBOR. [*Outside.*] That is Naisi. Strike him! [*Tumult. Deirdre crouches down on Naisi's cloak. Conchubor comes in hurriedly.*] They 've met their death—the three that stole you, Deirdre, and from this out you 'll be my queen in Emain.   [*A keen of men's voices is heard behind.*

DEIRDRE. [*Bewildered and terrified.*] It is not I will be a queen.

CONCHUBOR. Make your lamentation a short while if you will, but it isn't long till a day 'll come when you begin pitying a man is old and desolate, and High King also. . . . Let you not fear me, for it 's I 'm well pleased you have a store of pity for the three that were your friends in Alban

DEIRDRE. I have pity, surely. . . . It 's the way pity has me this night, when I think of Naisi, that I could set my teeth into the heart of a king.

CONCHUBOR. I know well pity 's cruel, when it was my pity for my own self destroyed Naisi.

DEIRDRE. [*More wildly.*] It was my words without pity gave Naisi a death will have no match until the ends of life and time. [*Breaking out into a keen.*] But who 'll pity Deirdre has lost the lips of Naisi from her neck and from her cheek for ever? Who 'll pity Deirdre has lost the twilight in the woods with Naisi, when beech-trees were silver and copper, and ash-trees were fine gold?

CONCHUBOR. [*Bewildered.*] It 's I 'll know the way to pity and care you, and I with a share of troubles has me thinking this night it would be a good bargain if it was I was in the grave, and Deirdre crying over me, and it was Naisi who was old and desolate. [*Keen heard.*

DEIRDRE. [*Wild with sorrow.*] It is I who am desolate; I, Deirdre, that will not live till I am old.

CONCHUBOR. It 's not long you 'll be desolate, and I seven years saying: 'It 's a bright day for Deirdre in the woods of Alban'; or saying again: 'What way will Deirdre be sleeping this night, and wet leaves and branches driving from the north?' Let you not break the thing I 've set my life on, and you giving yourself up to your sorrow when it 's joy and sorrow do burn out like straw blazing in an east wind.

DEIRDRE. [*Turning on him.*] Was it that way with your sorrow, when I and Naisi went northward from Slieve Fuadh and let raise our sails for Alban?

CONCHUBOR. There 's one sorrow has no end surely—that 's being old and lonesome. [*With extraordinary pleading.*] But you and I will have a little peace in Emain, with harps playing, and old men telling stories at the fall of the night. I 've let build rooms for our two selves, Deirdre, with red gold upon the walls and ceilings that are set with bronze. There was never a queen in the east had a house the like of your house, that 's waiting for yourself in Emain.

SOLDIER. [*Running in.*] Emain is in flames. Fergus has come back, and is setting fire to the world. Come up. Conchubor, or your state will be destroyed!

CONCHUBOR. [*Angry and regal again.*] Are the Sons of Usna buried?

SOLDIER. They are in their grave, but no earth is thrown.

CONCHUBOR. Let me see them. Open the tent! [*Soldier opens back of tent and shows grave.*] Where are my fighters?

SOLDIER. They are gone to Emain.

CONCHUBOR. [*To Deirdre.*] There are none to harm you. Stay here until I come again.

> [*Goes out with soldier. Deirdre looks round for a moment, then goes up slowly and looks into grave. She crouches down and begins swaying herself backwards and forwards, keening softly. At first her words are not heard, then they become clear.*

DEIRDRE. It 's you three will not see age or death coming —you that were my company when the fires on the hill-tops were put out and the stars were our friends only. I 'll turn my thoughts back from this night, that 's pitiful for want of pity, to the time it was your rods and cloaks made a little tent for me where there 'd be a birch-tree making shelter and a dry stone; though from this day my own fingers will be making a tent for me, spreading out my hairs and they knotted with the rain.

> [*Lavarcham and Old Woman come in stealthily on right.*

DEIRDRE. [*Not seeing them.*] It is I, Deirdre, will be crouching in a dark place; I, Deirdre, that was young with Naisi, and brought sorrow to his grave in Emain.

OLD WOMAN. Is that Deirdre broken down that was so light and airy?

LAVARCHAM. It is, surely, crying out over their grave.

> [*She goes to Deirdre.*

DEIRDRE. It will be my share from this out to be making lamentation on his stone always, and I crying for a love will be the like of a star shining on a little harbour by the sea.

LAVARCHAM. [*Coming forward.*] Let you rise up, Deirdre, and come off while there are none to heed us, the way I 'll find you shelter and some friend to guard you.

DEIRDRE. To what place would I go away from Naisi? What are the woods without Naisi or the seashore?

LAVARCHAM. [*Very coaxingly.*] If it is that way you 'd be, come till I find you a sunny place where you 'll be a great wonder they 'll call the queen of sorrows; and you 'll begin taking a pride to be sitting up pausing and dreaming when the summer comes.

DEIRDRE. It was the voice of Naisi that was strong in summer—the voice of Naisi that was sweeter than pipes playing, but from this day will be dumb always.

LAVARCHAM. [*To Old Woman.*] She doesn't heed us at all. We 'll be hard set to rouse her.

OLD WOMAN. If we don't the High King will rouse her, coming down beside her with the rage of battle in his blood, for how could Fergus stand against him?

LAVARCHAM. [*Touching Deirdre with her hand.*] There 's a score of woman's years in store for you, and you 'd best choose will you start living them beside the man you hate, or being your own mistress in the west or south?

DEIRDRE. It is not I will go on living after Ainnle and after Ardan. After Naisi I will not have a lifetime in the world.

OLD WOMAN. [*With excitement.*] Look, Lavarcham! There 's a light leaving the Red Branch. Conchubor and his lot will be coming quickly with a torch of bog-deal for her marriage, throwing a light on her three comrades.

DEIRDRE. [*Startled.*] Let us throw down clay on my three comrades. Let us cover up Naisi along with Ainnle and Ardan, they that were the pride of Emain. [*Throwing in clay.*] There is Naisi was the best of three, the choicest of the choice of many. It was a clean death was your share, Naisi; and it is not I will quit your head, when it 's many a dark night among the snipe and plover that you and I were whispering together. It is not I will quit your head, Naisi, when it 's many a night we saw the stars among the clear trees of Glen da Ruadh, or the moon pausing to rest her on the edges of the hills.

OLD WOMAN. Conchubor is coming surely.   I see the glare of flames throwing a light upon his cloak.

LAVARCHAM. [*Eagerly.*] Rise up, Deirdre, and come to Fergus, or be the High King's slave for ever!

DEIRDRE. [*Imperiously.*] I will not leave Naisi, who has left the whole world scorched and desolate. I will not go away when there is no light in the heavens, and no flower in the earth under them, but is saying to me that it is Naisi who is gone for ever.

CONCHUBOR. [*Behind.*] She is here. Stay a little back. [*Lavarcham and Old Woman go into the shadow on left as Conchubor comes in. With excitement to Deirdre.*] Come forward and leave Naisi the way I've left charred timber and a smell of burning in Emain Macha, and a heap of rubbish in the storehouse of many crowns.

DEIRDRE. [*More awake to what is round her.*] What are crowns and Emain Macha, when the head that gave them glory is this place, Conchubor, and it stretched upon the gravel will be my bed to-night?

CONCHUBOR. Make an end with talk of Naisi, for I've come to bring you to Dundealgan since Emain is destroyed.

[*Conchubor makes a movement towards her.*

DEIRDRE. [*With a tone that stops him.*] Draw a little back from Naisi, who is young for ever. Draw a little back from the white bodies I am putting under a mound of clay and grasses that are withered—a mound will have a nook for my own self when the end is come.

CONCHUBOR. [*Roughly.*] Let you rise up and come along with me in place of growing crazy with your wailings here.

DEIRDRE. It's yourself has made a crazy story, and let you go back to your arms, Conchubor, and to councils where your name is great, for in this place you are an old man and a fool only.

CONCHUBOR. If I've folly I've sense left not to lose the thing I've bought with sorrow and the deaths of many.

[*He moves towards her.*

DEIRDRE. Do not raise a hand to touch me.

CONCHUBOR. There are other hands to touch you. My fighters are set round in among the trees.

DEIRDRE. Who'll fight the grave, Conchubor, and it opened on a dark night?

LAVARCHAM. [*Eagerly.*] There are steps in the wood. I hear the call of Fergus and his men.

CONCHUBOR. [*Furiously.*] Fergus cannot stop me. I am more powerful than he is, though I am defeated and old.

FERGUS. [*Comes in to Deirdre; a red glow is seen behind the grave.*] I have destroyed Emain, and now I'll guard you all times, Deirdre, though it was I, without knowledge, brought Naisi to his grave.

CONCHUBOR. It's not you will guard her, for my whole armies are gathering. Rise up, Deirdre, for you are mine surely.

FERGUS. [*Coming between them.*] I am come between you.

CONCHUBOR. [*Wildly.*] When I've killed Naisi and his brothers, is there any man that I will spare? And is it you will stand against me, Fergus, when it's seven years you've seen me getting my death with rage in Emain?

FERGUS. It's I, surely, will stand against a thief and traitor.

DEIRDRE. [*Stands up and sees the light from Emain.*] Draw a little back with the squabbling of fools when I am broken up with misery. [*She turns round.*] I see the flames of Emain starting upward in the dark night; and because of me there will be weasels and wild cats crying on a lonely wall where there were queens and armies and red gold, the way there will be a story told of a ruined city and a raving king and a woman will be young for ever. [*She looks round.*] I see the trees naked and bare, and the moon shining. Little moon, little moon of Alban, it's lonesome you'll be this night, and to-morrow night, and long nights after, and you pacing the woods beyond Glen Laoi, looking every place for Deirdre and Naisi, the two lovers who slept so sweetly with each other.

FERGUS. [*Going to Conchubor's right and whispering.*] Keep back, or you will have the shame of pushing a bolt on a queen who is out of her wits.

CONCHUBOR. It is I who am out of my wits, with Emain in flames, and Deirdre raving, and my own heart gone within me.

DEIRDRE. [*In a high and quiet tone.*] I have put away sorrow like a shoe that is worn out and muddy, for it is I have had a life that will be envied by great companies. It was not by a low birth I made kings uneasy, and they sitting in the halls of Emain. It was not a low thing to be chosen by Conchubor, who was wise, and Naisi had no match for bravery. It is not a small thing to be rid of grey hairs, and the loosening of the teeth. [*With a sort of triumph.*] It was the choice of lives we had in the clear woods, and in the grave we 're safe, surely. . . .

CONCHUBOR. She will do herself harm.

DEIRDRE. [*Showing Naisi's knife.*] I have a little key to unlock the prison of Naisi you 'd shut upon his youth for ever. Keep back, Conchubor; for the High King who is your master has put his hands between us. [*She half turns to the grave.*] It was sorrows were foretold, but great joys were my share always; yet it is a cold place I must go to be with you, Naisi; and it 's cold your arms will be this night that were warm about my neck so often. . . . It 's a pitiful thing to be talking out when your ears are shut to me. It 's a pitiful thing, Conchubor, you have done this night in Emain; yet a thing will be a joy and triumph to the ends of life and time.

> [*She presses knife into her heart and sinks into the grave.
> Conchubor and Fergus go forward. The red glow
> fades, leaving stage very dark.*

FERGUS. Four white bodies are laid down together; four clear lights are quenched in Ireland. [*He throws his sword into the grave.*] There is my sword that could not shield you—my four friends that were the dearest always. The flames of Emain have gone out: Deirdre is dead and there is none to keen her. That is the fate of Deirdre and the Children of Usna, and for this night, Conchubor, our war is ended.   [*He goes out.*

LAVARCHAM. I have a little hut where you can rest, Conchubor; there is a great dew falling.

CONCHUBOR. [*With the voice of an old man.*] Take me with you. I 'm hard set to see the way before me.

OLD WOMAN. This way, Conchubor.   [*They go out.*

LAVARCHAM. [*Beside the grave.*] Deirdre is dead, and Naisi is dead; and if the oaks and stars could die for sorrow, it 's a dark sky and a hard and naked earth we 'd have this night in Emain.

CURTAIN

POEMS AND TRANSLATIONS

PREFACE

I have often thought that at the side of the poetic diction, which every one condemns, modern verse contains a great deal of poetic material, using poetic in the same special sense.   The poetry of exaltation will be always the highest; but when men lose their poetic feeling for ordinary life, and cannot write poetry of ordinary things, their exalted poetry is likely to lose its strength of exaltation, in the way men cease to build beautiful churches when they have lost happiness in building shops.

Many of the older poets, such as Villon and Herrick and Burns, used the whole of their personal life as their material, and the verse written in this way was read by strong men, and thieves, and deacons, not by little cliques only.   Then, in the town writing of the eighteenth century, ordinary life was put into verse that was not poetry, and when poetry came back with Coleridge and Shelley, it went into verse that was not always human.

In these days poetry is usually a flower of evil or good; but it is the timber of poetry that wears most surely, and there is no timber that has not strong roots among the clay and worms.

Even if we grant that exalted poetry can be kept successful by itself, the strong things of life are needed in poetry also, to show that what is exalted or tender is not made by feeble blood.   It may almost be said that before verse can be human again it must learn to be brutal.

The poems which follow were written at different times during the last sixteen or seventeen years, most of them before the views just stated, with which they have little to do, had come into my head.

The translations are sometimes free, and sometimes almost literal, according as seemed most fitting with the form of language I have used.

J. M. S.

GLENAGEARY, *December* 1908.

POEMS

QUEENS

SEVEN dog-days we let pass
Naming Queens in Glenmacnass
All the rare and royal names
Wormy sheepskin yet retains:
Etain, Helen, Maeve, and Fand,
Golden Deirdre's tender hand;
Bert, the big-foot, sung by Villon.
Cassandra, Ronsard found in Lyon.
Queens of Sheba, Meath, and Connaught.
Coifed with crown, or gaudy bonnet;
Queens whose finger once did stir men,
Queens were eaten of fleas and vermin,
Queens men drew like Monna Lisa,
Or slew with drugs in Rome and Pisa.
We named Lucrezia Crivelli,
And Titian's lady with amber belly,
Queens acquainted in learned sin,
Jane of Jewry's slender shin:
Queens who cut the boss of Glanna,
Judith of Scripture, and Gloriana,
Queens who wasted the East by proxy,
Or drove the ass-cart, a tinker's doxy.
Yet these are rotten—I ask their pardon—
And we 've the sun on rock and garden;
These are rotten, so you 're the Queen
Of all are living, or have been.

IN KERRY

WE heard the thrushes by the shore and sea,
And saw the golden stars' nativity,
Then round we went the lane by Thomas Flynn,
Across the church where bones lie out and in;
And there I asked beneath a lonely cloud
Of strange delight, with one bird singing loud,
What change you 'd wrought in graveyard, rock, and sea,
This new wild paradise to wake for me. . . .
Yet know no more than knew those merry sins
Had built this stack of thigh-bones, jaws, and shins.

A WISH

MAY seven tears in every week
Touch the hollow of your cheek,
That I—signed with such a dew—
For a lion's share may sue
Of the roses ever curled
Round the May-pole of the world.

Heavy riddles lie in this,
Sorrow 's sauce for every kiss.

THE 'MERGENCY MAN

He was lodging above in Coom,
And he 'd the half of the bailiff's room.

Till a black night came in Coomasaharn,
A night of rains you 'd swamp a star in.

'To-night,' says he, 'with the devil's weather
The hares itself will quit the heather.

'I 'll catch my boys with a latch on the door,
And serve my process on near a score.'

The night was black at the fording place,
And the flood was up in a whitened race,
But devil a bit he 'd turn his face.

Then the peelers said, 'Now mind your lepping,
How can you see the stones for stepping?

'We 'll wash our hands of your bloody job.'
'Wash and welcome,' says he, 'begob.'

He made two leps with a run and dash,
Then the peelers heard a yell and splash;

And the 'mergency man in two days and a bit
Was found in the ebb tide stuck in a net.

DANNY

ONE night a score of Erris men,
A score I 'm told and nine,
Said, 'We 'll get shut of Danny's noise
Of girls and widows dyin'.

'There 's not his like from Binghamstown
To Boyle and Ballycroy,
At playing hell on decent girls,
At beating man and boy.

'He 's left two pairs of female twins
Beyond in Killacreest,
And twice in Crossmolina fair
He 's struck the parish priest.

'But we 'll come round him in the night
A mile beyond the Mullet;
Ten will quench his bloody eyes,
And ten will choke his gullet.'

It wasn't long till Danny came,
From Bangor making way,
And he was damning moon and stars
And whistling grand and gay.

Till in a gap of hazel glen—
And not a hare in sight—
Out lepped the nine-and-twenty lads
Along his left and right.

Then Danny smashed the nose on Byrne,
He split the lips on three,
And bit across the right-hand thumb
On one Red Shawn Magee.

But seven tripped him up behind,
And seven kicked before,
And seven squeezed around his throat
Till Danny kicked no more.

Then some destroyed him with their heels,
Some tramped him in the mud,
Some stole his purse and timber pipe,
And some washed off his blood.

·   ·   ·   ·   ·

And when you 're walking out the way
From Bangor to Belmullet,
You 'll see a flat cross on a stone,
Where men choked Danny's gullet.

PATCH-SHANEEN

SHANEEN and Maurya Prendergast
Lived west in Carnareagh,
And they 'd a cur-dog, a cabbage plot,
A goat, and cock of hay.

He was five foot one or two,
Herself was four foot ten,
And he went travelling asking meal
Above through Caragh Glen.

She 'd pick her bag of carrageen
Or perries through the surf,
Or loan an ass of Foxy Jim
To fetch her creel of turf.

Till on one windy Samhain night,
When there 's stir among the dead,
He found her perished, stiff and stark,
Beside him in the bed.

And now when Shaneen travels far
From Droum to Ballyhyre,
The women lay him sacks or straw,
Beside the seed of fire.

And when the grey cocks crow and flap
And winds are in the sky,
'Oh, Maurya, Maurya, are you dead?'
You 'll hear Patch-Shaneen cry.

ON AN ISLAND

You 've plucked a curlew, drawn a hen,
Washed the shirts of seven men,
You 've stuffed my pillow, stretched the sheet,
And filled the pan to wash your feet,
You 've cooped the pullets, wound the clock,
And rinsed the young men's drinking crock;
And now we 'll dance to jigs and reels,
Nailed boots chasing girls' naked heels,
Until your father 'll start to snore,
And Jude, now you 're married, will stretch on the floor.

BEG-INNISH

BRING Kateen-Beug and Maurya Jude
To dance in Beg-Innish,
And when the lads (they 're in Dunquin)
Have sold their crabs and fish,
Wave fawny shawls and call them in,
And call the little girls who spin,
And seven weavers from Dunquin,
To dance in Beg-Innish.

I 'll play you jigs, and Maurice Kean,
Where nets are laid to dry,
I 've silken strings would draw a dance
From girls are lame or shy;
Four strings I 've brought from Spain and France
To make your long men skip and prance,
Till stars look out to see the dance
Where nets are laid to dry.

We 'll have no priest or peeler in
To dance in Beg-Innish;
But we 'll have drink from M'riarty Jim
Rowed round while gannets fish,
A keg with porter to the brim,
That every lad may have his whim,
Till we up with sails with M'riarty Jim
And sail from Beg-Innish.

EPITAPH

After reading Ronsard's lines from Rabelais

IF fruits are fed on any beast
Let vine-roots suck this parish priest,
For while he lived, no summer sun
Went up but he 'd a bottle done,
And in the starlight beer and stout
Kept his waistcoat bulging out.

Then Death that changes happy things
Damned his soul to water springs.

THE PASSING OF THE SHEE

After looking at one of Æ's pictures

ADIEU, sweet Angus, Maeve, and Fand,
Ye plumed yet skinny Shee,
That poets played with hand in hand
To learn their ecstasy.

We 'll stretch in Red Dan Sally's ditch,
And drink in Tubber fair,
Or poach with Red Dan Philly's bitch
The badger and the hare.

ON AN ANNIVERSARY

After reading the dates in a book of Lyrics

WITH Fifteen-ninety or Sixteen-sixteen
We end Cervantes, Marot, Nashe, or Green:
Then Sixteen-thirteen till twoscore and nine,
Is Crashaw's niche, that honey-lipped divine.
And so when all my little work is done
They 'll say I came in Eighteen-seventy-one,
And died in Dublin . . . What year will they write
For my poor passage to the stall of night?

TO THE OAKS OF GLENCREE

My arms are round you, and I lean
Against you, while the lark
Sings over us, and golden lights, and green
Shadows are on your bark.

There 'll come a season when you 'll stretch
Black boards to cover me:
Then in Mount Jerome I will lie, poor wretch,
With worms eternally.

A QUESTION

I ASKED if I got sick and died, would you
With my black funeral go walking too,
If you 'd stand close to hear them talk or pray
While I 'm let down in that steep bank of clay.

And, No, you said, for if you saw a crew
Of living idiots pressing round that new
Oak coffin—they alive, I dead beneath
That board—you 'd rave and rend them with your teeth.

DREAD

BESIDE a chapel I 'd a room looked down,
Where all the women from the farms and town,
On Holy-days and Sundays used to pass
To marriages, and christenings, and to Mass.

Then I sat lonely watching score and score,
Till I turned jealous of the Lord next door. . . .
Now by this window, where there 's none can see,
The Lord God 's jealous of yourself and me.

IN GLENCULLEN

THRUSH, linnet, stare, and wren,
Brown lark beside the sun,
Take thought of kestrel, sparrow-hawk,
Birdlime and roving gun.

You great-great-grandchildren
Of birds I 've listened to,
I think I robbed your ancestors
When I was young as you.

I 'VE THIRTY MONTHS

I 'VE thirty months, and that 's my pride,
Before my age 's a double score,
Though many lively men have died
At twenty-nine or little more.

I 've left a long and famous set
Behind some seven years or three,
But there are millions I 'd forget
Will have their laugh at passing me.

25, IX, 1908.

EPITAPH

A SILENT sinner, nights and days,
No human heart to him drew nigh,
Alone he wound his wonted ways,
Alone and little loved did die.

And autumn Death for him did choose,
A season dank with mists and rain,
And took him, while the evening dews
Were settling o'er the fields again.

PRELUDE

STILL south I went and west and south again,
Through Wicklow from the morning till the night,
And far from cities, and the sights of men,
Lived with the sunshine, and the moon's delight.

I knew the stars, the flowers, and the birds,
The grey and wintry sides of many glens,
And did but half remember human words,
In converse with the mountains, moors, and fens.

IN MAY

In a nook
That opened south,
You and I
Lay mouth to mouth.

A snowy gull
And sooty daw
Came and looked
With many a caw;

'Such,' I said,
'Are I and you,
When you 've kissed me
Black and blue!'

ON A BIRTHDAY

Friend of Ronsard, Nashe, and Beaumont,
Lark of Ulster, Meath, and Thomond,
Heard from Smyrna and Sahara
To the surf of Connemara,
Lark of April, June, and May,
Sing loudly this my Lady-day.

WINTER

With little money in a great city

THERE 's snow in every street
Where I go up and down,
And there 's no woman, man, or dog
That knows me in the town.

I know each shop, and all
These Jews, and Russian Poles,
For I go walking night and noon
To spare my sack of coals.

THE CURSE

*To a sister of an enemy of the author's who disapproved of
'The Playboy'*

LORD, confound this surly sister,
Blight her brow with blotch and blister,
Cramp her larynx, lung, and liver,
In her guts a galling give her.

Let her live to earn her dinners
In Mountjoy with seedy sinners:
Lord, this judgment quickly bring,
And I 'm Your servant, J. M. Synge.

TRANSLATIONS FROM PETRARCH

SONNETS FROM *LAURA IN DEATH*

LAURA BEING DEAD, PETRARCH FINDS TROUBLE IN ALL THE THINGS OF THE EARTH

LIFE is flying from me, not stopping an hour, and death is making great strides following my track. The days about me, and the days passed over me, are bringing me desolation, and the days to come will be the same surely.

All things that I am bearing in mind, and all things I am in dread of, are keeping me in troubles, in this way one time, in that way another time, so that if I wasn't taking pity on my own self it 's long ago I 'd have given up my life.

If my dark heart has any sweet thing it is turned away from me, and then farther off I see the great winds where I must be sailing. I see my good luck far away in the harbour, but my steersman is tired out, and the masts and the ropes on them are broken, and the beautiful lights where I would be always looking are quenched.

HE ASKS HIS HEART TO RAISE ITSELF UP TO GOD

WHAT is it you 're thinking, lonesome heart? For what is it you 're turning back ever and always to times that are gone away from you? For what is it you 're throwing sticks on the fire where it is your own self that is burning?

The little looks and sweet words you 've taken one by one and written down among your songs, are gone up into the heavens, and it 's late, you know well, to go seeking them on the face of the earth.

Let you not be giving new life every day to your own destruction, and following a fool's thoughts for ever. Let you seek heaven when there is nothing left pleasing on the earth, and it a poor thing if a great beauty, the like of her, would be destroying your peace and she living or dead.

HE WISHES HE MIGHT DIE AND FOLLOW LAURA

In the years of her age the most beautiful and the most flowery —the time Love has his mastery—Laura, who was my life, has gone away leaving the earth stripped and desolate. She has gone up into the heavens, living and beautiful and naked, and from that place she is keeping her lordship and her reign upon me, and I crying out: Ohone, when will I see that day breaking that will be my first day with herself in paradise?

My thoughts are going after her, and it is that way my soul would follow her, lightly, and airily, and happily, and I would be rid of all my great troubles. But what is delaying me is the proper thing to lose me utterly, to make me a greater weight on my own self.

Oh, what a sweet death I might have died this day three years to-day!

LAURA IS EVER PRESENT TO HIM

If the birds are making lamentation, or the green banks are moved by a little wind of summer, or you can hear the waters making a stir by the shores that are green and flowery,

That 's where I do be stretched out thinking of love, writing my songs, and herself that heaven shows me though hidden in the earth I set my eyes on, and hear the way that she feels my sighs and makes an answer to me.

'Alas,' I hear her say, 'why are you using yourself up before the time is come, and pouring out a stream of tears so sad and doleful.

'You 'd do right to be glad rather, for in dying I won days that have no ending, and when you saw me shutting up my eyes I was opening them on the light that is eternal.'

HE CEASES TO SPEAK OF HER GRACES AND HER VIRTUES
WHICH ARE NO MORE

THE eyes that I would be talking of so warmly, and the arms, and the hands, and the feet, and the face, that are after calling me away from myself and making me a lonesome man among all people;

The hair that was of shining gold, and brightness of the smile that was the like of an angel's surely, and was making a paradise of the earth, are turned to a little dust that knows nothing at all.

And yet I myself am living; it is for this I am making a complaint, to be left without the light I had such a great love for, in good fortune and bad, and this will be the end of my songs of love, for the vein where I had cleverness is dried up, and everything I have is turned to complaint only.

HE IS JEALOUS OF THE HEAVENS AND THE EARTH

WHAT a grudge I am bearing the earth that has its arms about her, and is holding that face away from me, where I was finding peace from great sadness.

What a grudge I am bearing the heavens that are after taking her, and shutting her in with greediness, the heavens that do push their bolt against so many.

What a grudge I am bearing the blessed saints that have got her sweet company, that I am always seeking; and what a grudge I am bearing against death, that is standing in her two eyes and will not call me with a word.

THE FINE TIME OF THE YEAR INCREASES PETRARCH'S SORROW

THE south wind is coming back, bringing the fine season, and the flowers, and the grass, her sweet family, along with her. The swallow and the nightingale are making a stir, and the spring is turning white and red in every place.

There is a cheerful look on the meadows, and peace in the sky, and the sun is well pleased, I 'm thinking, looking downward, and the air and the waters and the earth herself are full of love, and every beast is turning back looking for its mate.

And what a coming to me is great sighing and trouble, which herself is drawing out of my deep heart, herself that has taken the key of it up to heaven.

And it is this way I am, that the singing birds, and the flowers of the earth, and the sweet ladies, with their grace and comeliness, are the like of a desert to me, and wild beasts astray in it.

HE UNDERSTANDS THE GREAT CRUELTY OF DEATH

MY flowery and green age was passing away, and I feeling a chill in the fires had been wasting my heart, for I was drawing near the hillside that is above the grave.

Then my sweet enemy was making a start, little by little, to give over her great wariness, the way she was wringing a sweet thing out of my sharp sorrow. The time was coming when Love and Decency can keep company, and lovers may sit together and say out all things are in their hearts. But Death had his grudge against me, and he got up in the way, like an armed robber, with a pike in his hand.

THE SIGHT OF LAURA'S HOUSE REMINDS HIM OF THE GREAT HAPPINESS HE HAS LOST

Is this the nest in which my phoenix put on her feathers of gold and purple, my phoenix that did hold me under her wing, and she drawing out sweet words and sighs from me? Oh, root of my sweet misery, where is that beautiful face, where light would be shining out, the face that did keep my heart like a flame burning? She was without a match upon the earth, I hear them say, and now she is happy in the heavens.

And she has left me after her dejected and lonesome, turning back all times to the place I do be making much of for her sake only, and I seeing the night on the little hills where she took her last flight up into the heavens, and where one time her eyes would make sunshine and it night itself.

HE SENDS HIS RHYMES TO THE TOMB OF LAURA TO PRAY HER TO CALL HIM TO HER

Let you go down, sorrowful rhymes, to the hard rock is covering my dear treasure, and then let you call out till herself that is in the heavens will make answer, though her dead body is lying in a shady place.

Let you say to her that it is tired out I am with being alive, with steering in bad seas, but I am going after her step by step, gathering up what she let fall behind her.

It is of her only I do be thinking, and she living and dead, and now I have made her with my songs so that the whole world may know her, and give her the love that is her due.

May it please her to be ready for my own passage that is getting near; may she be there to meet me, herself in the heavens, that she may call me, and draw me after her.

ONLY HE WHO MOURNS HER AND HEAVEN THAT POSSESSES HER KNEW HER WHILE SHE LIVED

AH, Death, it is you that have left the world cold and shady, with no sun over it. It 's you have left Love without eyes or arms to him, you 've left liveliness stripped, and beauty without a shape to her, and all courtesy in chains, and honesty thrown down into a hole. I am making lamentation alone, though it isn't myself only has a cause to be crying out; since you, Death, have crushed the first seed of goodness in the whole world, and with it gone what place will we find a second?

The air and the earth and seas would have a good right to be crying out—and they pitying the race of men that is left without herself, like a meadow without flowers or a ring robbed of jewellery.

The world didn't know her the time she was in it, but I myself knew her—and I left now to be weeping in this place; and the heavens knew her, the heavens that are giving an ear this day to my crying out.

LAURA WAITS FOR HIM IN HEAVEN

THE first day she passed up and down through the heavens, gentle and simple were left standing, and they in great wonder, saying one to the other:

'What new light is that? What new beauty at all? The like of herself hasn't risen up these long years from the common world.'

And herself, well pleased with the heavens, was going forward, matching herself with the most perfect that were before her, yet one time, and another, waiting a little, and turning her head back to see if myself was coming after her. It 's for that I 'm lifting up all my thoughts and will into the heavens, because I do hear her praying that I should be making haste for ever.

TRANSLATIONS FROM VILLON
AND OTHERS

VILLON

PRAYER OF THE OLD WOMAN, VILLON'S MOTHER

MOTHER of God that 's Lady of the Heavens, take myself, the poor sinner, the way I 'll be along with them that 's chosen.

Let you say to your own Son that He 'd have a right to forgive my share of sins, when it 's the like He 's done, many 's the day, with big and famous sinners. I 'm a poor aged woman, was never at school, and is no scholar with letters, but I 've seen pictures in the chapel with paradise on one side, and harps and pipes in it, and the place on the other side, where sinners do be boiled in torment; the one gave me great joy, the other a great fright and scaring; let me have the good place, Mother of God, and it 's in your faith I 'll live always.

It 's yourself that bore Jesus, that has no end or death, and He the Lord Almighty, that took our weakness and gave Himself to sorrows, a young and gentle man. It 's Himself is our Lord surely, and it 's in that faith I 'll live always.

AN OLD WOMAN'S LAMENTATIONS

THE man I had a love for—a great rascal would kick me in the gutter—is dead thirty years and over it, and it is I am left behind, grey and aged. When I do be minding the good days I had, minding what I was one time, and what it is I 'm come to, and when I do look on my own self, poor and dry, and pinched together, it wouldn't be much would set me raging in the streets.

Where is the round forehead I had, and the fine hair, and the two eyebrows, and the eyes with a big gay look out of them would bring folly from a great scholar? Where is my straight, shapely nose, and two ears, and my chin with a valley in it, and my lips were red and open?

Where are the pointed shoulders were on me, and the long arms and nice hands to them? Where is my bosom was as white as any, or my straight rounded sides?

It 's the way I am this day—my forehead is gone away into furrows, the hair of my head is grey and whitish, my eyebrows are tumbled from me, and my two eyes have died out within my head—those eyes that would be laughing to the men—my nose has a hook on it, my ears are hanging down, and my lips are sharp and skinny.

That 's what 's left over from the beauty of a right woman —a bag of bones, and legs the like of two shrivelled sausages going beneath it.

It 's of the like of that we old hags do be thinking, of the good times are gone away from us, and we crouching on our hunkers by a little fire of twigs, soon kindled and soon spent, we that were the pick of many.

COLIN MUSSET, AN OLD POET, COMPLAINS TO HIS PATRON

From the Old French

I 'M getting old in your big house, and you 've never stretched your hand with a bit of gold to me, or a day's wages itself. By my faith in Mary, it 's not that way I 'll serve you always, living on my pocket, with a few coppers only, and a small weight in my bag. You 've had me to this day, singing on your stairs before you, but I 'm getting a good mind to be going off, when I see my purse flattened out, and my wife does be making a fool of me from the edge of the door.

It 's another story I hear when I come home at night and herself looks behind me, and sets her eye on my bag stuffed to bursting, and I maybe with a grey, decent coat on my back. It 's that time she 's not long leaving down her spinning and coming with a smile, ready to choke me with her two hands squeezing my neck. It 's then my sons have a great rage to be rubbing the sweat from my horse, and my daughter isn't long wringing the necks on a pair of chickens, and making a stew in the pot. It 's that day my youngest will bring me a towel, and she with nice manners. . . . It 's a full purse, I tell you, makes a man lord in his own house.

WALTER VON DER VOGELWEIDE

I NEVER set my two eyes on a head was so fine as your head, but I 'd no way to be looking down into your heart.

It 's for that I was tricked out and out—that was the thanks I got for being so steady in my love.

I tell you, if I could have laid my hands on the whole set of the stars, the moon and the sun along with it, by Christ I 'd have given the lot to her. No place have I set eyes on the like of her; she 's bad to her friends, and gay and playful with those she 'd have a right to hate. I ask you can that behaviour have a good end come to it?

LEOPARDI

SILVIA

Are you bearing in mind that time when there was a fine look out of your eyes, and yourself, pleased and thoughtful, were going up the boundaries that are set to childhood? That time the quiet rooms, and the lanes about the house, would be noisy with your songs that were never tired out; the time you 'd be sitting down with some work that is right for women, and well pleased with the hazy coming times you were looking out at in your own mind.

May was sweet that year, and it was pleasantly you 'd pass the day.

Then I 'd leave my pleasant studies, and the paper I had smudged with ink where I would be spending the better part of the day, and cock my ears from the sill of my father's house, till I 'd hear the sound of your voice, or of your loom when your hands moved quickly. It 's then I would set store of the quiet sky and the lanes and little places, and the sea was far away in one place and the high hills in another.

There is no tongue will tell till the judgment what I feel in myself those times.

THE ARAN ISLANDS

These passages from *The Aran Island.* have been selected from the four parts of the complete work, published in two volumes by George Allen & Unwin Ltd. The headings are the Editor's.

INTRODUCTION

The geography of the Aran Islands is very simple, yet it may need a word to itself. There are three islands, Aranmor, the north island, about nine miles long; Inishmaan, the middle island, about three miles and a half across, and nearly round in form; and the south island, Inisheer—in Irish, east island—like the middle island but slightly smaller. They lie about thirty miles from Galway, up the centre of the bay, but they are not far from the cliffs of County Clare, on the south, or the corner of Connemara on the north.

Kilronan, the principal village on Aranmor, has been so much changed by the fishing industry, developed there by the Congested Districts Board, that it has now very little to distinguish it from any fishing village on the west coast of Ireland. The other islands are more primitive, but even on them many changes are being made, that it was not worth while to deal with in the text.

In the pages that follow I have given a direct account of my life on the islands, and of what I met with among them, inventing nothing and changing nothing that is essential. As far as possible, however, I have disguised the identity of the people I speak of, by making changes in their names, and in the letters I quote, and by altering some local and family relationships. I have had nothing to say about them that was not wholly in their favour, but I have made this disguise to keep them from ever feeling that a too direct use had been made of their kindness and friendship, for which I am more grateful than it is easy to say.

THE ARAN ISLANDS

SELECTIONS FROM NOTE-BOOKS

ARANMOR

I AM in Aranmor, sitting over a turf fire, listening to a murmur of Gaelic that is rising from a little public house under my room.

The steamer which comes to Aran sails according to the tide, and it was six o'clock this morning when we left the quay of Galway in a dense shroud of mist.

A low line of shore was visible at first on the right between the movement of the waves and fog, but when we came further it was lost sight of, and nothing could be seen but the mist curling in the rigging, and a small circle of foam.

There were few passengers; a couple of men going out with young pigs tied loosely in sacking, three or four young girls who sat in the cabin with their heads completely twisted in their shawls, and a builder, on his way to repair the pier at Kilronan, who walked up and down and talked with me.

In about three hours Aran came in sight. A dreary rock appeared at first sloping up from the sea into the fog; then, as we drew nearer, a coastguard station and the village.

A little later I was wandering out along the one good roadway of the island, looking over low walls on either side into small flat fields of naked rock. I have seen nothing so desolate. Grey floods of water were sweeping everywhere upon the limestone, making at times a wild torrent of the road, which twined continually over low hills and cavities in the rock or passed between a few small fields of potatoes or grass hidden away in corners that had shelter. Whenever the cloud lifted I could see the edge of the sea below me on the right, and the naked ridge of the island above me on the other side. Occasionally I passed a lonely chapel or school-house, or a line of stone pillars with crosses above them and inscriptions asking a prayer for the soul of the person they commemorated.

I met few people; but here and there a band of tall girls passed me on their way to Kilronan, and called out to me with humorous wonder, speaking English with a slight foreign intonation that differed a good deal from the brogue of Galway. The rain and cold seemed to have no influence on their vitality, and as they hurried past me with eager laughter and great talking in Gaelic, they left the wet masses of rock more desolate than before.

A little after midday when I was coming back one old half-blind man spoke to me in Gaelic, but, in general, I was surprised at the abundance and fluency of the foreign tongue.

In the afternoon the rain continued, so I sat here in the inn looking out through the mist at a few men who were unlading hookers that had come in with turf from Conne-mara, and at the long-legged pigs that were playing in the surf. As the fishermen came in and out of the public house underneath my room, I could hear through the broken panes that a number of them still used the Gaelic, though it seems to be falling out of use among the younger people of this village.

The old woman of the house had promised to get me a teacher of the language, and after a while I heard a shuffling on the stairs, and the old dark man I had spoken to in the morning groped his way into the room. I brought him over to the fire, and we talked for many hours. . . .

As we talked he sat huddled together over the fire, shaking and blind, yet his face was indescribably pliant, lighting up with an ecstasy of humour when he told me anything that had a point of wit or malice, and growing sombre and desolate again when he spoke of religion or the fairies.

.   .   .   .

Afterwards he told me how one of his children had been taken by the fairies.

One day a neighbour was passing, and she said, when she saw it on the road: 'That's a fine child.'   Its mother tried to say: 'God bless it,' but something choked the words in her throat.   A while later they found a wound on its neck, and for three nights the house was filled with noises.

'I never wear a shirt at night,' he said, 'but I got up out of my bed, all naked as I was, when I heard the noises in the house, and lighted a light, but there was nothing in it.'

Then a dummy came and made signs of hammering nails in a coffin.

The next day the seed potatoes were full of blood, and the child told his mother that he was going to America.

That night it died, and 'Believe me,' said the old man, 'the fairies were in it.'

•   •   •   •

The rain has cleared off, and I have had my first real introduction to the island and its people.

I went out through Killeany—the poorest village in Aranmor—to a long neck of sandhill that runs out into the sea towards the south-west.   As I lay there on the grass the clouds lifted from the Connemara mountains and, for a moment, the green undulating foreground, backed in the distance by a mass of hills, reminded me of the country near Rome.   Then the dun topsail of a hooker swept above the edge of the sandhill and revealed the presence of the sea.

•   •   •   •

OLD MOURTEEN

In spite of the charm of my teacher, the old blind man I met the day of my arrival, I have decided to move on to Inishmaan, where Gaelic is more generally used, and the life is perhaps the most primitive that is left in Europe.

I spent all this last day with my blind guide, looking at

the antiquities that abound in the west or north-west of the island.

As we set out I noticed among the groups of girls who smiled at our fellowship—old Mourteen says we are like the cuckoo with its pipit—a beautiful oval face with the singularly spiritual expression that is so marked in one type of the West Ireland women. Later in the day, as the old man talked continually of the fairies and women they have taken, it seemed that there was a possible link between the wild mythology that is accepted on the islands and the strange beauty of the women.

At midday we rested near the ruins of a house, and two beautiful boys came up and sat near us. Old Mourteen asked them why the house was in ruins, and who had lived in it.

'A rich farmer built it a while since,' they said, 'but after two years he was driven away by the fairy host.'

The boys came on with us some distance to the north to visit one of the ancient beehive dwellings that is still in perfect preservation. When we crawled in on our hands and knees, and stood up in the gloom of the interior, old Mourteen took a freak of earthly humour and began telling what he would have done if he could have come in there when he was a young man and a young girl along with him.

Then he sat down in the middle of the floor, and began to recite old Irish poetry with an exquisite purity of intonation that brought tears to my eyes, though I understood but little of the meaning.

．　　．　　．　　．

Then we talked about Inishmaan.

'You 'll have an old man to talk with you over there,' he said, 'and tell you stories of the fairies, but he 's walking about with two sticks under him this ten year. Did ever you hear what it is goes on four legs when it is young, and on two legs after that, and on three legs when it does be old?'

I gave him the answer.

'Ah, master,' he said, 'you 're a cute one, and the blessing

of God be on you.   Well, I 'm on three legs this minute,
but the old man beyond is back on four; I don't know if
I 'm better than the way he is; he 's got his sight and I 'm
only an old dark man.'

INISHMAAN

I AM settled at last on Inishmaan in a small cottage with a
continual drone of Gaelic coming from the kitchen that
opens into my room.

Early this morning the man of the house came over for
me with a four-oared curagh—that is, a curagh with four
rowers and four oars on either side, as each man uses two
—and we set off a little before noon.

It gave me a moment of exquisite satisfaction to find
myself moving away from civilization in this rude canvas
canoe of a model that has served primitive races since men
first went on the sea.

A small sail was run up in the bow, and we set off
across the sound with a leaping oscillation that had no resem-
blance to the heavy movement of a boat.

The sail is only used as an aid, so the men continued to
row after it had gone up, and as they occupied the four
cross-seats I lay on the canvas at the stern and the frame of
shelter laths, which bent and quivered as the waves passed
under them.

When we set off it was a brilliant morning of April,
and the green, glittering waves seemed to toss the canoe
among themselves; yet as we drew nearer this island a
sudden thunder-storm broke out behind the rocks we were
approaching, and lent a momentary tumult to this still vein
of the Atlantic.

We landed at a small pier, from which a rude track leads
up to the village between small fields and bare sheets of rock
like those in Aranmor.   The youngest son of my boatman,
a boy of about seventeen, who is to be my teacher and guide,
was waiting for me at the pier and guided me to his house,

while the men settled the curagh and followed slowly with my baggage.

My room is at one end of the cottage, with a boarded floor and ceiling, and two windows opposite each other. Then there is the kitchen with earth floor and open rafters, and two doors opposite each other opening into the open air, but no windows. Beyond it there are two small rooms of half the width of the kitchen, with one window apiece.

The kitchen itself, where I will spend most of my time, is full of beauty and distinction. The red dresses of the women who cluster round the fire on their stools give a glow of almost eastern richness, and the walls have been toned by the turf smoke to a soft brown that blends with the grey earth colour of the floor. Many sorts of fishing tackle, and the nets and oilskins of the men, are hung upon the walls or among the open rafters; and right overhead, under the thatch, there is a whole cow-skin from which they make pampooties.

Every article on these islands has an almost personal character, which gives this simple life, where all art is unknown, something of the artistic beauty of medieval life. The curaghs and spinning wheels, the tiny wooden barrels that are still much used in the place of earthenware, the home-made cradles, churns, and baskets, are all full of individuality, and being made from materials that are common here, yet to some extent peculiar to the island, they seem to exist as a natural link between the people and the world that is about them.

The simplicity and unity of the dress increases in another way the local air of beauty. The women wear red petticoats and jackets of the island wool stained with madder, to which they usually add a plaid shawl twisted round their chests and tied at the back. When it rains they throw another petticoat over their heads with the waistband round their faces, or, if they are young, they use a heavy shawl like those worn in Galway. Occasionally other wraps are worn, and during the thunder-storm I arrived in I saw several girls with men's waistcoats buttoned round their bodies. Their skirts do not come much below the knee, and show their powerful legs in the heavy indigo stockings with which they are all provided.

The men wear three colours: the natural wool, indigo, and a grey flannel that is woven of alternate threads of indigo and the natural wool. In Aranmor many of the younger men have adopted the usual fisherman's jersey, but I have only seen one on this island.

* * * *

PAT DIRANE

WHEN I was going out this morning to walk round the island with Michael, the boy who is teaching me Irish, I met an old man making his way down to the cottage. He was dressed in miserable black clothes which seemed to have come from the mainland, and was so bent with rheumatism that, at a little distance, he looked more like a spider than a human being.

Michael told me it was Pat Dirane, the story-teller old Mourteen had spoken of on the other island. I wished to turn back, as he appeared to be on his way to visit me, but Michael would not hear of it.

'He will be sitting by the fire when we come in,' he said; 'let you not be afraid, there will be time enough to be talking to him by and by.'

He was right. As I came down into the kitchen some hours later old Pat was still in the chimney corner, blinking with the turf smoke.

* * * *

PAMPOOTIES

MICHAEL walks so fast when I am out with him that I cannot pick my steps, and the sharp-edged fossils which abound in the limestone have cut my shoes to pieces.

The family held a consultation on them last night, and in the end it was decided to make me a pair of pampooties, which I have been wearing to-day among the rocks.

They consist simply of a piece of raw cow-skin, with the hair outside, laced over the toe, and round the heel with two ends of fishing line that work round and are tied above the instep.

In the evening, when they are taken off, they are placed in a basin of water, as the rough hide cuts the foot and stocking if it is allowed to harden. For the same reason the people often step into the surf during the day, so that their feet are continually moist.

At first I threw my weight upon my heels, as one does naturally in a boot, and was a good deal bruised; but after a few hours I learned the natural walk of man, and could follow my guide in any portion of the island.

In one district below the cliffs, towards the north, one goes for nearly a mile jumping from one rock to another without a single ordinary step; and here I realized that toes have a natural use, for I found myself jumping towards any tiny crevice in the rock before me, and clinging with an eager grip in which all the muscles of my feet ached from their exertion.

The absence of the heavy boot of Europe has preserved to these people the agile walk of the wild animal, while the general simplicity of their lives has given them many other points of physical perfection.

• • • •

THE TIME OF DAY

WHILE I am walking with Michael someone often comes to me to ask the time of day. Few of the people, however, are sufficiently used to modern time to understand in more than a vague way the convention of the hours, and when I tell them what o'clock it is by my watch they are not satisfied, and ask how long is left them before the twilight.

The general knowledge of time on the island depends, curiously enough, on the direction of the wind. Nearly all the cottages are built, like this one, with two doors opposite each other, the more sheltered of which lies open all day to give light to the interior. If the wind is northerly the south door is opened, and the shadow of the door-post moving across the kitchen floor indicates the hour; as soon, however, as the wind changes to the south the other door is opened, and the people, who never think of putting up a primitive dial, are at a loss.

This system of doorways has another curious result. It usually happens that all the doors on one side of the village pathway are lying open with women sitting about on the thresholds, while on the other side the doors are shut and there is no sign of life. The moment the wind changes everything is reversed, and sometimes when I come back to the village after an hour's walk there seems to have been a general flight from one side of the way to the other.

In my own cottage the change of the doors alters the whole tone of the kitchen, turning it from a brilliantly lighted room looking out on a yard and laneway to a sombre cell with a superb view of the sea.

When the wind is from the north the old woman manages my meals with fair regularity; but on the other days she often makes my tea at three o'clock instead of six. If I refuse it she puts it down to simmer for three hours in the turf, and then brings it in at six o'clock full of anxiety to know if it is warm enough.

The old man is suggesting that I should send him a clock when I go away. He 'd like to have something from me in the house, he says, the way they wouldn't forget me, and wouldn't a clock be as handy as another thing, and they 'd be thinking on me whenever they 'd look on its face.

The general ignorance of any precise hours in the day makes it impossible for the people to have regular meals.

They seem to eat together in the evening, and sometimes in the morning a little after dawn, before they scatter for their work; but during the day they simply drink a cup of tea and eat a piece of bread, or some potatoes, whenever they are hungry.

For men who live in the open air they eat strangely little. Often when Michael has been out weeding potatoes for eight or nine hours without food, he comes in and eats a few slices of home-made bread, and then he is ready to go out with me and wander for hours about the island.

They use no animal food except a little bacon and salt fish. The old woman says she would be very ill if she ate fresh meat.

Some years ago, before tea, sugar, and flour had come into general use, salt fish was much more the staple article of diet than at present, and, I am told, skin diseases were very common, though they are now rare on the islands.

No one who has not lived for weeks among these grey clouds and seas can realize the joy with which the eye rests on the red dresses of the women, especially when a number of them are to be found together, as happened early this morning.

I heard that the young cattle were to be shipped for a fair on the mainland, which is to take place in a few days, and I went down on the pier, a little after dawn, to watch them.

The bay was shrouded in the greys of coming rain, yet the thinness of the cloud threw a silvery light on the sea, and an unusual depth of blue to the mountains of Connemara.

As I was going across the sandhills one dun-sailed hooker glided slowly out to begin her voyage, and another beat up to the pier. Troops of red cattle, driven mostly by the women, were coming up from several directions, forming, with the green of the long tract of grass that separates the sea from the rocks, a new unity of colour.

The pier itself was crowded with bullocks and a great number of the people. I noticed one extraordinary girl in the throng who seemed to exert an authority on all who came near her. Her curiously formed nostrils and narrow chin gave her a witch-like expression, yet the beauty of her hair and skin made her singularly attractive.

When the empty hooker was made fast its deck was still many feet below the level of the pier, so the animals were slung down by a rope from the mast-head, with much struggling and confusion.   Some of them made wild efforts to escape, nearly carrying their owners with them into the sea, but they were handled with wonderful dexterity, and there was no mishap.

When the open hold was filled with young cattle, packed as tightly as they could stand, the owners, with their wives or sisters, who go with them to prevent extravagance in Galway, jumped down on the deck, and the voyage was begun. Immediately afterwards a rickety old hooker beat up with turf from Connemara, and while she was unlading all the men sat along the edge of the pier and made remarks upon the rottenness of her timber till the owners grew wild with rage.

The tide was now too low for more boats to come to the pier, so a move was made to a strip of sand towards the south-east, where the rest of the cattle were shipped through the surf.   Here the hooker was anchored about eighty yards from the shore, and a curagh was rowed round to tow out the animals.   Each bullock was caught in its turn and girded with a sling of rope by which it could be hoisted on board.   Another rope was fastened to the horns and passed out to a man in the stern of the curagh.   Then the animal was forced down through the surf and out of its depth before it had much time to struggle.   Once fairly swimming, it was towed out to the hooker and dragged on board in a half-drowned condition.

The freedom of the sand seemed to give a stronger spirit of revolt, and some of the animals were only caught after a dangerous struggle.   The first attempt was not always successful, and I saw one three-year-old lift two men with his horns, and drag another fifty yards along the sand by his tail before he was subdued.

While this work was going on a crowd of girls and women collected on the edge of the cliff and kept shouting down a confused babble of satire and praise.

When I came back to the cottage I found that among the women who had gone to the mainland was a daughter of the old woman's, and that her baby of about nine months had been left in the care of its grandmother.

As I came in she was busy getting ready my dinner, and old Pat Dirane, who usually comes at this hour, was rocking the cradle. It is made of clumsy wicker-work, with two pieces of rough wood fastened underneath to serve as rockers, and all the time I am in my room I can hear it bumping on the floor with extraordinary violence. When the baby is awake it sprawls on the floor, and the old woman sings it a variety of lullabies that have much musical charm.

Another daughter, who lives at home, has gone to the fair also, so the old woman has both the baby and myself to take care of, as well as a crowd of chickens that live in a hole beside the fire. Often when I want tea, or when the old woman goes for water, I have to take my own turn at rocking the cradle.

One of the largest duns, or pagan forts, on the islands, is within a stone's throw of my cottage, and I often stroll up there after a dinner of eggs or salt pork, to smoke drowsily on the stones. The neighbours know my habit, and not infrequently someone wanders up to ask what news there is in the last paper I have received, or to make inquiries about the American war. If no one comes I prop my book open with stones touched by the Fir-bolgs, and sleep for hours in the delicious warmth of the sun. The last few days I have almost lived on the round walls, for, by some miscalculation, our turf has come to an end, and the fires are kept up with dried cow-dung—a common fuel on the island—the smoke from which filters through into my room and lies in blue layers above my table and bed.

Fortunately the weather is fine, and I can spend my days in the sunshine. When I look round from the top of these walls I can see the sea on nearly every side, stretching away to distant ranges of mountains on the north and south. Underneath me to the east there is the one inhabited district of the island, where I can see red figures moving above the cottages, sending up an occasional fragment of conversation or of the old island melodies.

The baby is teething, and has been crying for several days. Since his mother went to the fair they have been feeding him with cow's milk, often slightly sour, and giving him, I think, more than he requires.

This morning, however, he seemed so unwell they sent out to look for a foster-mother in the village, and before long a young woman, who lives a little way to the east, came in and restored him his natural food.

A few hours later, when I came into the kitchen to talk to old Pat, another woman performed the same kindly office, this time a person with a curiously whimsical expression.

PAT'S STORY

PAT told me a story of an unfaithful wife, which I will give further down, and then broke into a moral dispute with the visitor, which caused immense delight to some young men who had come down to listen to the story. Unfortunately it was carried on so rapidly in Gaelic that I lost most of the points.

This old man talks usually in a mournful tone about his ill health, and his death, which he feels to be approaching, yet he has occasional touches of humour that remind me of old Mourteen on the north island. To-day a grotesque twopenny doll was lying on the floor near the old woman. He picked it up and examined it as if comparing it with her. Then he held it up: 'Is it you is after bringing that thing into the world,' he said, 'woman of the house?'

Here is his story:

One day I was travelling on foot from Galway to Dublin, and the darkness came on me and I ten miles from the town I was wanting to pass the night in. Then a hard rain began to fall and I was tired walking, so when I saw a sort of a house with no roof on it up against the road, I got in the way the walls would give me shelter.

As I was looking round I saw a light in some trees two perches off, and thinking any sort of a house would be better than where I was, I got over a wall and went up to the house to look in at the window.

I saw a dead man laid on a table, and candles lighted, and a woman watching him. I was frightened when I saw him, but it was raining hard, and I said to myself, if he was dead he couldn't hurt me. Then I knocked on the door and the woman came and opened it.

'Good evening, ma'am,' says I.

'Good evening kindly, stranger,' says she. 'Come in out of the rain.'

Then she took me in and told me her husband was after dying on her, and she was watching him that night.

'But it's thirsty you'll be, stranger,' says she. 'Come into the parlour.'

Then she took me into the parlour—and it was a fine clean house—and she put a cup, with a saucer under it, on the table before me, with fine sugar and bread.

When I'd had a cup of tea I went back into the kitchen where the dead man was lying, and she gave me a fine new pipe off the table with a drop of spirits.

'Stranger,' says she, 'would you be afeard to be alone with himself?'

'Not a bit in the world, ma'am,' says I; 'he that's dead can do no hurt.'

Then she said she wanted to go over and tell the neighbours the way her husband was after dying on her, and she went out and locked the door behind her.

I smoked one pipe, and I leaned out and took another off the table. I was smoking it with my hand on the back of my chair — the way you are yourself this minute, God bless you!—and I looking on the dead man, when he opened his eyes as wide as myself and looked at me.

'Don't be afeard, stranger,' said the dead man; 'I'm not

dead at all in the world.   Come here and help me up, and
I 'll tell you all about it.'

Well, I went up and took the sheet off of him, and I
saw that he had a fine clean shirt on his body, and fine flannel
drawers.

He sat up then, and says he:

'I 've got a bad wife, stranger, and I let on to be dead the
way I 'd catch her goings on.'

Then he got two fine sticks he had to keep down his wife,
and he put them at each side of his body, and he laid himself
out again as if he was dead.

In half an hour his wife came back, and a young man
along with her.   Well, she gave him his tea, and she told
him he was tired, and he would do right to go and lie down
in the bedroom.

The young man went in, and the woman sat down to
watch by the dead man.   A while after she got up, and
'Stranger,' says she, 'I 'm going in to get the candle out of
the room; I 'm thinking the young man will be asleep by
this time.'   She went into the bedroom, but the divil a bit
of her came back.

Then the dead man got up, and he took one stick, and he
gave the other to myself.   We went in and we saw them
lying together with her head on his arm.

The dead man hit him a blow with the stick so that the
blood out of him leapt up and hit the gallery.

That is my story.

·   ·   ·   ·

ARAN BIRDS

It has cleared, and the sun is shining with a luminous warmth
that makes the whole island glisten with the splendour of a
gem, and fills the sea and sky with a radiance of blue
light.

I have come out to lie on the rocks, where I have the
black edge of the north island in front of me; Galway Bay,

too blue almost to look at, on my right, the Atlantic on my left, a perpendicular cliff under my ankles, and over me innumerable gulls that chase each other in a white cirrus of wings.

A nest of hooded crows is somewhere near me, and one of the old birds is trying to drive me away by letting itself fall like a stone every few moments, from above forty yards above me to within reach of my hand.

Gannets are passing up and down above the sound, swooping at times after a mackerel, and further off I can see the whole fleet of hookers coming out from Kilronan for a night's fishing in the deep water to the west.

As I lie here hour after hour, I seem to enter into the wild pastimes of the cliff and to become a companion of the cormorants and crows.

Many of the birds display themselves before me with the vanity of barbarians, forming in strange evolutions as long as I am in sight, and returning to their ledge of rock when I am gone. Some are wonderfully expert, and cut graceful figures for an unconceivable time without a flap of their wings, growing so absorbed in their own dexterity that they often collide with one another in their flight, an incident always followed by a wild outburst of abuse. Their language is easier than Gaelic, and I seem to understand the greater part of their cries, though I am not able to answer. There is one plaintive note which they take up in the middle of their usual babble with extraordinary effect, and pass on from one to another along the cliff with a sort of an inarticulate wail, as if they remembered for an instant the horror of the mist.

On the low sheets of rock to the east I can see a number of red and grey figures hurrying about their work. The continual passing in this island between the misery of last night and the splendour of to-day, seems to create an affinity between the moods of these people and the moods of varying rapture and dismay that are frequent in artists, and in certain forms of alienation. Yet it is only in the intonation of a few sentences or some old fragment of melody that I catch

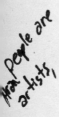
than people are artists,

the real spirit of the island, for in general the men sit together and talk with endless iteration of the tides and fish, and of the price of kelp in Connemara.

THE WAKE AND THE KEENING

AFTER Mass this morning an old woman was buried. She lived in the cottage next mine, and more than once before noon I heard a faint echo of the keen. I did not go to the wake for fear my presence might jar upon the mourners, but all last evening I could hear the strokes of a hammer in the yard, where, in the middle of a little crowd of idlers, the next of kin laboured slowly at the coffin. To-day, before the hour for the funeral, poteen was served to a number of men who stood about upon the road, and a portion was brought to me in my room. Then the coffin was carried out, sewn loosely in sailcloth, and held near the ground by three cross-poles lashed upon the top. As we moved down to the low eastern portion of the island, nearly all the men, and all the oldest women, wearing petticoats over their heads came out and joined in the procession.

While the grave was being opened the women sat down among the flat tombstones, bordered with a pale fringe of early bracken, and began the wild keen, or crying for the dead. Each old woman, as she took her turn in the leading recitative, seemed possessed for the moment with a profound ecstasy of grief, swaying to and fro, and bending her forehead to the stone before her, while she called out to the dead with a perpetually recurring chant of sobs.

All round the graveyard other wrinkled women, looking out from under the deep red petticoats that cloaked them, rocked themselves with the same rhythm and intoned the inarticulate chant that is sustained by all as an accompaniment.

The morning had been beautifully fine, but as they lowered the coffin into the grave, thunder rumbled overhead and hailstones hissed among the bracken.

In Inishmaan one is forced to believe in a sympathy between man and nature, and at this moment, when the thunder sounded a death peal of extraordinary grandeur above the voices of the women, I could see the faces near me stiff and drawn with emotion.

When the coffin was in the grave, and the thunder had rolled away across the hills of Clare, the keen broke out again more passionately than before.

This grief of the keen is no personal complaint for the death of one woman over eighty years, but seems to contain the whole passionate rage that lurks somewhere in every native of the island. In this cry of pain the inner consciousness of the people seems to lay itself bare for an instant, and to reveal the mood of beings who feel their isolation in the face of a universe that wars on them with winds and seas. They are usually silent, but in the presence of death all outward show of indifference or patience is forgotten, and they shriek with pitiable despair before the horror of the fate to which they all are doomed.

Before they covered the coffin an old man kneeled down by the grave and repeated a simple prayer for the dead.

There was an irony in these words of atonement and Catholic belief spoken by voices that were still hoarse with the cries of pagan desperation.

A little beyond the grave I saw a line of old women who had recited in the keen sitting in the shadow of a wall beside the roofless shell of the church. They were still sobbing and shaken with grief, yet they were beginning to talk again of the daily trifles that veil from them the terrors of the world.

When we had all come out of the graveyard, and two men had rebuilt the hole in the wall through which the coffin had been carried in, we walked back to the village, talking of anything, and joking of anything, as if merely coming from the boat-slip or the pier.

One man told me of the poteen-drinking that takes place at some funerals.

'A while since,' he said, 'there were two men fell down

in the graveyard while the drink was on them. The sea was rough that day, the way no one could go to bring the doctor, and one of the men never woke again, and found death that night.'

·　　·　　·　　·

MAKING KELP

THE work needed to form a ton of kelp is considerable. The seaweed is collected from the rocks after the storms of autumn and winter, dried on fine days, and then made up into a rick, where it is left till the beginning of June.

It is then burnt in low kilns on the shore, an affair that takes from twelve to twenty-four hours of continuous hard work, though I understand the people here do not manage well, and spoil a portion of what they produce by burning it more than is required.

The kiln holds about two tons of molten kelp, and when full is loosely covered with stones, and left to cool. In a few days the substance is as hard as the limestone, and has to be broken with crowbars before it can be placed in curaghs for transport to Kilronan, where it is tested to determine the amount of iodine it contains, and paid for accordingly. In former years good kelp would bring seven pounds a ton, now four pounds are not always reached.

In Aran even manufacture is of interest. The low flame-edged kiln, sending out dense clouds of creamy smoke, with a band of red- and grey-clothed workers moving in the haze, and usually some petticoated boys and women who come down with drink, forms a scene with as much variety and colour as any picture from the East.

The men feel in a certain sense the distinction of their island, and show me their work with pride. One of them said to me yesterday: 'I 'm thinking you never saw the like of this work before this day?'

'That is true,' I answered, 'I never did.'

'Bedad, then,' he said, 'isn't it a great wonder that you 've seen France and Germany, and the Holy Father, and never seen a man making kelp till you come to Inishmaan.'

THE HORSES

ALL the horses from this island are put out on grass among the hills of Connemara from June to the end of September, as there is no grazing here during the summer.

Their shipping and transport is even more difficult than that of the horned cattle. Most of them are wild Connemara ponies, and their great strength and timidity make them hard to handle on the narrow pier, while in the hooker itself it is not easy to get them safely on their feet in the small space that is available. They are dealt with in the same way as for the bullocks I have spoken of already, but the excitement becomes much more intense, and the storm of Gaelic that rises the moment a horse is shoved from the pier, till it is safely in its place, is indescribable. Twenty boys and men howl and scream with agitation, cursing and exhorting, without knowing, most of the time, what they are saying.

Apart, however, from this primitive babble, the dexterity and power of the men are displayed to more advantage than in anything I have seen hitherto. I noticed particularly the owner of a hooker from the north island that was loaded this morning. He seemed able to hold up a horse by his single weight when it was swinging from the mast-head, and preserved a humorous calm even in moments of the wildest excitement. Sometimes a large mare would come down sideways on the backs of the other horses, and kick there till the hold seemed to be filled with a mass of struggling centaurs, for the men themselves often leap down to try and save the foals from injury. The backs of the horses put in first are often a good deal cut by the shoes of the others that arrive on top of them; but otherwise they do not seem to be much the worse, and as they are not on their way to a fair, it is not of much consequence in what condition they come to land.

There is only one bit and saddle in the island, which are

used by the priest, who rides from the chapel to the pier when he has held the service on Sunday.

The islanders themselves ride with a simple halter and a stick, yet sometimes travel, at least in the larger island, at a desperate gallop. As the horses usually have panniers, the rider sits sideways over the withers, and if the panniers are empty they go at full speed in this position without anything to hold to.

More than once in Aranmor I met a party going out west with empty panniers from Kilronan. Long before they came in sight I could hear the clatter of hoofs, and then a whirl of horses would come round a corner at full gallop with their heads out, utterly indifferent to the slender halter that is their only check. They generally travel in single file with a few yards between them, and as there is no traffic there is little fear of an accident.

Sometimes a woman and a man ride together; but in this case a man sits in the usual position, and the woman sits sideway behind him, and holds him round the waist.

THE FAIRIES

OLD Pat Dirane continues to come up every day to talk to me, and at times I turn the conversation to his experiences of the fairies.

He has seen a good many of them, he says, in different parts of the island, especially in the sandy districts north of the slip. They are about a yard high, with caps like the 'peelers' pulled down over their faces. On one occasion he saw them playing ball in the evening just above the slip, and he says I must avoid that place in the morning or after nightfall, for fear they might do me mischief.

He has seen two women who were 'away' with them, one a young married woman, the other a girl. The woman was standing by a wall, at a spot he described to me with great care, looking out towards the north.

Another night he heard a voice crying out in Irish: 'A

mháthair tá mé marbh' ('O Mother, I'm killed'), and in the morning there was blood on the wall of his house, and a child in a house not far off was dead.

Yesterday he took me aside, and said he would tell me a secret he had never yet told to any person in the world.

'Take a sharp needle,' he said, 'and stick it in under the collar of your coat, and not one of them will be able to have power on you.'

Iron is a common talisman with barbarians; but in this case the idea of exquisite sharpness was probably present also, and, perhaps, some feeling for the sanctity of the instrument of toil, a folk-belief that is common in Brittany.

* * * *

WHILE THE CURAGHS ARE OUT

WHILE the curaghs are out I am left with a few women and very old men who cannot row. One of those old men, whom I often talk with, has some fame as a bone-setter, and is said to have done remarkable cures, both here and on the mainland. Stories are told of how he has been taken off by the quality in their carriages through the hills of Connemara, to treat their sons and daughters, and come home with his pockets full of money.

Another old man, the oldest on the island, is fond of telling me anecdotes—not folk-tales—of things that have happened here in his lifetime.

He often tells me about a Connaught man who killed his father with the blow of a spade when he was in a passion, and then fled to this island and threw himself on the mercy of some of the natives with whom he was said to be related. They hid him in a hole—which the old man has shown me— and kept him safe for weeks, though the police came and searched for him, and he could hear their boots grinding on the stones over his head. In spite of a reward which was offered, the island was incorruptible, and after much trouble the man was safely shipped to America.

This impulse to protect the criminal is universal in the west. It seems partly due to the association between justice and the hated English jurisdiction, but more directly to the primitive feeling of these people—who are never criminals yet always capable of crime—that a man will not do wrong unless he is under the influence of a passion which is as irresponsible as a storm on the sea. If a man has killed his father, and is already sick and broken with remorse, they can see no reason why he should be dragged away and killed by the law.

Such a man, they say, will be quiet all the rest of his life, and if you suggest that punishment is needed as an example, they ask: 'Would any one kill his father if he was able to help it?'

*   *   *   *

INISHEER

YESTERDAY—a Sunday—three young men rowed me over to Inisheer, the south island of the group.

The stern of the curagh was occupied, so I was put in the bow with my head on a level with the gunwale. A considerable sea was running in the sound, and when we came out from the shelter of this island, the curagh rolled and vaulted in a way not easy to describe.

At one moment, as we went down into the furrow, green waves curled and arched themselves above me; then in an instant I was flung up into the air and could look down on the heads of the rowers, as if we were sitting on a ladder, or out across a forest of white crests to the black cliff of Inishmaan.

The men seemed excited and uneasy, and I thought for a moment that we were likely to be swamped. In a little while, however, I realized the capacity of the curagh to raise its head among the waves, and the motion became strangely exhilarating. Even, I thought, if we were dropped into the blue chasm of the waves, this death, with the fresh sea saltness in one's teeth, would be better than most deaths one is likely to meet.

When we reached the other island it was raining heavily, so that we could not see anything of the antiquities or people. For the greater part of the afternoon we sat on the tops of empty barrels in the public house, talking of the destiny of Gaelic. We were admitted as travellers, and the shutters of the shop were closed behind us, letting in only a glimmer of grey light, and the tumult of the storm. Towards evening it cleared a little and we came home in a calmer sea, but with a dead head-wind that gave the rowers all they could do to make the passage.

    •   •   •   •

LEAVING INISHMAAN

I AM leaving in two days, and old Pat Dirane has bidden me good-bye. He met me in the village this morning, and took me into 'his little tint,' a miserable hovel where he spends the night.

I sat for a long time on his threshold, while he leaned on a stool behind me, near his bed, and told me the last story I shall have from him—a rude anecdote not worth recording. Then he told me with careful emphasis how he had wandered when he was a young man, and lived in a fine college, teaching Irish to the young priests!

They say on the island that he can tell as many lies as four men; perhaps the stories he has learned have strengthened his imagination.

When I stood up in the doorway to give him God's blessing, he leaned over on the straw that forms his bed, and shed tears. Then he turned to me again, lifting up one trembling hand, with the mitten worn to a hole on the palm from the rubbing of his crutch.

'I 'll not see you again,' he said, with tears trickling on his face, 'and you 're a kindly man. When you come back next year I won't be in it. I won't live beyond the winter.

But listen now to what I 'm telling you; let you put insurance on me in the city of Dublin, and it 's five hundred pounds you 'll get on my burial.'

This evening, my last in the island, is also the evening of the 'Pattern'—a festival something like 'Pardons' of Brittany.

I waited specially to see it, but a piper who was expected did not come, and there was no amusement.   A few friends and relations came over from the other island and stood about the public house in their best clothes, but without music dancing was impossible.

I believe on some occasions, when the piper is present, there is a fine day of dancing and excitement, but the Galway piper is getting old, and is not easily induced to undertake the voyage.

Last night, St John's Eve, the fires were lighted and boys ran about with pieces of the burning turf, though I could not find out if the idea of lighting the house fires from the bonfire is still found on the island.

●   ●   ●   ●

THE RETURN

I RETURNED to the middle island this morning, in the steamer to Kilronan, and on here in a curagh that had gone over with salt fish.   As I came up from the slip the doorways in the village filled with women and children, and several came down on the roadway to shake hands and bid me a thousand welcomes.

Old Pat Dirane is dead, and several of my friends have gone to America; that is all the news they have to give me after an absence of many months.

When I arrived at the cottage I was welcomed by the old people, and great excitement was made by some little presents I had brought them—a pair of folding scissors for the old woman, a strop for her husband, and some other trifles.

Then the youngest son, Columb who is still at home,

went into the inner room and brought out the alarm clock I sent them last year when I went away.

'I am very fond of this clock,' he said, patting it on the back; 'it will ring for me any morning when I want to go out fishing. Bedad, there are no two cocks in the island that would be equal to it.'

I had some photographs to show them that I took here last year, and while I was sitting on a little stool near the door of the kitchen, showing them to the family, a beautiful young woman I had spoken to a few times last year slipped in, and after a wonderfully simple and cordial speech of welcome, she sat down on the floor beside me to look on also.

The complete absence of shyness or self-consciousness in most of these people gives them a beautiful charm, and when this young and beautiful woman leaned across my knees to look nearer at some photograph that pleased her, I felt more than ever the strange simplicity of the island life.

.   .   .   .   .

'GREEN DELIRIUM'

THERE has been a storm for the last twenty-four hours, and I have been wandering on the cliffs till my hair is stiff with salt. Immense masses of spray were flying up from the base of the cliff, and were caught at times by the wind and whirled away to fall at some distance from the shore. When one of these happened to fall on me, I had to crouch down for an instant, wrapped and blinded by a white hail of foam.

The waves were so enormous that when I saw one more than usually large coming towards me, I turned instinctively to hide myself, as one blinks when struck upon the eyes.

After a few hours the mind grows bewildered with the endless change and struggle of the sea, and an utter despondency replaces the first moment of exhilaration.

At the south-west corner of the island I came upon a number of people gathering the seaweed that is now thick on the rocks. It was raked from the surf by the men, and then carried up to the brow of the cliff by a party of young girls.

In addition to their ordinary clothing these girls wore a raw sheepskin on their shoulders, to catch the oozing sea-water, and they looked strangely wild and seal-like with the salt caked upon their lips and wreaths of seaweed in their hair.

For the rest of my walk I saw no living thing but one flock of curlews, and a few pipits hiding among the stones.

About sunset the clouds broke and the storm turned to a hurricane. Bars of purple cloud stretched across the sound, where immense waves were rolling from the west, wreathed with snowy phantasies of spray. Then there was the bay full of green delirium, and the Twelve Pins touched with mauve and scarlet in the east.

The suggestion from this world of inarticulate power was immense, and now at midnight, when the wind is abating, I am still trembling and flushed with exultation.

I have been walking through the wet lanes in my pam-pooties in spite of the rain, and I have brought on a feverish cold.

The wind is terrific. If anything serious should happen to me I might die here and be nailed in my box, and shoved down into a wet crevice in the graveyard before any one could know it on the mainland.

∙ ∙ ∙ ∙ ∙

AN IRISH LETTER

An Irish letter has come to me from Michael. I will translate it literally.

DEAR NOBLE PERSON,

I write this letter with joy and pride that you found the way to the house of my father the day you were on the steamship. I am thinking there will not be loneliness on you, for there will be the fine beautiful Gaelic League, and you will be learning powerfully.

I am thinking there is no one in life walking with you now but your own self from morning till night, and great is the pity.

What way are my mother and my three brothers and my sisters, and do not forget white Michael, and the poor little child and the old grey woman, and Rory. I am getting a forgetfulness on all my friends and kindred.—I am your friend. . . .

It is curious how he accuses himself of forgetfulness after asking for all his family by name. I suppose the first home-sickness is wearing away, and he looks on his independent well-being as a treason towards his kindred.

One of his friends was in the kitchen when the letter was brought to me, and, by the old man's wish, he read it out loud as soon as I had finished it. When he came to the last sentence, he hesitated for a moment, and then omitted it altogether.

This young man had come up to bring me a copy of the *Love Songs of Connaught*, which he possesses, and I persuaded him to read, or rather chant me, some of them. When he had read a couple I found that the old woman knew many of them from her childhood, though her version was often not the same as what was in the book. She was rocking herself on a stool in the chimney corner beside a pot of indigo, in which she was dyeing wool, and several times when the young man finished a poem she took it up again and recited the verses with exquisite musical intonation, putting a wistfulness and passion into her voice that seemed to give it all the cadences that are sought in the profoundest poetry.

The lamp had burned low, and another terrible gale was howling and shrieking over the island. It seemed like a dream that I should be sitting here among these men and women, listening to this rude and beautiful poetry that is filled with the oldest passions of the world.

·   ·   ·   ·

A YOUNG-OLD GIRL

In some ways these men and women seem strangely far away from me. They have the same emotions that I have, and the animals have; yet I cannot talk to them when there is much to say, more than to the dog that whines beside me in a mountain fog.

There is hardly an hour I am with them that I do not feel the shock of some inconceivable idea, and then again the shock of some vague emotion that is familiar to them and to me. On some days I feel this island as a perfect home and resting-place; on other days I feel that I am a waif among the people. I can feel more with them than they can feel with me, and while I wander among them, they like me sometimes, and laugh at me sometimes, yet never know what I am doing.

In the evenings I sometimes meet with a girl who is not yet half through her teens, yet seems in some ways more consciously developed than any one else that I have met here. She has passed part of her life on the mainland, and the disillusion she found in Galway has coloured her imagination.

As we sit on stools on either side of the fire I hear her voice going backwards and forwards, in the same sentence, from the gaiety of a child to the plaintive intonation of an old race that is worn with sorrow. At one moment she is a simple peasant, at another she seems to be looking out at the world with a sense of prehistoric disillusion, and to sum up in the expression of her grey-blue eyes the whole external despondency of the clouds and sea.

Our conversation is usually disjointed. One evening we talked of a town on the mainland.

'Ah, it 's a queer place,' she said; 'I wouldn't choose to live in it. It 's a queer place, and indeed I don't know the place that isn't.'

Another evening we talked of the people who live on the island or come to visit it.

'Father —— is gone,' she said; 'he was a kind man but

a queer man.   Priests is queer people, and I don't know who isn't.'

Then after a long pause she told me with seriousness, as if speaking of a thing that surprised herself, and should surprise me, that she was very fond of the boys.

In our talk, which is sometimes full of the innocent realism of childhood, she is always pathetically eager to say the right thing and be engaging.

One evening I found her trying to light a fire in the little side room of her cottage, where there is an ordinary fire-place. I went in to help her and showed her how to hold up a paper before the mouth of the chimney to make a draught, a method she had never seen.   Then I told her of men who lived alone in Paris and make their own fires that they may have no one to bother them.   She was sitting in a heap on the floor staring into the turf and as I finished she looked up with surprise.

'They 're like me so,' she said; 'would any one have thought that!'

Below the sympathy we feel there is still a chasm between us.

'Musha,' she muttered, as I was leaving her this evening, 'I think it 's to hell you 'll be going by and by.'

Occasionally I meet her also in a kitchen where young men go to play cards after dark and a few girls slip in to share the amusement.   At such times her eyes shine in the light of the candles, and her cheeks flush with the first tumult of youth, till she hardly seems the same girl who sits every evening droning to herself over the turf.

·   ·   ·   ·

ARANMOR AGAIN

I AM in the north island again, looking out with a singular sensation to the cliffs across the sound.   It is hard to believe that those hovels I can just see in the south are filled with people whose lives have the strange quality that is found in

the oldest poetry and legend. Compared with them the falling
off that has come with the increased prosperity of this island
is full of discouragement. The charm which the people
over there share with the birds and flowers has been replaced
here by the anxiety of men who are eager for gain. The eyes
and expressions are different, though the faces are the same,
and even the children here seem to have an indefinable
modern quality that is absent from the men of Inishmaan.

My voyage from the middle island was wild. The morning was so stormy that in ordinary circumstances I would
not have attempted the passage, but as I had arranged to
travel with a curagh that was coming over for the parish
priest—who is to hold stations on Inishmaan—I did not like
to draw back.

I went out in the morning and walked up to the cliffs
as usual. Several men I fell in with shook their heads when
I told them I was going away, and said they doubted if a
curagh could cross the sound with the sea that was in it.

$$\cdot \qquad \cdot \qquad \cdot \qquad \cdot$$

At last it was decided we should go, and I started for the
pier in a wild shower of rain with the wind howling in the
walls. The schoolmaster and a priest who was to have gone
with me came out as I was passing through the village and
advised me not to make the passage; but my crew had gone
on towards the sea, and I thought it better to go after them.
The eldest son of the family was coming with me, and I
considered that the old man, who knew the waves better
than I did, would not send out his son if there was more
than reasonable danger.

I found my crew waiting for me under a high wall below
the village, and we went on together. The island had never
seemed so desolate. Looking out over the black limestone
through the driving rain to the gulf of struggling waves, an
indescribable feeling of dejection came over me.

$$\cdot \qquad \cdot \qquad \cdot \qquad \cdot$$

OLD MOURTEEN

OLD MOURTEEN is keeping me company again, and I am now able to understand the greater part of his Irish.

He took me out to-day to show me the remains of some cloghauns, or beehive dwellings, that are left near the central ridge of the island. After I had looked at them we lay down in the corner of a little field, filled with the autumn sunshine and the odour of withering flowers, while he told me a long folk-tale which took more than an hour to narrate.

He is so blind that I can gaze at him without discourtesy, and after a while the expression of his face made me forget to listen, and I lay dreamily in the sunshine, letting the antique formulas of the story blend with the suggestions from the prehistoric masonry I lay on. The glow of childish transport that came over him when he reached the nonsense ending—so common in these tales—recalled me to myself, and I listened attentively while he gabbled with delighted haste: 'They found the path and I found the puddle. They were drowned, and I was found. If it 's all one to me to-night, it wasn't all one to them the next night. Yet, if it wasn't itself, not a thing did they lose but an old back tooth'— or some such gibberish.

As I led him home through the paths he described to me— it is thus we get along—lifting him at times over the low walls he is too shaky to climb, he brought the conversation to the topic they are never weary of—my views on marriage.

He stopped as we reached the summit of the island, with the stretch of the Atlantic just visible behind him.

'Whisper, noble person,' he began; 'do you never be thinking on the young girls? The time I was a young man, the divil a one of them could I look on without wishing to marry her.'

'Ah, Mourteen,' I answered, 'it 's a great wonder you 'd be asking me. What at all do you think of me yourself?'

'Bedad, noble person, I 'm thinking it 's soon you 'll be getting married. Listen to what I 'm telling you: a man who is not married is no better than an old jackass. He goes into his sister's house, and into his brother's house; he eats a bit in this place and a bit in another place, but he has no home for himself; like an old jackass straying on the rocks.'

THE SEA BETWEEN

I HAVE left Aran. The steamer had a more than usually heavy cargo, and it was after four o'clock when we sailed from Kilronan.

Again I saw the three low rocks sink down into the sea with a moment of inconceivable distress. It was a clear evening, and as we came out into the bay the sun stood like an aureole behind the cliffs of Inishmaan. A little later a brilliant glow came over the sky, throwing out the blue of the sea and of the hills of Connemara.

When it was quite dark, the cold became intense, and I wandered about the lonely vessel that seemed to be making her own way across the sea. I was the only passenger, and all the crew, except one boy who was steering, were huddled together in the warmth of the engine room.

Three hours passed, and no one stirred. The slowness of the vessel and the lamentation of the cold sea about her sides became almost unendurable. Then the lights of Galway came in sight, and the crew appeared as we beat up slowly to the quay.

* * * *

THE NIGHTS OF INISHMAAN

I HAVE been down sitting on the pier till it was quite dark. I am only beginning to understand the nights of Inishmaan and the influence they have had in giving distinction to these men, who do most of their work after nightfall.

I could hear nothing but a few curlews and other wild-fowl whistling and shrieking in the seaweed, and the low rustling of the waves.   It was one of the dark sultry nights peculiar to September, with no light anywhere except the phosphorescence of the sea, and an occasional rift in the clouds that showed the stars behind them.

The sense of solitude was immense.   I could not see or realize my own body, and I seemed to exist merely in my perception of the waves and of the crying birds, and of the smell of seaweed.

When I tried to come home I lost myself among the sand-hills, and the night seemed to grow unutterably cold and dejected, as I groped among slimy masses of seaweed and wet crumbling walls.

After a while I heard a movement in the sand, and two grey shadows appeared beside me.   They were two men who were going home from fishing.   I spoke to them and knew their voices, and we went home together.

THRESHING AND THATCHING

In the autumn season the threshing of the rye is one of the many tasks that fall to the men and boys.   The sheaves are collected on a bare rock, and then each is beaten separately on a couple of stones placed on end one against the other. The land is so poor that a field hardly produces more grain than is needed for seed the following year, so the rye growing is carried on merely for the straw, which is used for thatching.

The stooks are carried to and from the threshing field, piled on donkeys that one meets everywhere at this season, with their black, unbridled heads just visible beneath a pinnacle of golden straw.

While the threshing is going on sons and daughters keep turning up with one thing and another till there is a little crowd on the rocks, and any one who is passing stops for an hour or two to talk on his way to the sea, so that, like the kelp burning in the summer time, this work is full of sociability.

When the threshing is over the straw is taken up to the cottages and piled up in an outhouse, or more often in a corner of the kitchen, where it brings a new liveliness of colour.

A few days ago, when I was visiting a cottage where there are the most beautiful children on the island, the eldest daughter, a girl of about fourteen, went and sat down on a heap of straw by the doorway. A ray of sunlight fell on her and on a portion of the rye, giving her figure and red dress with the straw under it a curious relief against the nets and oilskins and forming a natural picture of exquisite harmony and colour.

In our own cottage the thatching—it is done every year—has just been carried out. The rope twisting was done partly in the lane, partly in the kitchen when the weather was uncertain. Two men usually sit together at this work, one of them hammering the straw with a heavy block of wood, the other forming the rope, the main body of which is twisted by a boy or girl with a bent stick specially formed for this employment.

In wet weather, when the work must be done indoors, the person who is twisting recedes gradually out of the door, across the lane, and sometimes across a field or two beyond it. A great length is needed to form the close network which is spread over the thatch, as each piece measures about fifty yards. When this work is in progress in half the cottages of the village, the road has a curious look, and one has to pick one's steps through a maze of twisting ropes that pass from the dark doorways on either side into the fields.

When four or five immense balls of rope have been completed, a thatching party is arranged, and before dawn some morning they come down to the house, and the work is taken in hand with such energy that it is usually ended within the day.

Like all work that is done in common on the island, the thatching is regarded as a sort of festival. From the moment a roof is taken in hand there is a whirl of laughter and talk till it is ended; and, as the man whose house is being covered is a host instead of an employer, he lays himself out to please the men who work with him.

The day our own house was thatched the large table was taken into the kitchen from my room, and high teas were given every few hours. Most of the people who came along the road turned down into the kitchen for a few minutes, and the talking was incessant. Once when I went into the window I heard Michael retailing my astronomical lectures from the apex of the gable; but usually their topics have to do with the affairs of the island.

•   •   •   •

THE CURAGHS

LATE this evening I saw a three-oared curagh with two old women in her besides the rowers, landing at the slip through a heavy roll. They were coming from Inisheer, and they rowed up quickly enough till they were within a few yards of the surf line, where they spun round and waited with the prow towards the sea, while wave after wave passed underneath them and broke on the remains of the slip. Five minutes passed; ten minutes; and still they waited with the oars just paddling in the water, and their heads turned over their shoulders.

I was beginning to think that they would have to give up and row round to the lee side of the island, when the curagh seemed suddenly to turn into a living thing. The prow was again towards the slip, leaping and hurling itself through the spray. Before it touched, the man in the bow wheeled round, two white legs came out over the prow like the flash of a sword, and before the next wave arrived he had dragged the curagh out of danger.

This sudden and united action in men without discipline shows well the education that the waves have given them. When the curagh was in safety the two old women were carried up through the surf and slippery seaweed on the backs of their sons.

In this broken weather, a curagh cannot go out without danger, yet accidents are rare and seem to be nearly always caused by drink. Since I was here last year four men have been drowned on their way home from the large island. First a curagh belonging to the south island, which put off with two men in her heavy with drink, came to shore here the next evening dry and uninjured, with the sail half set, and no one in her.

More recently a curagh from this island with three men, who were the worse for drink, was upset on its way home. The steamer was not far off, and saved two of the men, but could not reach the third.

Now a man has been washed ashore in Donegal with one pampooty on him, and a striped shirt with a purse in one of the pockets, and a box for tobacco.

For three days the people here have been trying to fix his identity. Some think it is the man from this island, others think that the man from the south answers the description more exactly. To-night as we were returning from the slip, we met the mother of the man who was drowned from this island, still weeping and looking out over the sea. She stopped the people who had come over from the south island to ask them with a terrified whisper what is thought over there.

Later in the evening, when I was sitting in one of the cottages, the sister of the dead man came in through the rain with her infant, and there was a long talk about the rumours that had come in. She pieced together all she could remember about his clothes, and what his purse was like, and where he had got it, and the same for his tobacco box, and his stockings. In the end there seemed little doubt that it was her brother.

'Ah!' she said, 'it's Mike sure enough, and please God they'll give him a decent burial.'

Then she began to keen slowly to herself. She had loose yellow hair plastered round her head with the rain, and as she sat by the door suckling her infant, she seemed like a type of the women's life upon the islands.

For a while the people sat silent, and one could hear nothing but the lips of the infant, the rain hissing in the yard, and the breathing of four pigs that lay sleeping in one corner. Then one of the men began to talk about the new boats that have been sent to the south island, and the conversation went back to its usual round of topics.

· · · ·

A BALLAD SINGER OF THE INISHEER

The mode of reciting ballads in this island is singularly harsh. I fell in with a curious man to-day beyond the east village, and we wandered out on the rocks towards the sea. A wintry shower came on while we were together, and we crouched down in the bracken, under a loose wall. When we had gone through the usual topics he asked me if I was fond of songs, and began singing to show what he could do.

The music was much like what I have heard before on the islands—a monotonous chant with pauses on the high and low notes to mark the rhythm; but the harsh nasal tone in which he sang was almost intolerable. His performance reminded me, in general effect, of a chant I once heard from a party of Orientals I was travelling with in a third-class carriage from Paris to Dieppe, but the islander ran his voice over a much wider range.

His pronunciation was lost in the rasping of his throat, and, though he shrieked into my ear to make sure that I understood him above the howling of the wind, I could only make out that it was an endless ballad telling the fortune of a young man who went to sea and had many adventures. The English nautical terms were employed continually in describing his life on the ship, but the man seemed to feel that they were not in their place, and stopped short when one of them occurred to give me a poke with his finger and explain jib, topsail, and bowsprit, which were for me the most intelligible features of the poem. Again, when the scene changed to Dublin, 'glass of whisky,' 'public house,' and such things were in English.

When the shower was over he showed me a curious cave hidden among the cliffs a short distance from the sea. On our way back he asked me the three questions I am met with on every side—whether I am a rich man, whether I am married, and whether I have ever seen a poorer place than these islands.

When he heard that I was not married he urged me to come back in the summer so that he might take me over in a curagh to the Spa in County Clare, where there is 'spree mor agus go leor ladies' (a big spree and plenty of ladies).

Something about the man repelled me while I was with him, and though I was cordial and liberal he seemed to feel that I abhorred him. We arranged to meet again in the evening, but when I dragged myself with an inexplicable loathing to the place of meeting, there was no trace of him.

It is characteristic that this man who is probably a drunkard and shebeener and certainly in penury—refused the chance of a shilling because he felt that I did not like him. He had a curiously mixed expression of hardness and melancholy. Probably his character has given him a bad reputation on the island, and he lives here with the restlessness of a man who has no sympathy with his companions.

INISHMAAN

I HAVE come over again to Inishmaan, and this time I had fine weather for my passage. The air was full of luminous sunshine from the early morning, and it was almost a summer's day when I set sail at noon with Michael and two other men who had come over for me in a curagh.

The wind was in our favour, so the sail was put up and Michael sat in the stern to steer with an oar, while I rowed with the others.

We had had a good dinner and drink, and were wrought up by this sudden revival of summer to a dreamy voluptuous gaiety that made us shout with exultation to hear our voices passing out across the blue twinkling of the sea.

Even after the people of the south island, these men of the Inishmaan seemed to be moved by strange archaic sympathies with the world. Their mood accorded itself with wonderful fineness to the suggestions of the day, and their ancient Gaelic seemed so full of divine simplicity that I would have liked to turn the prow to the west and row with them for ever.

I told them I was going back to Paris in a few days to sell my books and my bed, and that then I was coming back to grow as strong and simple as they were among the islands of the west.

Confirmed

When our excitement sobered down, Michael told me that one of the priests had left his gun at our cottage and given me leave to use it till he returned to the island. There was another gun and a ferret in the house also, and he said that as soon as we got home he was going to take me out fowling on rabbits.

A little later in the day we set off, and I nearly laughed to see Michael's eagerness that I should turn out a good shot.

We put the ferret down in a crevice between two bare sheets of rock, and waited. In a few minutes we heard rushing paws underneath us, then a rabbit shot up straight into the air from the crevice at our feet and set off for a wall that was a few feet away. I threw up the gun and fired.

'Buail tu é,' screamed Michael at my elbow as he ran up the rock. I had killed it.

We shot seven or eight more in the next hour, and Michael was immensely pleased. If I had done badly I think I should have had to leave the islands. The people would have despised me. A 'duine uasal' who cannot shoot seems to these descendants of hunters a fallen type who is worse than an apostate.

THE WOMEN

THE women of this island are before conventionality, and share some of the liberal features that are thought peculiar to the women of Paris and New York.

Many of them are too contented and too sturdy to have more than a decorative interest, but there are others full of curious individuality.

This year I have got to know a wonderfully humorous girl, who has been spinning in the kitchen for the last few days with the old woman's spinning wheel. The morning she began I heard her exquisite intonation almost before I awoke, brooding and cooing over every syllable she uttered.

I have heard something similar in the voices of German and Polish women, but I do not think men—at least European men—who are always further than women from the simple animal emotions, or any speakers who use languages with weak gutturals, like French or English, can produce this inarticulate chant in their ordinary talk.

She plays continual tricks with her Gaelic in the way girls are fond of, piling up diminutives and repeating adjectives with a humorous scorn of syntax. While she is here the talk never stops in the kitchen. To-day she has been asking me many questions about Germany, for it seems one of her sisters married a German husband in America some years ago, who kept her in great comfort, with a fine 'capull glas' (grey horse) to ride on, and this girl has decided to escape in the same way from the drudgery of the island.

This was my last evening on my stool in the chimney corner, and I had a long talk with some neighbours who came in to bid me prosperity, and lay about on the floor with their heads on low stools and their feet stretched out to the embers of the turf. The old woman was at the other side of the fire, and the girl I have spoken of was standing at her spinning wheel, talking and joking with every one. She says when I go away now I am to marry a rich wife with plenty of money, and if she dies on me I am to come back here and marry herself for my second wife.

I have never heard talk so simple and so attractive as the talk of these people. This evening they began disputing about their wives, and it appeared that the greatest merit they see in a woman is that she should be fruitful and bring them many children. As no money can be earned by children on the island this one attitude shows the immense difference between these people and the people of Paris.

The direct sexual instincts are not weak on the island, but they are so subordinated to the instincts of the family that they rarely lead to irregularity. The life here is still at an almost patriarchal stage, and the people are nearly as far from the romantic moods of love as they are from the impulsive life of the savage.

THE STEAMER

THE wind was so high this morning that there was some doubt whether the steamer would arrive, and I spent half the day wandering about with Michael watching the horizon.

At last, when we had given her up, she came in sight far away to the north, where she had gone to have the wind with her where the sea was at its highest.

I got my baggage from the cottage and set off for the slip with Michael and the old man, turning into a cottage here and there to say good-bye.

In spite of the wind outside, the sea at the slip was as calm as a pool. The men who were standing about while the steamer was at the south island wondered for the last time whether I would be married when I came back to see them. Then we pulled out and took our place in the line. As the tide was running hard the steamer stopped a certain distance from the shore, and gave us a long race for good places at her side. In the struggle we did not come off well, so I had to clamber across two curaghs, twisting and fumbling with the roll, in order to get on board.

It seemed strange to see the curaghs full of well-known faces turning back to the slip without me, but the roll in the sound soon took off my attention. Some men were on board whom I had seen on the south island, and a good many Kilronan people on their way home from Galway, who told me that in one part of their passage in the morning they had come in for heavy seas.

As is usual on Saturday, the steamer had a large cargo of flour and porter to discharge at Kilronan, and, as it was nearly four o'clock before the tide could float her at the pier, I felt some doubt about our passage to Galway.

The wind increased as the afternoon went on, and when I came down in the twilight I found that the cargo was not yet all unladen, and that the captain feared to face the gale that was rising. It was some time before he came to a final decision, and we walked backwards and forwards from the village with heavy clouds flying overhead and the wind howling in the walls. At last he telegraphed to Galway to know if he was wanted the next day, and we went into a public house to wait for the reply.

The kitchen was filled with men sitting closely on long forms ranged in lines at each side of the fire. A wild-looking but beautiful girl was kneeling on the hearth talking loudly to the men, and a few natives of Inishmaan were hanging about the door, miserably drunk. At the end of the kitchen the bar was arranged, with a sort of alcove beside it, where some older men were playing cards. Overhead there were the open rafters, filled with turf and tobacco smoke.

This is the haunt so much dreaded by the women of the other islands, where the men linger with their money till they go out at last with reeling steps and are lost in the sound. Without this background of empty curaghs, and bodies floating naked with the tide, there would be something almost absurd about the dissipation of this simple place where men sit, evening after evening, drinking bad whisky and porter, and talking with endless repetition of fishing, and kelp, and of the sorrows of purgatory.

When we had finished our whisky word came that the boat might remain.

With some difficulty I got my bags out of the steamer and carried them up through the crowd of women and donkeys that were still struggling on the quay in an inconceivable medley of flour bags and cases of petroleum. When I reached the inn the old woman was in great good humour, and I spent some time talking by the kitchen fire. Then I groped my way back to the harbour, where, I was told, the old net mender, who came to see me on my first visit to the islands, was spending the night as watchman.

It was quite dark on the pier, and a terrible gale was blowing. There was no one in the little office where I expected to find him, so I groped my way further on towards a figure I saw moving with a lantern.

It was the old man, and he remembered me at once when I hailed him and told him who I was. He spent some time arranging one of his lanterns and then he took me back to his office—a mere shed of planks and corrugated iron, put up for the contractor of some work which is in progress on the pier.

When we reached the light I saw that his head was rolled up in an extraordinary collection of mufflers to keep him from the cold, and that his face was much older than when I saw him before, though still full of intelligence.

·   ·   ·   ·

ANOTHER JOURNEY

No two journeys to these islands are alike. This morning I sailed with the steamer a little after five o'clock in a cold night air, with the stars shining on the bay. A number of Claddagh fishermen had been out all night fishing not far from the harbour, and without thinking, or perhaps caring to think, of the steamer, they had put out their nets in the channel where she was to pass. Just before we started the mate sounded the steam whistle repeatedly to give them warning, saying as he did so:

'If you were out now in the bay, gentlemen, you 'd hear some fine prayers being said.'

When we had gone a little way we began to see the light from the turf fires carried by the fishermen flickering on the water, and to hear a faint noise of angry voices. Then the outline of a large fishing boat came in sight through the darkness, with the forms of three men who stood on the deck shrieking and howling at us to alter our course. The captain feared to turn aside, as there are sand banks near the channel; so the engines were stopped, and we glided over the nets without doing them harm. As we passed close to the boat the crew could be seen plainly on the deck, one of them holding the bucket of red turf, and their abuse could be distinctly heard. It changed continually, from profuse Gaelic maledictions to the simpler curses they know in English. As they spoke they could be seen writhing and twisting themselves with passion against the light which was beginning to turn on the ripple of the sea. Soon afterwards another set of voices began in front of us, breaking out in strange contrast with the dwindling stars and the silence of the dawn.

Further on we passed many boats that let us go by without a word, as their nets were not in the channel. Then day came on rapidly, with cold showers that turned golden in the first rays from the sun, filling the troughs of the sea with curious transparencies and light.

THE DANCING

THIS year I have brought my fiddle with me so that I may have something new to keep up the interest of the people. I have played for them several tunes; but as far as I can judge they do not feel modern music, though they listen eagerly from curiosity. Irish airs like *Eileen Aroon* please them better; but it is only when I play some jig like the *Black*

Rogue—which is known on the island—that they seem to respond to the full meaning of the notes.   Last night I played for a large crowd which had come together for another purpose from all parts of the island.

About six o'clock I was going into the schoolmaster's house, and I heard a fierce wrangle going on between a man and a woman near the cottages to the west, that lie below the road.   While I was listening to them several women came down to listen also from behind the wall, and told me that the people who were fighting were near relations who lived side by side and often quarrelled about trifles, though they were as good friends as ever the next day.   The voices sounded so enraged that I thought mischief would come of it, but the women laughed at the idea.   Then a lull came, and I said that they seemed to have finished at last.

'Finished!' said one of the women; 'sure they haven't rightly begun. It's only playing they are yet.'

It was just after sunset, and the evening was bitterly cold, so I went into the house and left them.

An hour later the old man came down from my cottage to say that some of the lads and the 'fear lionta' (the man of the nets—a young man from Aranmore who is teaching net mending to the boys) were up at the house, and had sent him down to tell me they would like to dance, if I would come up and play for them.

I went out at once, and as soon as I came into the air I heard the dispute going on still to the west more violently than ever.   The news of it had gone about the island, and little bands of girls and boys were running along the lanes towards the scene of the quarrel as eagerly as if they were going to a racecourse.

I stopped for a few minutes at the door of our cottage to listen to the volume of abuse that was rising across the stillness of the island.   Then I went into the kitchen and began tuning the fiddle, as the boys were impatient for my music. At first I tried to play standing, but on the upward stroke my bow came in contact with the salt fish and oilskins that hung from the rafters; so I settled myself at last on a table in the corner, where I was out of the way, and got one of the people to hold up my music before me, as I had no stand. I played a French melody first, to get myself used to the people and the qualities of the room, which has little resonance between the earth floor and the thatch overhead. Then I struck up the *Black Rogue*, and in a moment a tall man bounded out from his stool under the chimney and began flying round the kitchen with peculiarly sure and graceful bravado.

The lightness of the pampooties seems to make the dancing on this island lighter and swifter than anything I have seen on the mainland, and the simplicity of the men enables them to throw a naïve extravagance into their steps that is impossible in places where the people are self-conscious.

The speed, however, was so violent that I had some difficulty in keeping up, as my fingers were not in practice, and I could not take off more than a small part of my attention to watch what was going on. When I finished I heard a commotion at the door, and the whole body of people who had gone down to watch the quarrel filed into the kitchen and arranged themselves around the walls, the women and girls, as is usual, forming themselves in one compact mass, crouching on their heels near the door.

I struck up another dance—*Paddy get up*—and the 'fear lionta' and the first dancer went through it together, with additional rapidity and grace, as they were excited by the presence of the people who had come in. Then word went round that an old man, known as 'Little Roger,' was outside, and they told me he was once the best dancer on the island.

For a long time he refused to come in, for he said he was too old to dance, but at last he was persuaded, and the people brought him in and gave him a stool opposite me. It was some time longer before he would take his turn, and when he did so, though he was met with great clapping of hands, he only danced for a few moments. He did not know the dances in my book, he said, and did not care to dance to music he was not familiar with. When the people pressed him again he looked across to me.

'John,' he said, in shaking English, 'have you got *Larry Grogan*, for it is an agreeable air?'

I had not, so some of the young men danced again to the *Black Rogue*, and then the party broke up. The altercation was still going on at the cottage below us, and the people were anxious to see what was coming of it.

About ten o'clock a young man came in and told us that the fight was over.

'They have been at it for four hours,' he said, 'and now they're tired. Indeed it is time they were, for you'd rather be listening to a man killing a pig than to the noise they were letting out of them.'

After the dancing and excitement we were too stirred up to be sleepy, so we sat for a long time round the embers of the turf, talking and smoking by the light of a candle.

From ordinary music we came to talk of the music of the fairies, and they told me this story, when I had told them some stories of my own:

A man who lives in the other end of the village got his gun one day and went out to look for rabbits in a thicket near the small dun. He saw a rabbit sitting up under a tree, and he lifted his gun to take aim at it, but just as he had it covered he heard a kind of music over his head, and he looked up into the sky. When he looked back for the rabbit, not a bit of it was to be seen.

He went on after that, and he heard the music again.

Then he looked over a wall, and he saw a rabbit sitting up by the wall with a sort of flute in its mouth, and it playing on it with its two fingers!

．　　．　　．　　．

THE SORROWS

A YOUNG married woman I used often to talk with is dying of a fever—typhus, I am told—and her husband and brother have gone off in a curagh to get the doctor and the priest from the north island, though the sea is rough.

I watched them from the dun for a long time after they had started.   Wind and rain were driving through the sound, and I could see no boats or people anywhere except this one black curagh splashing and struggling through the waves. When the wind fell a little I could hear people hammering below me to the east.   The body of a young man who was drowned a few weeks ago came ashore this morning, and his friends have been busy all day making a coffin in the yard of the house where he lived.

After a while the curagh went out of sight into the mist, and I came down to the cottage shuddering with cold and misery.

The old woman was keening by the fire.

'I have been to the house where the young man is,' she said, 'but I couldn't go to the door with the air was coming out of it.   They say his head isn't on him at all, and indeed it isn't any wonder and he three weeks in the sea.   Isn't it great danger and sorrow is over every one on this island?'

I asked her if the curagh would soon be coming back with the priest.

'It will not be coming soon or at all to-night,' she said. 'The wind has gone up now, and there will come no curagh to this island for maybe two days or three.   And wasn't it a cruel thing to see the haste was on them, and they in danger all the time to be drowned themselves?'

Then I asked her how the woman was doing.

'She's nearly lost,' said the old woman; 'she won't be alive at all to-morrow morning.   They have no boards to make her a coffin, and they 'll want to borrow the boards that a man below has had this two years to bury his mother, and she alive still.   I heard them saying there are two more women with the fever, and a child that 's not three.   The Lord have mercy on us all!'

I went out again to look over the sea, but night had fallen and the hurricane was howling over the dun.   I walked down the lane and heard the keening in the house where the young man was.   Further on I could see a stir about the door of the cottage that had been last struck by typhus.

Then I turned back again in the teeth of the rain, and sat over the fire with the old man and woman talking of the sorrows of the people till it was late in the night.

This evening the old man told me a story he had heard long ago on the mainland:

There was a young woman, he said, and she had a child. In a little time the woman died and they buried her the day after. That night another woman—a woman of the family —was sitting by the fire with the child on her lap, giving milk to it out of a cup. Then the woman they were after burying opened the door, and came into the house. She went over to the fire, and she took a stool and sat down before the other woman. Then she put out her hand and took the child on her lap, and gave it her breast. After that she put the child in the cradle and went over to the dresser and took milk and potatoes off it, and ate them. Then she went out. The other woman was frightened, and she told the man of the house when he came back, and two young men. They said they would be there the next night, and if she came back they would catch hold of her. She came the next night and gave the child her breast, and when she got up to go to the dresser, the man of the house caught hold of her, but he fell down on the floor. Then the two young men caught hold of her and they held her. She told them she was away with the fairies, and they could not keep her that night, though she was eating no food with the fairies, the way she might be able to come back to her child. Then she told them they would all be leaving that part of the country on the Oidhche Shamhna, and that there would be four or five hundred of them riding on horses, and herself would be on a grey horse, riding behind a young man. And she told them to go down to a bridge they would be crossing that night, and to wait at the head of it, and when she would be coming up she would slow the horse and they would be able to throw something on her and on the young man, and they would fall over on the ground and be saved.

She went away then, and on the Oidhche Shamhna the men went down and got her back. She had four children after that, and in the end she died.

It was not herself they buried at all the first time, but some old thing the fairies put in her place.

'There are people who say they don't believe in these things,' said the old woman, 'but there are strange things, let them say what they will. There was a woman went to bed at the lower village a while ago, and her child along with her. For a time they did not sleep, and then something came to the window, and they heard a voice, and this is what it said:

'"It is time to sleep from this out."

'In the morning the child was dead, and indeed it is many get their death that way on the island.'

The young man has been buried, and his funeral was one of the strangest scenes I have met with. People could be seen going down to his house from early in the day, yet when I went there with the old man about the middle of the afternoon, the coffin was still lying in front of the door, with the men and women of the family standing round beating it, and keening over it, in a great crowd of people. A little later every one knelt down and a last prayer was said. Then the cousins of the dead man got ready two oars and some pieces of rope—the men of his own family seemed too broken with grief to know what they were doing—the coffin was tied up, and the procession began. The old women walked close behind the coffin, and I happened to take a place just after them, among the first of the men. The rough lane to the graveyard slopes away towards the east, and the crowd of women going down before me in their red dresses, cloaked with red petticoats, with the waistband that is held round the head just seen from behind, had a strange effect, to which the white coffin and the unity of colour gave a nearly cloistral quietness.

This time the graveyard was filled with withered grass and bracken instead of the early ferns that were to be seen everywhere at the other funeral I have spoken of, and the grief of the people was of a different kind, as they had come to bury a young man who had died in his first manhood, instead of an old woman of eighty. For this reason the keen lost a part of its formal nature, and was recited as the expression of intense personal grief by the young men and women of the man's own family.

When the coffin had been laid down near the grave that was to be opened, two long switches were cut out from the brambles among the rocks, and the length and breadth of the coffin were marked on them. Then the men began their work, clearing off stones and thin layers of earth, and breaking up an old coffin that was in the place into which the new one had to be lowered. When a number of blackened boards and pieces of bone had been thrown up with the clay, a skull was lifted out and placed upon a gravestone. Immediately the old woman, the mother of the dead man, took it up in her hands, and carried it away by herself. Then she sat down and put it in her lap—it was the skull of her own mother—and began keening and shrieking over it with the wildest lamentation.

As the pile of mouldering clay got higher beside the grave a heavy smell began to rise from it, and the men hurried with their work, measuring the hole repeatedly with the two rods of bramble. When it was nearly deep enough the old woman got up and came back to the coffin, and began to beat on it, holding the skull in her left hand. This last moment of grief was the most terrible of all. The young women were nearly lying among the stones, worn out with their passion of grief, yet raising themselves every few moments to beat with magnificent gestures on the boards of the coffin. The young men were worn out also, and their voices cracked continually in the wail of the keen.

When everything was ready the sheet was unpinned from the coffin, and it was lowered into its place. Then an old man took a wooden vessel with holy water in it, and a wisp of bracken, and the people crowded round him while he splashed the water over them. They seemed eager to get as much of it as possible, more than one old woman crying out with a humorous voice:

'Tabhair dham braon eile, a Mhourteen' (Give me another drop, Martin).

When the grave was half filled in, I wandered round towards the north watching two seals that were chasing each other near the surf.   I reached the Sandy Head as the light began to fail, and found some of the men I knew best fishing there with a sort of drag-net.   It is a tedious process, and I sat for a long time on the sand watching the net being put out, and then drawn in again by eight men working together with a slow rhythmical movement.

As they talked to me and gave me a little poteen and a little bread when they thought I was hungry, I could not help feeling that I was talking with men who were under a judgment of death.   I knew that every one of them would be drowned in the sea in a few years and battered naked on the rocks, or would die in his own cottage and be buried with another fearful scene in the graveyard I had come from.

·   ·   ·   ·

Everyman
A selection of titles

*indicates volumes available in paperback

Complete lists of Everyman's Library and Everyman Paperbacks
are available from the Sales Department, J.M. Dent and Sons Ltd,
Aldine House, 33 Welbeck Street, London W1M 8LX.

BIOGRAPHY

Bligh, William. *A Book of the 'Bounty'*
Boswell, James. *The Life of Samuel Johnson*
Byron, Lord. *Letters*
*Chesterfield, Lord. *Letters to His Son and others*
Cibber, Colley. *An Apology for the Life of Colly Cibber*
*De Quincey, Thomas. *Confessions of an English Opium-Eater*
Forster, John. *Life of Charles Dickens* (2 vols)
*Gaskell, Elizabeth. *The Life of Charlotte Brontë*
*Gilchrist, Alexander. *The Life of William Blake*
*Hudson, W.H. *Far Away and Long Ago*
*Johnson, Samuel. *Lives of the English Poets: a selection*
Pepys, Samuel. *Diary* (3 vols)
Thomas, Dylan
    Adventures in the Skin Trade
    Portrait of the Artist as a Young Dog
Tolstoy. *Childhood, Boyhood and Youth*

FICTION

*American Short Stories of the Nineteenth Century
Austen, Jane
    Emma
    Mansfield Park
    Northanger Abbey
    Persuasion
    Pride and Prejudice
    Sense and Sensibility
*Australian Short Stories